Topical Reference Series

White Papers on Club Management

Issues 1-6

00881TXT01ENCM01
PP-1336

Topical Reference Series

White Papers on Club Management

Issues 1-6

Bridgette M. Redman

Club Managers
Association of America

American
Hotel & Lodging
Educational Institute

Disclaimer

This publication is designed to provide accurate and authoritative information in regard to the subject matter covered. It is sold with the understanding that the publisher is not engaged in rendering legal, accounting, or other professional service. If legal advice or other expert assistance is required, the services of a competent professional person should be sought.

> *— From the* Declaration of Principles *jointly adopted by the American Bar Association and a Committee of Publishers and Associations.*

Nothing contained in this publication shall constitute a standard, an endorsement, or a recommendation of the Club Managers Association of America (CMAA), the American Hotel & Lodging Educational Institute (the Institute), or the American Hotel & Lodging Association (AH&LA). CMAA, AH&LA and the Institute, disclaim any liability with respect to the use of any information, procedure, or product, or reliance thereon by any member of the hospitality industry.

© Copyright 1997 by the
AMERICAN HOTEL & LODGING
EDUCATIONAL INSTITUTE
2113 N. High Street
Lansing, Michigan 48906
and
CLUB MANAGERS ASSOCIATION OF AMERICA
1733 King Street
Alexandria, Virginia 22314

Printed in the United States of America

Library of Congress Cataloging-in-Publication Data
Redman, Bridgette M. (Bridgette Michele), 1968-
    White papers on club management/written by Bridgette M. Redman.
        p. cm. — (Topical reference series)
    Includes bibliographical references.
    Contents: v. 1. Issues 1 to 6.
    ISBN 978-0-86612-164-4 (alk. paper)
    1. Clubs—United States—Management. I. American Hotel & Motel Association. Educational Institute. II. Club Managers Association of America. III. Title IV. Series.
HS2723.R43   1997
367'.068—dc21   97-25551
                                                                                     CIP

CMAA advisors: Alyson Austin
                        Kathi Driggs
                        Joe Perdue, CCM, CHE
                        Tamara Tyrell

Editors: Paul Madden
                        Jim Purvis
                        Jean Raber

Contents

Preface

Premier Club Services was founded in 1993 — a department of the Club Managers Association of America (CMAA) devoted to supporting and encouraging the utmost in efficient, sound, and successful club operations.

Demographic and economic evidence indicates that clubs are facing unprecedented pressure to provide exceptional service to its members. To accomplish this successfully, the club manager must continually strive to improve club operations, as well as deal with a rapidly changing work force.

In 1995, Premier Club Services introduced the Topical Reference Series to club managers. This series is a collection of white papers that examines issues relevant to club managers and their boards. The TRS compiles the best in current industry knowledge on topics of importance to club management and governance.

The TRS issues are mailed on a quarterly basis to Premier Club Services subscribers. Each issue takes a practical look at specific issues and topics that club managers have identified as important.

This volume contains a compilation of the first six issues: Board and Committee Orientation, Club Bylaws, Club Rules, Effective Meetings, Roles and Responsibilities of Board and Committee Members, and Ethics. Added to the issue are review questions, activities, and case studies as a bonus to those who would like to use these issues in classrooms, club training sessions, or CMAA education meetings.

One of the key questions asked of managers when a Topical Reference Series issue is being written is, "What are the five most important questions that you would want answered after reading an article on (the current topic)?" The answers to that question help immediately focus the issue on the practical concerns that affect the club management industry.

Since every club is unique in its operations and policies, the Topical Reference Series does not dictate one single way to respond to a given issue. Instead, it offers advice from other managers in the industry.

One of the things that makes the Topical Reference Series unique in the club industry is that it is compiled from the expertise of practicing managers. The research for each issue centers on finding out what managers are doing in the field and then compiling that information to make it available to all. This keeps the issues practical and of value.

After each issue in this book are case studies that focus on the real problems and situations club managers face. Three club experts were selected to come to the Educational Institute and work with staff writers to create practical, realistic case studies. These experts spent two intensive days discussing scenarios, debating responses to hospitality dilemmas, and providing detailed information for the writers to use in developing cases. Particular thanks are extended to those devoted experts: **Cathy Gustafson, CCM**, University of South Carolina, Columbia, South Carolina; **Kurt D. Kuebler, CCM**, Vice President, General Manager, The Desert Highlands Association, Scottsdale, Arizona; and **William A. Schulz, MCM**, General Manager, Houston Country Club, Houston, Texas.

Club Board and Committee Orientation

Welcome to the Club Managers Association of America's Premier Club Services' Topical Reference Series. This issue can be a valuable resource for general managers, chief operating officers, club board members, club committee members, or anyone else who plans and implements club orientations.

The focus of this issue is on conducting orientations for new board and committee members. Have you ever wondered why you should bother orienting new members? This issue can help answer this question. This issue will also discuss the part you — whether you are a committee chair or the general manager/chief operating officer (GM/COO) — can play in orientation.

Many clubs suffer from a lack of commitment from board members but don't understand why. This issue will discuss what clubs do to successfully orient new members and will show the wide variety of orientation strategies used by GMs/COOs responsible for the function.

This issue will also cover the basic types of orientation activities, formats, agendas, and materials. Finally, you'll find a checklist to help you prepare for your own orientations.

What is an Orientation?

The volunteers who sit on the club's boards and committees make decisions that govern the long-term direction of the organization. Considering the crucial role that they play in determining the club's future, it is important that new board and committee members fully understand their new responsibilities.

Orientations — meetings or a series of meetings that introduce the new members to the board or committee — can help volunteers make a successful transition from neophyte to contributor. How can board and committee orientations help members understand their responsibilities?

- They set forth a clear role for new board and committee members.

- They can help secure the future of the club.

- They can provide new members with the materials they need to govern effectively.

- They can shorten the learning curve of new members and help them more quickly become productive members.

- They can help new members understand what is and what is not expected of them.

- They can give current members, board or committee leaders, and the GM/COO a chance to welcome the new members and to share their collective knowledge.

What Do Orientations Accomplish?

One GM/COO said his orientations help make sure that all committee members are reading from the same sheet of music so that the first meeting won't be a "discordant cacophony of competing scores."

Successful club orientation is not very different from the orientation new employees receive. Like new employees who have been through interviews and have researched their new employer, new board and committee members may have some idea of what they're getting into. After all, they've probably been club members for some time. However, without adequate orientation, the new board and committee members will lack the essential knowledge of what the club's mission is and what role they are to play in fulfilling that mission.

The upfront attention of an orientation can well determine whether the board or committee is a productive, energetic one that contributes to the success of the club, or one that merely meets according to schedule and carries out only the status quo.

Orientations Vary Among Clubs

There is almost as much variety in types of club orientations as there is in types of clubs. An orientation session may be a formal session involving from two to twenty people, or may be an informal session between a long-standing board or committee member and the newcomer. Programs can last from 15 minutes to several hours and can even be spread out over several weeks.

According to successful club orientation planners, the best orientation program must meet the unique needs of the club. The message communicated to new members during orientation sessions will be the unique message of a particular club. It will speak of the personality, the mission, and the objectives of the club, its boards, and its committees. The orientation session can range from a short, restrained meeting, to a glitzy, multimedia presentation. However it is done, new members should walk away with a clear vision of their role and their responsibilities.

Board and Committee Orientation — Is It Really Necessary?

Successful orientations can nourish the excitement new board and committee members bring with them to the first day of their term. When done well, orientations can also accomplish several other objectives.

Orientation experts most frequently cite these five objectives to orientation:

- Bring new members up to speed
- Build loyalty and enthusiasm
- Communicate the club's mission
- Teach policies and procedures
- Introduce formal and informal networks

This section will discuss each of these primary objectives in detail.

If orientations are not held, new board and committee members could find themselves in a threatening, suddenly unfamiliar environment. The following is a situation all clubs want to avoid:

Peter Johnson Joins the Board

Peter Johnson was excited about his first board meeting. Peter had been a member of Centercity Country Club for 10 years and had become a board member the previous week. He showed up at 5:45 p.m. and found everyone already seated and going over the previous meeting's minutes.

After taking a seat next to a golf partner, he whispered, "I thought the meeting started at 6 p.m."

His partner raised an eyebrow and whispered back, "It does, but we always wrap up old business before the meeting starts — and you'll want to go sit in that chair at the far end of the table. All new members sit there until they get up to speed on things."

Peter uncomfortably picked up his notepad and membership manual and shuffled to the chair at the end of the table.

However, his enthusiasm soon waxed again as the board began to discuss making the new dining room accessible to people with disabilities. Peter had recently renovated his business to meet the requirements of the Americans with Disabilities Act and had a lot of ideas on the topic. After getting the attention of the president, Peter spoke up, "We should remember to make all areas of our formal dining room accessible to individuals who use wheelchairs. Building a ramp to the upper level of seating should be considered."

Peter's voice trailed off as he noticed his long-time friends on the board shifting uncomfortably. The president waved his hand impatiently, "Thank you, Peter, but we already discussed that option at some length last quarter. It's been referred to committee. Perhaps you can tell us more when the report is ready, but for now, we really need to stay on schedule."

Peter stayed silent for the rest of the meeting, except to cast his votes where required. When the next board meeting came up, Peter remained quiet, commenting only when he was called on.

Peter, a longtime, loyal club member, thought he knew everything he needed to know to be a board member — and no one told him otherwise.

A successful orientation would have told Peter what meeting procedures were, what the major issues under consideration were, and what actions had already been taken. If Centercity Country Club had taken the time to orient Peter to the board, the club would probably still have an enthusiastic board member. Now, they'll be lucky if Peter performs any but the most perfunctory of membership duties.

Orient to Bring New Members Up to Speed

One of the primary reasons to hold orientations is to make sure new board and committee members are able to make immediate contributions.

An effective orientation session will let new members know what to expect in the first meeting so that they can come prepared and ready to participate. It will also help prevent new members from covering issues the board has already closed on.

Orientations sessions can bring new members up to speed by giving them minutes of meetings for the past year, by briefing them on major issues, and by answering their questions.

Orient to Build Loyalty and Enthusiasm

An orientation session can show new board or committee members that they are important. The club is really saying that it is willing to invest time and effort into these new board or committee members.

When new board or committee members see that the current members are willing to invest in them, then the new members will be eager to invest more time and show more commitment to the board or committee.

Orient to Communicate the Club's Mission

Every board and committee has a purpose. Even if a board or committee does not have a written mission statement, there should still be clear-cut responsibilities that it fulfills.

It can be risky to assume that just because someone applied for a position on a committee or the board that he or she understands its mission. The new member may have a very different concept of the goals and responsibilities of the body. For example, a new member on a golf committee may think it is part of his or her job to correct the caddy who arrives improperly groomed. Board and committee leaders can use the orientation session to communicate the difference between governing and managing, and, thereby, head off many uncomfortable situations.

Many GMs/COOs say the most important thing they want to accomplish in an orientation is to help new members understand what they are and are *not* responsible for. An orientation can be the ideal time to bring up specific examples of recent board or committee actions and to explain which were appropriate and which were not appropriate.

The orientation is also a time to share with new members any confidential information that they probably wouldn't have had access to as a regular members but will need to know to govern effectively. This may include an explanation of membership selection or a list of delinquent member accounts. Whatever information is needed, an orientation session can provide a sensitive environment to share sensitive information.

Orient to Teach Policies and Procedures

Like an employee orientation, a board or committee member orientation should cover policies and procedures that new members need to know. At the orientation a president or committee chair can say whether members should submit agenda items before the meeting, can discuss how he or she conducts meetings, or can review the club bylaws.

The orientation is also an opportunity to acquaint new members with the legal duties of the club and of the governing body. The issue of board and committee liability is a growing one and one that members should understand upfront. Orientation sessions can let members know not only what their liability is, but also what actions they can take to avoid liability.

Members should be informed of liability insurance that the club holds to protect officers and directors and what that coverage includes and does not include.

This can also be an appropriate time to spell out the duties members must fulfill to avoid liability. While these duties vary from state to state, they usually include:

- *Duty of Care:* Board members must take the same precautions that an "ordinarily prudent" person would take.
- *Duty of Loyalty (or Good Faith):* Board members must put the interests of the board ahead of their own personal interests.
- *Duty of Obedience:* Board members must remain faithful to the mission of the club.

A good resource for developing information on common duties is *The Legal Obligations of Nonprofit Boards: A Guidebook for Board Members* by Jacqueline Covey Leifer and Michael B. Glomb, published by the National Center for Nonprofit Boards. (See the Additional Resources at the end of this issue.)

Most new board and committee members become familiar with the club's major policies when they first join. However, they may not understand the reasoning behind the policies. The orientation session can be an opportunity to explain this reasoning. There also may be issues surrounding these policies that the board is dealing with on an ongoing basis. New members should be made aware of these issues and told which issues have the highest priority.

Orient to Introduce Informal and Formal Networks

The most valuable resource to new board or committee members is often the informal contacts they make throughout the club. The orientation can help introduce them to all the board and committee members and to the officers of each group. It can also introduce them to the club staff employees and managers.

One GM/COO said the orientation is especially important because the members then learn to use him as a resource person throughout their term. He uses the orientation period as a time to provide the new members all the information they need and to become a partner with each of them.

Other important, more formal resources to introduce new members to are professional associations such as the Club Managers Association of America (CMAA) that provide information, materials, and services to clubs. For example, the services provided by CMAA range from professional development opportunities for management to the Club Issues Forum where directors and managers are able to meet together to obtain and discuss information critical to the operation of private clubs.

Who Conducts Orientation?

There are no set rules about the best person to conduct orientation. At some clubs, the manager is the only person who participates in orientation, at others a panel of officers or staff may participate.

What is most important is that the person conducting the orientation has planned for it and is able to answer whatever questions the new board or committee members might ask. Later sections in this issue contain tips for planning and conducting an orientation.

Many people find that the most effective orientations are those that involve several people. Each person involved can bring his or her unique perspectives to the new members. Also, having several short presentations by different people can usually keep a new member's attention longer than having one person make one long presentation.

The orientation may include individuals such as:

- GM/COO
- Club attorney
- Club board president
- Other board members
- Other staff members

For example, a pro shop committee orientation may include the golf pro or pro shop manager. Traditionally, however, the major roles in orientation are taken by the board president or committee chairman, board or committee members, and the GM/COO.

Role of Board President or Committee Chair

The job of the board president or committee chairman begins before the formal orientation session. As soon as a new board or committee member is named to his or her position, the board president or committee chairman should send a letter welcoming the new member to the position and inviting him or her to the orientation session. The letter should also explain how the board president or committee chair can be reached whenever the member has questions or information.

Participation by the club board president or committee chairman in the orientation session can pave the way for future cooperation. Those who chair meetings have their own standards, methods, and quirks. Orientation gives the club board president or committee chairman the opportunity to communicate the way he or she does business.

It is also important that the board president or committee chair follow up with a phone call or letter to new members after the orientation session. There is often so much information presented during the session it may take a few days for new members to formulate questions about what they have learned.

Role of Board or Committee Members

While current board and committee members rarely take a formal role in most board and committee orientations, they nonetheless play important informal roles. It is their collective knowledge, skills, and experience that make the board or committee effective. It is their support and assistance that will help new board and committee members take an active part in future proceedings.

Whenever possible and convenient, new members should be introduced to the current members during the orientation period. The introduction should go beyond names and

Figure 1: Introductions

Sample Board Member Introductions

"I'm Trevor Carrington. I've been on the club's board for two terms now. This year, I'm chairing the membership commitee, but I've also chaired the pension committee and the wine committee. I'm a third generation club member; my grandfather joined this club right after World War I. Personally, I've watched it grow from a 20-man smoking circle when I was a child to the luxurious athletic and dining facility that it is today. When I'm not at the club or at home, I'm managing the business accounts for a statewide transportation company."

• • •

"Welcome to the Board! I'm Ryanne McPherson, chairwoman of the house committee. When I was first invited to join the club six years ago, I was somewhat nervous about being the first female full member. However, I was welcomed so warmly by everyone here that I knew I had to give back to this wonderful organization. Although being CEO of a local employment agency takes up a good deal of my time, I've always found the work here to be enjoyable and rewarding. I'd be happy to explain more about the major projects of the house committee."

---

titles. Encourage current board or committee members to give a short biography that emphasizes their strengths and what perspective they bring to the board or committee. (See Figure 1: Introductions.)

Board and committee members should reach out to new members as much as possible. Frequently, the best source of information about the workings of the governing body can come from a peer. At some clubs, an experienced member may be asked to "adopt" (or mentor) a new member for the first year of the new member's tenure.

Role of GM/COO

The bulk of planning and conducting the orientation usually falls to the GM/COO since he or she is frequently the person with the most intimate knowledge of the workings of the club and its boards and committees. This expertise makes the GM/COO the ideal person to conduct orientations and to establish an orientation program format that can then be followed each year.

The first step is planning the orientation. The GM/COO may have a set agenda or outline that he or she uses each year. One GM/COO said computers have helped him produce a consistent, but snazzy orientation each year. He stores most materials on disk, updating them as members or rules change. He is then able to print out a customized handbook for each member. This helps to ensure that everyone gets basically the same information from year to year.

A key decision that must be made early on is where the orientation session will be held. The GM/COO and president may decide to hold it on-premises or off-premises. Holding it on-premises allows the session to include a tour of the facilities, it also provides easy access to additional resource material. However, holding the session off-premises may provide a more comfortable environment for the new member. At a different site, everyone is more relaxed and there may be fewer interruptions or barriers to communication.

As mentioned, the GM/COO frequently schedules and sets up the orientation. If it is a group session, it may mean coordinating the schedules of everyone involved. The manager will also need to make sure that all materials and equipment needed for the orientation are in place.

Format of an Orientation

Orientations, as noted earlier, can take several different formats. The format often depends on the size of the board or committee, how frequently it meets, how many new members are being inducted, and what the style of the board or committee is.

The type and amount of information that needs to be passed along will also dictate the activities planned for an orientation. An orientation planner should select the most effective techniques and activities to communicate the club's board or committee needs.

Orientations, no matter their format, should always be time-efficient, effective, and useful. Whenever possible, they should also be entertaining. Plan carefully to make sure the orientation meets these objectives. The following sections can help determine what will work best for a club's orientation.

Types of Orientations

When developing an orientation program, decide early just what type of orientation is desired and how many people are going to be involved in it.

It is not uncommon for orientation types to vary from year to year depending on the person who does the orienting. Just as every club has its own style, every board president or committee chair has his or her own style. One may place a high priority on orientations while another may not have the time to make it a high priority.

Some common orientation types include:

- Group sessions
- Individual sessions
- Self-orientation
- Mentor sessions

Each orientation type has its advantages and disadvantages depending on the club's circumstances. (See Figure 2: Types of Orientation.) There may even be times when orientation planner will want to use more than one type of orientation.

Group Sessions

A group orientation brings all the new members together at the same time, and the orientation planner will conduct any orientation activities at the same time for all new members. Usually group sessions are very structured and new members are given a schedule of speakers and how long each activity will last.

Group sessions are one of the most common methods of orientation because they are time-efficient. The people conducting the orientation session have to present the material only once.

Figure 2: Types of Orientation

Type of Orientation	Description	Advantages	Disadvantages
Group session	Two or more new members are oriented at the same time.	• Saves time for the manager, the president, etc. • Helps new members form a team. • Provides consistency for all new members.	• Can be difficult to schedule. • Provides little individual attention. • May not answer questions of all members.
Individual session	The president or GM/COO meets individually with the new member to conduct orientations.	• New member can set the pace of the orientation. • Easy to schedule. • Gives individualized information to each new member.	• Can be time-consuming for the presenter if there are a lot of people who must be oriented. • Does not ensure that all new members receive the same information.
Self-orientation	The club president mails the orientation material to the new member and tells the new member to call if there are questions.	• Saves time for those conducting the orientation. • Allows new member to set the pace of his or her learning. • Opens a door for communication between president and new member	• Does not provide for any face-to-face question and answer period. • No one is able to explain especially complex or sensitive issues unless member asks about them. • Can leave the new member feeling slightly insecure.
Mentor sessions	An experienced board or committee member is paired with the new member and helps the new member learn whatever is necessary.	• Starts an ongoing relationship that can be beneficial to both parties. • Gives the new member ongoing support throughout the entire term. • Helps experienced member brush up on skills and knowledge.	• Orientations lack consistency. • Quality of orientation depends upon the mentor selected. • Time consuming on the part of the mentor and the new member.

The preparation time is reduced, as is the presentation time. For clubs that involve several people in conducting orientations, it means only having to coordinate their schedules once.

Another advantage of the group session format is that it gives new members a chance to meet each other. They can immediately begin to form a team and start working together. They can even help answer each other's questions and share common concerns. This can also help new members feel more secure at their first board or committee meeting.

Group sessions also help orientation planners ensure that all new members receive the same information. Because everyone is together at the same time, question and answer sessions can benefit all members, not just the person who asked the question.

Unfortunately, group sessions can be difficult to schedule. Club members are usually busy people. The person planning the orientation is faced with the unenviable job of coordinating several schedules of several very busy people. However, most people who have made a commitment to serve on a board or committee are willing to set aside the time in order to get themselves up to speed.

By definition, group sessions cannot provide the same degree of individual attention that other orientation types might. A group session cannot be tailored to the individual needs of each new member. The person conducting the orientation must assume that the participants don't know much about the board or committee and he or she must cover all the information needed.

More than one club solves the problem of group sessions not being able to provide individualized information by breaking the orientation into two meetings. The first meeting is a general session for all new members. The second meeting is for specific committees; for example, the golf and dining room committees hold separate orientation sessions.

Depending on the size of the group, there may not be time for everyone to ask all the questions that they have. Likewise, some members may be too embarrassed to ask questions in a group setting. In these instances, it is essential that there are good follow-up measures to answer questions.

Individual Sessions

Individual sessions may be the only option for clubs or committees that have only one new member each year. These sessions involve the new member meeting with the club president, committee chairperson, GM/COO, or any combination of those people. Typically the person conducting the orientation will hand out materials before or at the session and then discuss this information. New members can be encouraged to ask questions and the length of the session can be flexible enough to cover the materials and answer all questions.

Individual sessions can be very comfortable for the new member. He or she can set the pace of the meeting. The person conducting the orientation can then skip topics of which the member already has a good working knowledge and spend more time on information about which the new member seems confused or uncertain. If a new member has very little time available, the person conducting the orientation can go through the material very quickly.

The person conducting the orientation will probably find it much easier to schedule a session for one person than for many. He or she also has more flexibility as to where and when the orientation will take place. When only one person needs an orientation, it is much easier to schedule a meeting off-site, or in a club office, or over a meal.

Another advantage to individual orientations is that the club can provide personalized information to the new member. This is especially useful for committee orientations. There may be specific information that a swimming committee member needs to know that the house committee member does not.

Individual sessions can, however, be very taxing on the time of the person conducting the orientation. If there are several new members, the person conducting the orientation must then schedule several sessions of indeterminate length. It is often difficult to set a time limit on individual sessions. The person conducting the orientation cannot be sure whether the session will take fifteen minutes or three hours, and this can make scheduling especially difficult.

Another problem is that there is no guarantee that all new members are receiving the same information. Someone, for example, who has conducted several orientations may find that what he or she covered with the first new member may have been unintentionally overlooked with the next new member.

Self-Orientation

In self-orientation, the club provides new members with orientation material and a cover letter that refers them to the committee chair or board president for the answers to any questions on the material. A club that uses self-orientation typically has developed an orientation resource guide that covers the most important information. Because of the way the guide is used it must be written very clearly and must be self-explanatory.

Self-orientation can be the most time-effective way to conduct orientations for everyone involved. After the material has been compiled, there is very little that a board president, committee chairman, or GM/COO has to do. New members are able to pace their own orientation and learn the information in amounts that they are most comfortable with.

This method can also open a communication pathway between the board president or committee chair and the new members. This is especially true if the cover letter that goes out with the material is personalized. The new members are made aware that the governing body leaders will make themselves available to answer questions or listen to concerns.

Self-orientation does have some shortcomings. Because there is no face-to-face question and answer period, the new members may leave some questions unasked, feeling perhaps, that the question is too insignificant to interrupt another person's workday. There is also a danger that the members will assume that they understand something, only to be surprised later when they discover they have misinterpreted it.

In club governance, there are some issues that may be too sensitive to include in a written orientation package. While it is important for the member to understand the issue, a club may rightfully feel uncomfortable about sending such written information out without knowing that it will reach and remain only in the proper hands. Part of this danger can be alleviated by hand-delivering all orientation materials, but it does not always provide a full solution. Some sensitive issues may best be handled in confidential face-to-face conversations.

If a club has extensive orientation material, the volume can sap the enthusiasm of members suddenly confronted with hours of study. New members simply may not take the time to study carefully the orientation materials provided.

Mentor Sessions

Mentoring (making use of a trusted, experienced adviser) is growing in popularity in the workplace and in the general community. It is widely becoming recognized as a personalized way to communicate information, standards, and values to new board members.

Clubs that use mentors for orientation typically pair a more experienced member with an incoming member. The experienced member receives all of the orientation material and then shares it with the new member, also known as a "protege." Usually this relationship will continue through either the first year or the first term of the new member. The mentor is available on an ongoing basis to answer questions and follow up with other concerns the new member may have.

One of the reasons mentoring relationships are so popular is that both parties reap many benefits. The mentor and protege form a team and can learn from each other. The relationship can continue for as long as both parties need it to. Unlike traditional orientations, the assistance does not end after one session.

New members frequently find that they have additional questions a few days after the orientation session — after they've had time to absorb all of the new information. Mentoring relationships provide a built-in follow-up for members. The ongoing nature of the support also encourages new members to continue to think about the information presented so that they *will* have questions for their next session with their mentors.

The experienced member is also challenged and must stay up-to-date on new information and skills. Since the mentor is now a role model, he or she must uphold the standards that the board or committee expects. This can also motivate a long-serving board member whose initial enthusiasm is ebbing. And this newfound enthusiasm is often contagious for the new member.

Like individual orientations, mentoring sessions can lack consistency. Because there are a number of different mentors, each one is going to present the orientation material differently. There is little guarantee that the mentor has efficiently covered everything that needed to be covered.

Likewise, the quality of an orientation session rests solely on the shoulders of the mentor. If he or she is not particularly excited or committed to being a mentor, the orientation of the new member can suffer. The club board or committee must be very careful in selecting mentors to make certain that the mentor understands everything he or she needs to understand and that the mentor will be compatible with the protege.

Mentors and proteges must both be prepared to make the time investment that this type of relationship demands. Unlike the one or two sessions of the other types of orientations, mentoring is a long-term commitment requiring that both participants be available to each other.

Mentoring can also be effective when combined with other types of orientation. For example, mentoring can make an excellent follow-up to a group orientation. Combining types can give help reduce the short-comings of one type of orientation while greatly increasing the benefits.

Orientation Activities

Once the type of orientation that works best for the club is chosen, the orientation planner will need to decide which activities to include. Orientations can be as simple as a one-on-one discussion or as elaborate as a multimedia presentation with a panel discussion afterwards.

Some common activities to include in an orientation are:

- Tour of club
- Discussion/overview session
- Meal
- Slides or media presentation
- Panel discussions
- Distribution of printed material
- Question/answer session
- Board or committee meeting
- Follow-up actions

Each of these activities are discussed in more detail below.

Tour of Club

Even though the new board or committee members have probably spent several years in the club, that doesn't preclude a tour. The new members may find themselves looking at the club with new eyes — eyes that are now seeing something they are responsible for. Also, they may have never seen back-of-the house areas before.

During the tour, the person conducting the orientation can introduce new members to club staff members that they might be working with. The tour can also highlight areas of responsibility and illustrate the importance of the duties the new members have taken on.

Discussion/Overview Session

A discussion/overview session allows the person conducting the orientations to go over the mission, standards, and operating procedures of the board or committee. The intimacy of the discussion setting can also provide a safe environment for airing sensitive issues dealing with club governance.

Discussion sessions can vary in length from several minutes to several hours. It is very important that the person conducting the orientation have a detailed outline of what items need to be covered.

Meal

Throughout the ages, people have come together for fellowship over food. Eating a meal with someone can be the perfect icebreaker to begin developing professional relationships that can benefit all parties and ultimately produce better governance.

The meal included with the orientation can range from a small luncheon to an elegant banquet. Whatever the style of the meal, it will provide an opportunity for the new members and the people conducting the orientation to get to know each other better and to ask more informal questions.

However, the orientation planner probably does not want to make the meal the only activity in the orientation. The meal is not the most efficient or effective setting for reviewing printed material.

Media Presentations

Some clubs choose to present their board or committees in action. Media presentations can include video clips, slides, overhead transparencies, photographs and charts. The presentation can show the history of the club including interviews with past presidents along with previous activities and functions. The presentation can also illustrate the current financial status of the club and membership statistics. It can also present plans for expansion and renovation.

Clubs frequently design these presentations not just to be informative, but to inspire and motivate. A presentation can ground the new member in the roots of the club's history while vividly displaying how the club plans to grow in the future.

Panel Discussions

Panel discussions allow several people be involved in conducting the orientation in an organized and time-efficient manner. New members are able to listen to presentations from several people and then ask questions.

A typical panel might include the GM/COO, the board president, a committee chair, and the club attorney. Each person is usually given 10 to 15 minutes to discuss his or her area of expertise. During the question-and-answer session, new members can direct their questions to the person with the most knowledge in a particular area. The major advantage of this activity is that the subject-matter expert can directly answer most questions, and the panel reduces the amount of second-hand information.

Distribution of Printed Materials

The distribution of printed materials should be a key part of any orientation, whether it happens before, during, or after a formal presentation. At some clubs, distributing printed materials is the *only* orientation activity and while it is not ideal, it has been effective for some clubs.

The printed materials distributed might include an agenda for the orientation or a binder complete with mission statement, sample forms, calendars, etc. (See page 15 for more information about orientation materials and what should be included.)

Question/Answer Session

Giving the new members an opportunity to ask questions and get their individual questions answered is a critical activity for any orientation. When planning an orientation, there should always be time set aside for new members to ask questions. Without this time, the person conducting the orientation can only guess at whether the new member received and understood the information presented.

Though extremely important, the question/answer period does not have to be a formal, separate session. In fact, the most effective method can be to allot each orientation activity a time for questions and then to encourage new members to ask questions throughout the orientation period.

Board or Committee Meeting

While clubs do not want new members attending board or committee meetings before their orientation, orientation planners may schedule the orientation session immediately prior to such a meeting. New members can then immediately see the reality of things that were discussed during the orientation.

Whenever the first meeting is, allot time to introduce the new members to the current board or committee. Encourage current board or committee members to provide more than a name and title. They should provide a short biography of themselves, including which committees they've served on, their business or profession, and their particular interests and areas of expertise.

Follow Up Actions

While some board or committee members will need no further information after a thorough orientation, others will still have questions. The volume of new information presented during orientation can be overwhelming. After a few days, the new members usually have a much better grasp of the information. Even if new members don't have questions, following up with them can reinforce the idea that the board or committee leaders are there to support new members throughout their term.

One GM/COO conducts orientations for new board members on the Saturday before the first board meeting. During this orientation, he provides a board operations manual and reviews the information in it. The following Tuesday or Wednesday he calls the new members at their offices to ask if they have any further questions or if any of the information they received was unclear. By then, members have had a chance to read through all the material and have additional items to discuss.

Setting an Agenda

Once the orientation planner has determined the format of and activities for the orientation, he or she should write an agenda. This agenda can be used in future years by making minor changes in dates and times. (See Figure 3: Sample Agenda.)

Moreover, a well-planned agenda will make sure that the orientation planner covers all necessary information and has sufficient time for each of the planned activities. A printed agenda communicates to all participants in the orientation what to expect and what their role will be.

Orientation Materials

All new board or committee members should receive a manual containing the job descriptions of their positions and the resources they need to carry out their duties. This

Figure 3: Sample Agenda

City Club Orientation Agenda

9:00 a.m.	Welcome to all four new board members
	Peter Vinmore Joshua Seals Curtis Arbuckle Jamin Fords
9:10 a.m.	Show orientation video
9:30 a.m.	Tour of City Club/Introduction to staff
10:15 a.m.	Presentation by Board President Duke Yarl (club mission, meeting procedures and major issues)
10:30 a.m.	Presentation by GM/COO Diana Sanders (management philosophy, club rules and policies)
10:45 a.m.	Presentation by Treasurer Cass Peters (review financial statements)
11:15 a.m.	Break for lunch
12:30 p.m.	Presentation by Club Attorney Felicia Venn (liability insurance)
12:45 p.m.	Questions and answers
1:45 p.m.	Break
2:00 p.m.	Begin board meeting

manual will not only help with their initial orientation, but will also continue to be a valuable resource throughout their term.

Format of Materials

The amount and type of orientation material will determine its packaging. The orientation planner will want to choose packaging that is the most useful and convenient for the new board or committee members.

Three common formats for orientation materials include:

- File or pocket folders
- Three-ring binders
- Multiple binders

File or pocket folders are ideal if the club has very little material to distribute. They are easy to file and can fit easily into a briefcase. The club's logo and name may be printed on the folders.

Three-ring binders are a common way to distribute orientation materials. The binders can be stored on a bookshelf and readily accessed. Also, it is easy for a board president,

Figure 4: Orientation Material Checklist

Sample Resources

- ☐ Organization chart
- ☐ Mission statement
- ☐ Job descriptions
- ☐ Definition of responsibilities
- ☐ Club bylaws and articles of incorporation
- ☐ Club rules
- ☐ Club policies and procedures
- ☐ Club financial information
- ☐ Minutes of previous year's meetings
- ☐ Pending issues
- ☐ Calendar of events and meetings
- ☐ Names and biographies of board or committee
- ☐ Names of all committees and chairs
- ☐ Director's and officer's insurance information

- ☐ Meeting procedures and customs
- ☐ Club history
- ☐ Applicable state laws
- ☐ List of resources (CMAA, PGA, NGF, etc.)
- ☐ GM/COO responsibilities
- ☐ Guidelines for conducting effective meetings
- ☐ Sample forms
- ☐ Current news releases
- ☐ Long-range plans
- ☐ Conflict of interest policy
- ☐ Other:
- ☐
- ☐

---

committee chair, or GM/COO to update the binder with current information. Likewise, the members can add their own notes throughout their terms.

Some clubs use a two-binder approach to orientation material. The first binder contains resource materials such as the minutes of board or committee meetings of previous years, prior financial statements, liability insurance information, etc. The second binder should be brought to every board or committee meeting. It contains the documents that members on an ongoing basis such as purchase orders, club financial information, and names of all board and committee members.

Judith Grumman Nelson in *Six Keys to Recruiting, Orienting, and Involving Nonprofit Board Members* has suggestions for additional information that may be included in orientation materials. (See the list of resources at the end of this issue to find this and other books and pamphlets.)

Materials for New Members

Deciding what will be included in the orientation materials can be almost as time-consuming as gathering the materials. Figure 4 gives a sample checklist of materials that are commonly used in orientations. The orientation planner may want to customize the list to fit the needs of his or her club.

The following pages describe some of the materials that should be included in an orientation manual. However, each club will have its own priorities and each orientation manual will be unique. It is up to the orientation planner to decide what needs to be included and how it should be presented.

One GM/COO stresses the importance of giving members an opportunity to read the materials on their own. "We don't read (the materials) to them. We treat them as adults." Board and committee members are highly successful individuals. They will appreciate the information without the orientation planner reviewing or analyzing details for them.

Figure 5: Sample Club Organization Chart

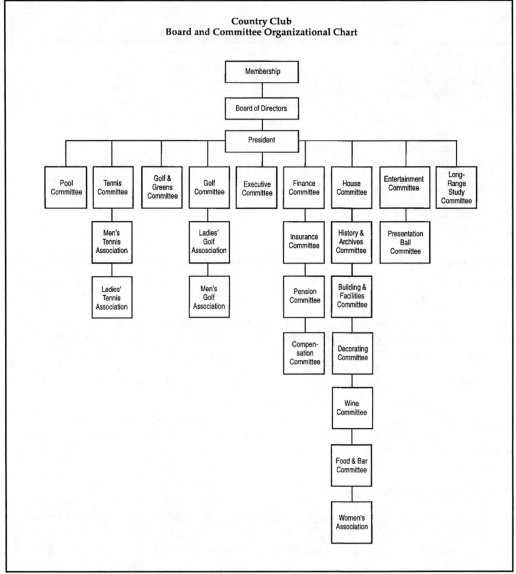

Source: "Club Operations Manual" CMAA.

Organization Chart

There are two main types of organization charts that clubs use and that are helpful in an orientation program. The first is an organization chart of the governing board. It starts with the members at the top and maps their relationship with the nominating committee, club board, president, officers, and each committee. (See Figure 5: Sample Club Organization

Figure 6: Sample Mission Statements

Board Mission Statement

The Board of Directors of _____ Country Club governs the strategic decisions of the _____ Country Club to provide each member the highest quality social and recreational experience.

House Committee Mission Statement

The House Committee is committed to providing the _____ Country Club Board of Directors with the best resources, information and recommendations concerning house matters.

Chart.) The second chart is an organization chart of the club staff. Some clubs combine these two charts to show the relationship of the governing body to the club staff.

Both charts can provide useful information for a new board or committee member. An organization chart can help new members understand immediately where they fit into club governance. It also visually represents their relationship to others within the club. Organization charts can be especially useful if they include the names of the people currently in each position. Many individuals with successful orientation programs say the organization chart is an essential component of their orientation materials.

Club's Mission Statement

There is a danger in orientations that the board president, committee chair, or GM/COO will inundate the new member with procedural information and only briefly mention the board or committee's role and mission. Making the mission statement a major part of the orientation can help keep the new members — and the entire board or committee — on track.

The Portable MBA Desk Reference defines mission statement in the following way:

> A short statement of the central purposes, strategies, and values of a company. Essentially, a company's mission statement should answer the question, "What business are we in?" A good mission statement should go beyond the obvious and deal with a number of issues that are vital to the company. They include the company's purpose...strategy...and values. (Paul A. Argenti, *The Portable MBA Desk Reference,* John Wiley & Sons, Inc. New York, 1994, page 282.)

The mission statement defines the role of the board or committee as a governing agent. When reviewing the mission statement, the person conducting the orientation can stress the difference between governing and managing and show how governing fulfills the club's mission. (See Figure 6: Sample Mission Statements.)

Definition of Responsibilities

New members often find a definition of their new responsibilities to be helpful. This definition can clearly illustrate exactly what the expectations are for board and committee members and what role they will play in governing the club.

Board and committee job descriptions are one way to define responsibilities. Other ways include more general statements about the duties of every member.

Club Bylaws and Articles of Incorporation

While most club members receive bylaws when they first join the club, these bylaws take on new meaning for board and committee members. Now the board and committee members are responsible for enforcing and evaluating these bylaws. The articles of incorporation have similar importance for board and committee members. This document can become key to their understanding of the mission and policies of the club.

These two basic documents form the groundwork for all of the club's governing actions. Even if they aren't immediately read, board and committee members need to have them as a reference.

Club Rules, Policies and Procedures

Club rules, policies, and procedures are important resources for the new board or committee member. The new members are now responsible for seeing that club rules, policies, and procedures are implemented. They will have to meet a higher standard in upholding them and will be expected to understand and explain them.

Club Financial Information

There are many financial documents that boards and committees use on a regular basis. It is important that new members be familiar with these documents and know how they can be used and interpreted to determine the current financial status of the club.

Financial information the orientation planner may include:

- Operating budgets
- Capital appropriation requests
- Capital budgets
- Statement of income and expense

Minutes of Board and Committee Meetings

Giving new members last year's minutes allows them to see which issues have been addressed, what steps have been taken, and who is responsible for each issue.

Also, the minutes give new members an idea of the kinds of issues they'll face and a feel for the club's philosophy regarding certain issues.

Pending Issues

New board and committee members need to know what issues are on the current and future agendas so that they will be prepared when these issues are discussed. Orientation materials may list the general issue or explain it in detail.

Calendar of Events

Calendars, while one of the most practical items in orientation materials, are frequently forgotten by orientation planners. If the same manual is used from year to year, the calendar must be updated — making it more time-consuming than the other items in the manual.

Nonetheless, new members will keep the orientation materials they receive, which is why it is the most logical place to put a calendar of events, meetings, schedules, etc.

Names and Biographies of Board Members

Orientation materials should contain the name and a short biography of each board member — whether the manual is for a new board member or a new committee member. If available, a picture may be included with each biography. This should help new members place names and faces with those they met during orientation, especially if the club is very large.

Names of All Committees and Chairs

While the organization chart may contain the names of all committees and committee chairs, this list should also outline areas of responsibility for each committee. For instance, it may list Rodney Jones as the chair of the entertainment committee, and state that the entertainment committee is responsible for overseeing the planning of major club social activities and for encouraging member participation in these activities.

Director's and Officer's Insurance

In a litigious society, all board and committee members have to be concerned about their personal liability. The orientation materials should provide information about the Director's and Officer's (D&O) insurance that is available for them and include its limits, loss coverage, etc. The orientation planner may also explain the difference between D&O insurance and liability insurance. D&O insurance does not cover liability for injuries or property damage done by a board member. For more information about liability vs. D&O insurance, see *The Jossey-Bass Handbook of Nonprofit Leadership and Management*, listed at the back of this issue.

Meeting Procedures and Customs

If specific meeting procedures and customs apply, these should be provided in the orientation materials. Specific information regarding expectations on participation and attendance at meetings is critical.

Club History

An important part of orientation is giving the new members a sense of ownership. This sense of ownership can be reinforced by showing them the history of the club and the tradition upon which they are to build.

Implementation Plan

Once the orientation planner has determined who will be involved in orientations, the fomat of the orientation, the activities to include, and the materials to distribute, then he or she must implement the orientation plan.

There are six basic steps to conducting an orientation:

- Setting orientation objectives
- Delivering orientation materials
- Planning the agenda
- Informing the involved parties
- Conducting the orientation
- Following up with new members

Each step has a subset of tasks. Using a checklist can help the orientation planner through each step. See Figure 7: Orientation Implementation Checklist to help prepare for orientations.

Making the Effort Pay Off

With all the time and effort it takes to plan and implement an effective orientation, is it worth it? Can the club be certain it isn't wasting the time of everyone involved?

Peter Tries Again

It has been several years since Peter's first term on the board of Centercity Country Club. He has been asked by the current president to complete the remaining term of a board member who has moved out of town.

The day after Peter is appointed, the board president, Harold, calls him, "Peter, I'm really glad you're on board. We're looking forward to an exciting year. CCC has a lot of fine projects planned, and I think you'll be able to contribute a lot to them."

Harold then invites Peter to an orientation meeting with himself and the GM/COO, Jose. Peter is happy to accept the invitation. About a week before the orientation meeting, Peter receives a board manual with the club bylaws, mission statement, organizational chart, and a variety of financial statements. It also, he's pleased to notice, contains minutes of the previous year's meetings and a listing of all the current issues before the board.

At the orientation meeting, the president and manager review important parts of the manual. Over lunch, they fill Peter in on some of the traditions of board meetings that aren't written in the manual. They also give him a directory of the other board members and tell him about their strengths and special interests.

At the end of the meeting, Jose tells Peter, "If you have any questions at all, now or any time during your term, please feel free to call me here at the club. I also hear you're quite the expert on accessibility issues; I'd like to be able to contact you about some of the renovations we're doing to the pro shop. Would that be all right?"

Peter gladly agrees and tells the manager and the president he will see them at next month's meeting. "You know, I think I'm going to like being on the board this time," Peter smiled to himself as he left the club. At the conclusion of a successful orientation, the club will have board members who understand how the board or committee works and who are ethusiastic about the role they will play in governing the club. The club will have created clear expectations for the new board members.

Figure 7: Orientation Implementation Checklist

Sample Orientation Planner

Setting Orientation Objectives

____ Write clear, measurable objectives for the orientation session
____ Compare objectives to previous years' objectives
____ Review materials to make sure they meet objectives
____ Update materials to reflect objectives

Delivering Materials

____ Send a welcoming letter to the new member
____ Compile all necessary materials (See Figure 4: Orientation Materials Checklist)
____ Mail or hand-deliver materials to new members

Planning the Agenda

____ Set a date (or dates) for the orientation session or sessions
____ List each orientation activity
     ____ Tour of club
     ____ Discussion/Overview session
     ____ Meal
     ____ Slides or media presentation
     ____ Panel discussions
     ____ Distribution of printed material
     ____ Question/Answer session
     ____ Board meeting
     ____ Other:
____ Assign a time to each activity
____ Prepare agenda and make copies

Informing the Involved Parties

____ Call or write individuals making presentations during the orientation
     ____ GM/COO
     ____ Board president
     ____ Committee chairman
     ____ Experienced board or committee member
     ____ Club attorney
     ____ Club controller
     ____ Other:
____ Call or write all new board or committee members
____ Schedule use of the room where orientation will be conducted, if necessary

Conducting the Orientation

____ Arrive at the orientation site early
____ Bring all necessary materials
____ Distribute the agenda
____ Begin on time

Following Up With New Members

____ Call a few days after the first orientation session
____ Call after the first board or committee meeting
____ Call a few months into the new member's term

By investing the time and hard work into an effective orientation the club will make an investment that will greatly benefit the new members, the board or committee, and the entire club.

ACKNOWLEDGEMENTS

The following individuals generously donated their expertise and time to make this issue possible:

Mr. Hardy Croom III, CCM
Mr. John Jordan, CCM
Mr. Willmoore M. "Bill" Kendall, CCM
Mr. C. Doug Postler, CCM

Additional Resources:

Judith Grummon Nelson, *Six Keys to Recruiting, Orienting, and Involving Nonprofit Board Members — A Guide to Building Your Board* National Center for Nonprofit Boards, Washington D.C., 1991.

Robert D. Herman & Associates, *The Jossey-Bass Handbook of Nonprofit Leadership and Management* Jossey-Bass, Inc. Publishers, California, 1994.

Cyril O. Houle, *Governing Boards,* Jossey-Bass, Inc. Publishers, California, 1989

John Carver, *Boards That Make a Difference — a New Design for Leadership in Nonprofit and Public Organizations,* Jossey-Bass, Inc. Publishers, California, 1990

Nancy R. Axelrod, *Booklet #2 The Chief Executive's Role in Developing the Nonprofit Board,* National Center for Nonprofit Boards, Washington D.C., 1988.

Richard T. Ingram, *Booklet #1 Ten Basic Responsibilities of Nonprofit Boards,* National Center for Nonprofit Boards, Washington D.C., 1988.

Richard P. Chait, *How to Help Your Board Govern More and Manage Less,* National Center for Nonprofit Boards, Washington D.C., 1993.

Jacqueline Covey Leifer and Michael B. Glomb, *The Legal Obligations of Nonprofit Boards: A Guidebook for Board Members,* National Center for Nonprofit Boards, Washington D.C., 1992.

Leadership Guide for Board Presidents and Committee Chairpersons, Aspen Publishers, Inc., Maryland, 1993.

1995 Board Member Manual, Aspen Publishers, Inc., Maryland, 1994.

Discussion Questions

1. How can orientations benefit the club? the board or committee member? the GM/COO?

2. Who might participate in an orientation?

3. What are some typical formats of orientations?

4. What types of materials can be included in an orientation?

Additional Activities

1. In small groups, develop an orientation program for a club committee. Determine timelines, who will be involved, what the format will be, and what materials will be included.

2. Invite a GM/COO to discuss his or her board orientation program. Discuss what works for that club that might not work at other clubs. Identify what elements of that orientation would be effective in many different types of clubs — country, city, athletic.

Case Study

Out-of-Control Board

Chris Miller is the new general manager of the Mountainview Country Club, a 1,000-member club just ten years old. The club's board fired the previous general manager because it was unhappy with the way the club was run. When Chris interviewed for the job, several board members mentioned that club operations seemed "chaotic" and that the club was bogged down with one problem after another. They wanted Chris to "turn things around." Despite some misgivings (Chris knew that he would be the club's fourth general manager in ten years), Chris took the position because he felt the club's potential was worth the risk.

It didn't take Chris long to realize that one of the biggest problems with the club was the board itself. At Chris's first monthly board meeting, he had been surprised at how Ted Fisher, the board's president, ran things. First, there was a generic agenda that consisted of an extremely simple outline: "Call meeting to order; Read previous minutes; Finance committee reports; House committee reports; Greens committee reports"; and so on. There were three new board members at the meeting, but they were not formally welcomed and they obviously had not been given any orientation because they looked lost throughout the meeting. The meeting itself wandered from subject to subject and took three hours to accomplish almost nothing. It was obvious that many of the committee chairs had nothing to report, but felt obligated to say something anyway. After the meeting, Chris had asked President Fisher about the generic agenda. "We always go in the same order," Fisher said, "so that's all we really need." What about the new board members—had they been given any orientation? "We've never bothered with that," Fisher said. "What is there to learn, really? They've been members for years."

After that first board meeting, Chris had asked his assistant manager, Linda, for some background information about the board and how it operated. Unfortunately, his worst suspicions were confirmed. Some of the board members are retired, Linda said, and have a lot of time on their hands, so they want to micromanage everything. On the other hand, many of the board members are very busy executives and they present an opposite problem: they are so pressed for time they hardly give the matters that come before the board any attention. Julia, the club's only female board member, had promised her friends that if she was elected to the board she would do something about the men-only Saturday-morning tee times. Her proposal to open the Saturday-morning tee times to women was defeated early in her term and she'd had a poor attitude ever since; she took scant interest in other club business and appeared to be just going through the motions until her term ended. Other board members, too, tended to focus on their pet projects to the exclusion of everything else.

Chris also learned that board members had a history of abusing their power in matters both large and small—not because they were deliberately trying to disrupt the club, but because they didn't know any better. Many board members habitually gave direct orders to club employees, for example. This bad habit had gotten started after the first general manager left the club and the club struggled without one for six months. Apparently the members didn't realize the havoc they caused when they contradicted a club manager's directives, or asked valets on duty to take them to the airport, or told a banquet server to drop what he was doing and drive by their house to pick up the wedding gift they forgot.

Some board members asked to be seated in the main dining room during busy periods without making reservations. Last year the club's dining room manager quit because she received a tongue-lashing and then a very harsh letter of reprimand from a board member. Her crime? She had refused to seat his party because some of his guests were wearing blue jeans and the club has a firm policy against blue jeans in the main dining room.

One of the board members tends to drink a little too much, Linda went on, and sometimes discusses with club bartenders things like the previous general manager's bonus plan and why the club fired its last golf pro. Around Christmas time an outbreak of food poisoning had occurred at the club, and a board member thought it would be helpful if he went to the media and explained the situation. Without the board's or anyone else's knowledge, he went to the local newspaper and told such a confused and contradictory tale that the newspaper launched a full-blown investigation and turned an unfortunate but minor incident into a front-page story. And last but not least, the board's vice president had almost gotten the club involved in a lawsuit because he repeatedly made inappropriate advances toward one of the club's female servers. Because this was another period when the club was between general managers, the server went directly to the board with her complaints, but the board ignored the problem. Soon afterwards the server graduated from college and landed another job, and it looked like she would not be pressing charges, but one never knew if the problem would reoccur more seriously.

All in all, it was a picture of an undisciplined board that was doing more harm than good to the club. Chris knew that if he was going to make positive changes at the club, he would have to start with the board, and he had his work cut out for him. Chris also knew from working at other clubs that timing was a critical factor. Since he had just been hired, he had the board's attention and a brief window of opportunity in which to address those issues that needed immediate action.

Discussion Questions

1. What challenges does Chris face with the club's board?

2. Which of these challenges should Chris address immediately (Priority A challenges), and which are not so critical and can be addressed over time (Priority B challenges)?

3. How should Chris address the immediate, Priority A challenges?

4. What can Chris do immediately to encourage the board president to run more effective meetings?

5. How can Chris help the board president see the need for an orientation program for new board members?

6. What elements should a new-board-member orientation program contain?

The following industry experts helped generate and develop this case: Cathy Gustafson, CCM, University of South Carolina; Kurt D. Kuebler, CCM, Vice President, General Manager, The Desert Highlands Association; and William A. Schulz, MCM, General Manager, Houston Country Club.

Club Bylaws: Determining the Need for Change

This issue of the Club Managers Association of America's Premier Club Services' Topical Reference Series addresses the topic of bylaw changes. It is a useful reference for clubs that are examining their bylaws to determine if revision is required.

This issue also analyzes current situations facing clubs and how their bylaws are affected. It includes case studies and sample bylaws — each with an analysis by experienced general managers/chief operating officers (GM/COOs). It is meant to help club management, board presidents and bylaw committees by identifying major concerns that clubs encounter when changing bylaws.

Bylaws govern all club boards. It is the bylaws that direct their meetings, the bylaws that direct the topics of their meetings and the bylaws that tell them even how they will conduct the meetings. But bylaws go beyond only board functions. According to one GM/COO, bylaws set the foundation for club rules. The bylaws are the backbone of the club. *Webster's Ninth New Collegiate Dictionary* says: "Bylaws are the rules adopted by an organization chiefly for the government of its members and the regulation of its affairs."

There is frequently a resistance to wholesale changes in bylaws because of the important roles history and tradition play in private social clubs. Nonetheless, few clubs remain static over the years and often find themselves with different needs than they had at their founding. This issue can help board members and bylaw committees plan systematic and meaningful changes in their bylaws.

Determining the Need for Change

It is important that clubs have bylaws that are responsive to the membership and its needs. Clubs that never review their bylaws sometimes end up burdened with antiquated bylaws that no longer reflect the club's mission, needs, or direction. Some clubs are facing membership shortages for the first time. For these and many other reasons, clubs are revising their bylaws.

As club boards blow the dust off old bylaws and attempt to alter them to meet the changing requirements of the club, they face a delicate task of making sure that any alterations stay in line with their mission and protect the club from future difficulties. They also must make certain that by meeting their current requirements, they do not ignore their long-term possibilities.

Clubs revising their bylaws sometimes struggle to balance modern demands with club traditions. No club can afford to ignore its traditions — nor would it want to. The club's heritage is part of what makes it special to its members. The argument "we've always done it that way" does have a place in private clubs.

However, clubs that have been around for a century or more sometimes face the questions: Can bylaws written in the mid-1800s still be relevant today? Is "the way we've always done it" still the right way? More often than not, the answer to both questions is "yes."

During the Great Depression, a club gathered to draw up its first set of bylaws. Acutely aware of the bank failures and the dangers of loans and investments, the members set forth that the board could not approve any capital loan for more than $10,000 without first getting an approval vote from the full membership. Sixty years later, notwithstanding the FDIC nor runaway inflation in the 40s and 70s, that bylaw still stood. The club members still respect the circumstances out of which that bylaw was written and are reluctant to change it — despite the fact that it severely ties the hands of the club in providing new services or even maintaining existing ones.

Yet another club had gone many years without reviewing its bylaws. When the club was built, it was in a secluded, quiet area. Over the years, changing demographics brought the membership closer to the club. As more people moved in, the area continued to develop. The club found that the use of its facilities had increased enormously. The board came to the conclusion that its bylaws did not accommodate this increased use of the facilities and revisited all of their bylaws in a major revision designed to provide better services to all of their members. The new bylaws changed the rules for use of facilities, membership categories and frequency of guest use.

Age alone, of course, does not make a document outdated. After all, the United States itself relies strongly on a document written in the 18th century — the U.S. Constitution. And that document is not only relevant, but is found to be continually robust. However, even the venerable U.S. Constitution has not been completely resistant to change. Over the years, 27 amendments have shaped the Constitution to keep pace with our changing society.

Some common reasons private clubs change their bylaws include:

- Change in membership demands
- Change in club mission
- Change in club operation
- Response to specific situations
- Practices that need documenting
- Change in social or legal environment

These reasons manifest themselves in a variety of bylaws covering a wide range of contemporary issues. Figure 1: Major Bylaw Issues lists some issues GM/COOs identified in a recent survey.

Change in Membership Demands

The most important reason to change bylaws is that members see a need for change. A club's foremost duty is to serve its members. The bylaws must remain responsive to the changing demands and makeup of the club membership.

The issues in which members recognize the need for change can cover the entire set of bylaws. Those which frequently affect the general membership are:

- Membership admissions
- Member, non-member and guest use of club facilities
- Membership categories

Figure 1: Major Bylaw Issues

The following are issues that several GM/COOs have said should be addressed in the bylaws:

- Use of the club by members, spouses and other family members
- Use of club by significant others
- Use of club by dates/escorts
- Gender-neutral wording
- New technology
- Discrimination
- Dress codes
- Simplified admissions process
- Membership categories, voting, death, divorce
- Election of members
- Club governance
- Stock or certificate of membership procedures
- Annual meeting time and procedures
- Board of directors: authority, elections, etc.
- Standing committees
- Resignations, non-payment of accounts
- Suspension or expulsion
- Indemnification of officers and directors
- Smoking restrictions

Many clubs have been revisiting their bylaws in light of new concerns surrounding these three issues.

Membership Admissions

In recent decades, many clubs have struggled against negative publicity, changing societal perceptions and declining memberships. Many clubs have sought to remarket themselves by making themselves more attractive to the various types of members they wish to have.

Clubs are now forced to face several issues surrounding membership admissions:

Simplifying membership application processes. The most common bylaw change made by clubs with declining membership is to simplify the membership application process. This poses a delicate challenge to clubs that must continue to maintain their high standards. They must recruit members of high caliber while making sure that they have sufficient members to cover their costs and provide the services members have come to expect. See Figure 2: Simplified Membership Admission for a revision one club made in its bylaws to simplify the application process.

Figure 2: Simplified Membership Admission

One club proposed the following bylaw change to "simplify the admissions procedure without compromising in any way the Club's high standards of admission." The amendment was intended to "remove what we believe to be unnecessary restrictions which are encumbering our admissions process."

The words underlined were added to the bylaw while the words struck through were deleted.

The proposal form shall then be completed and signed by the Proposer and the Seconder. The proposal form shall, among other things, name as references at least ~~six~~ _four_ ~~Regular~~ *Members,* ~~in addition to the Proposer and Seconder,~~ _who_ ~~(in the case of candidates for Regular Membership)~~ *know personally the candidate and the members of the candidate's immediate family.*

In the case of candidates for Regular membership, the references shall be either Regular Members or Non-Resident Members who have been Regular Members. In the case of candidates for Non-Resident membership, the references shall be either Regular Members or Non-Resident Members who need not have been Regular Members.

Ending discrimination based on race, gender, national origin, or religion. As society evolves in its views on free association versus discrimination, many clubs find themselves forced to either change their bylaws or face crippling negative publicity. See Figure 3 for examples of penalties clubs face when they do continue to discriminate. In 1987, Supreme Court nominee Anthony M. Kennedy was criticized for belonging to an all-white men's club. Members with political and social ambitions may withdraw from clubs that could cause them embarrassment through their discrimination policies. Because of this, many clubs are revisiting their admissions policies. Likewise, many clubs are striving to make their bylaws gender-neutral. While making the bylaws gender-neutral goes beyond mere language changes, Figure 4 gives some alternative word choices.

Converting from "blackball" approach to majority approval. The blackball method of membership voting has fallen from favor since its original use in British social clubs. Some clubs have switched their bylaws to require a certain percentage of approval votes rather than to dictate the number of nonapproval votes.

Member, Non-member and Guest Use of Club Facilities

Making a distinction among all the individuals who may be on the premises at a given time has never been an easy process for private clubs. And unless usage rules are clearly spelled out in bylaws, there are bound to be situations that raise the ire of members. They find that they don't have as much access as they thought or that they cannot use a facility because it's overcrowded with guests who don't pay dues.

Changes in our society have put pressure on traditional approaches to club use. Club members have different relationships today than they did a few decades ago and many clubs are trying to respond to the changing lifestyles of their members.

Some clubs have revised bylaws based on the following current situations:

Figure 3: Penalties for Discrimination

Clubs that choose to discriminate based on race, gender, national origin, or religion have paid increasingly higher penalties. Some of them include:

- *Loss of golf tournaments.* Most major golf organizations such as the PGA and the LPGA hesitate to schedule tournaments at clubs that discriminate.

- *Loss of liquor licenses.* Some states and localities will revoke liquor licenses if they find evidence of discrimination at a licensed establishment.

- *Increased property taxes.* A club puts its non-profit status at risk by discriminating. In doing so, the club becomes liable for higher assessments and taxes.

Significant others: If a full member is sharing a residence with his or her partner, but they are not married, should the club extend full privileges to the partner, the way they would to a spouse? As this situation becomes more common, club boards find that their current bylaws are often insufficient because they do not address this situation. It may be necessary for club boards to consult two different parts of their bylaws when these issues arise: guest use and spouse use.

Dates and escorts: Should a full member's date be restricted to the same club use as the in-town guest? Some clubs are expanding the privileges of dates and escorts as a way to encourage members to spend more time and money at the club.

Divorce: Clubs that do not have clear-cut bylaws covering what to do when members divorce find themselves in an awkward position during the divorce settlement. As club membership is considered an asset, both members of the marriage may want to retain club membership. With nearly 50 percent of all first-time marriages ending in divorce, clubs need to be prepared to decide objectively whether both member and spouse retain use of the club or not. It is also important that clubs set forth rules on the children's use of the club. Do privileges extend only to children who are in the custody of the full member? If the noncustodial parent is the full member, how often can the children use the club facilities?

Death: The bylaws should clearly address the policy for continued membership of surviving spouse and children. Clubs may wish to expedite the membership succession as a service to surviving spouses. See Figure 5: Letters of Condolence.

Membership Categories

Increasing the number and variety of membership categories is one way that clubs are changing their bylaws to respond to membership demands. According to *Club Management Operations* (CMAA, Kendall/Hunt Publishing Company, 1989, p. 6):

In a recent sampling of the bylaws of 50 clubs, all had a primary resident or regular membership, 91 percent had nonresident memberships; 93 percent had junior memberships; 91 percent, honorary memberships; 84 percent, social memberships; and 84 percent, senior memberships. The survey also identified some clubs with military, collegiate, widow and other classes.

Rare is the club that has only one membership category. Most find themselves with several, some with as many as 57. Membership categories are an extremely sensitive issue to

Figure 4: Gender-neutral Chart

Words to avoid	Gender-neutral terms
he	he or she
she	he or she
man	person or member
woman	person or member
wife	spouse or partner
husband	spouse or partner
widow/widower	surviving spouse
husband of former widow	spouse of <insert membership type>
sons/daughters	children
sportsman	athlete
bachelor/bachelorette	single, unmarried, unwed
barmaid	bartender, bar helper, bar server, cocktail server
barman	bartender, bar attendant, barkeep
boatman	boater, boat operator
seaman	sailor, crew member
bus boy	busser, busperson, dining room attendant, kitchen helper, dish carrier, server's assistant
businessman	executive, member of business community, professional
chairman	chair, moderator, committee head, presiding officer, coordinator, committee leader, organizer, facilitator, officiator
doorman	doorkeeper, door attendant
enlisted man	enlistee, service member, enlisted personnel
gamesman	gamester, games player
yachtsman	yachter
master	manager, director, chief, captain, authority, specialist
father/mother	parent
spokesman	representative, speaker
tradesman	storekeeper, merchant, small business owner, retailer, trades worker

Figure 5: Letters of Condolence

Letter One:	*Letter Two:*
Dear Mrs. Doe:	Dear Mr. Doe:
We were recently informed of the death of your husband. We would like to extend our sincere condolences to you and your family on this sad occasion.	The Board of Governors has asked me to convey to you and your family our deepest sympathy on the recent death of your wife.
We know that you are not thinking of the Club at this time. However, we would like to advise you that the Club and its facilities are at your disposal for six months without charge. At the end of this time, you will have the privilege of becoming one of our associate members without having to pay an initiation fee.	Mrs. Doe was a valued member of our Club. She will be missed.
	As a matter of Club policy, the surviving spouse of members automatically becomes an associate member upon the death of the other and continues to have membership privileges.
Sometime within the next six months, at your convenience, please be sure to contact us regarding this membership.	We have changed our records to reflect your status and welcome your continued association with the Club.
Again, please accept our deepest sympathy.	With Sympathy,
Sincerely,	
	General Manager
General Manager	

members. It is to fulfill the needs of the majority of members that categories were created in the first place. However, clubs with too many membership categories incur extra expense in maintaining each different type. Bylaw committees may wish to combine redundant categories to reduce the amount of paperwork the club has. For example, a club might choose to combine dining and social memberships, or golf and tennis memberships.

Other issues bylaw committees face in reference to membership categories are:

- Non-residents, boundaries and use rate
- Re-admitting members
- Transferring members from one category to another
- Age of junior members
- Lifetime membership

Change in Club Mission

The mission is the club's guiding beacon. However, the beacon can waver or even cast its light in a new direction. When a club changes its mission, the bylaws must change to stay on course with the new mission.

Sometimes the club's mission is contained in its charter or its articles of incorporation. It is a very weighty matter to change a club's charter. This move requires widespread membership support and, not infrequently, consultations with state licensing agencies. A change in a club's charter or articles of incorporation could affect not only the club members and club employees, but also the non-profit status of the club. However, charters *do* change and so do the bylaws that support the charter.

A club's mission may change even while the charter or articles of incorporation remain the same. The club may add buildings or land that alters the service and opportunities provided to club members. A club's mission may also change if it merges with another club or if it splits into two or more clubs.

Also, more clubs are engaging in strategic long-range planning to make sure they keep the vitality that originally produced their charter. As clubs form their strategic plans, they may find that their bylaws must also change to stay in harmony with these new directions.

For example, the acquisition of additional buildings or land may require the forming of bylaws to govern their uses. Additional services, while adding to the value of membership, frequently require additional internal regulations.

Change in Club Operation

Every governing body seeks to operate in a manner that reaps the greatest benefit for its members. To do this, the body must frequently re-evaluate the rules by which it governs. These operating issues make up the bulk of most bylaws.

Operating issues that may result in bylaw changes can be divided into those that affect:

- Club governance and meeting procedures
- Standing committees
- Club ownership procedures
- Indemnification of officers

Club Governance and Meeting Procedures

Clubs may decide that the way they choose their directors or run their meetings is ineffective. For example, a club that elects its president by the highest number of votes and the vice president by the second highest number of votes may decide that forcing two rivals to work that closely together may be counterproductive. Or a club may decide that its meetings would be run more efficiently by adopting Robert's Rules of Order.

In such situations, members seek ways to make the administration more effective, frequently by borrowing from ideas that are successful in corporate circles. As club members tend to be highly successful business people or athletes, they often bring to the club their skills, ideas and philosophies.

Figure 6: Case Study 1 — *Annual Membership Meeting* analyzes two bylaws written to establish membership meetings.

Figure 6: Case Study 1 — *Annual Membership Meeting*

A group of architects formed a social club that informally grew to more than 100 members. The original group decided to purchase land and incorporate as a country club. The original building was small, but plans were in the works for a larger facility. Until that time, the club decided to set a membership limit at 200. A bylaws committee was formed to draft the original set of bylaws for the club.

Two bylaws were drafted to address the scheduling of the annual membership meeting. They read:

1. *The Club shall hold its Annual Club Membership Meetings during the first week of March of each year at a time and place designated in the notice of such meeting. A quorum shall be reached when there are 100 members entitled to vote in attendance, in person, or by proxy — except for meetings where member assessments, certificates, or other fees are at issue. For these meetings, a quorum will be met when there are 150 voting members in attendance, in person, or by proxy.*

2. *The Board may call special meetings of members upon giving at least thirty (30) days written notice. The notice must state the purpose of the meeting. The Board shall also call a Special Meeting of the Club Membership upon written request of at least three voting members.*

While most of the GM/COOs who reviewed these bylaws thought they were a good start, they identified several problems with the bylaws as written.

1. The bylaws should mention a time frame in which meeting notice should be sent to the membership.

2. The date of the membership meeting is too specific. It is better to stipulate that the meeting should be held in the first three months of the calendar year.

3. Lower the numbers for a quorum. Setting a quorum at 50 percent and 75 percent is too high to effectively govern. "It will be almost impossible to have a meeting needing this percentage for a quorum," said one GM/COO.

4. Increase the number of members needed to call a special meeting. One GM/COO suggested 10 to 20 percent, warning, "With only three members, you could have a special meeting weekly."

5. Change the membership wording to "entitled to vote, represented in person or by proxy."

Standing Committees

Clubs may frequently change the purpose or makeup of a committee. If the bylaws spell out in detail the actions and authority of each committee, clubs may find themselves revising bylaws frequently. Most GM/COOs recommend that clubs make the bylaws that govern committees as general as possible, while still keeping them functional and relevant.

Bylaws affecting committees may change when a club decides to change the members of the committee, the requirements for committee members and committee chairmen, or the number of committees serving the club.

One club found that its immediate past president seldom attended meetings of the executive committee. The board members decided to amend the bylaws so that the immediate past president was still a member, but was now a non-voting member and was neither needed to help establish a quorum, nor required to attend meetings. The new bylaws added the chairman of another committee to the executive committee, thus keeping the balance of members.

Club Ownership Procedures

When clubs in the United States first began to form, the most common type of ownership was member ownership. When a person joined a club, he or she purchased stock in the club and was entitled to a refund upon termination of membership.

This arrangement creates liability for clubs. If the economy takes a turn for the worse and several club members withdraw their memberships, the club has an obligation to refund money to those members.

Because of this liability, many clubs are reducing or eliminating their refundable stock options and converting to issuing certificates of membership rather than stocks. Other clubs are reducing the percentage of the initiation fee that is refundable. Either change requires a revision of the bylaws and sometimes requires a revision of the club's charter.

Indemnification of Officers and Directors

In the early 1900s, few club officers or directors had to worry much about being sued for their club activities. Certainly, it was believed that a modicum of care and responsibility was all that was required to stay out of court.

In 1995, few people believe themselves immune to lawsuits. Even those who act in good faith may find themselves before the bar defending the actions of the club. Clubs especially have found themselves under fire over the procedures for membership selection, wrongful termination suits from employees, or discrimination of all types.

Many members are reluctant to serve on a board if the club does not offer indemnification for expenses incurred in a lawsuit. Volunteers today are much more conscious of the protection they need and the protection that is offered them.

Most clubs have altered their bylaws to reimburse their directors and officers for expenses incurred and for judgments or fines handed down against them while conducting club business. One such bylaw (CMAA, *Club* Hunt Publishing Company, Iowa, 1989, p. 71) reads:

> The Club shall pay the expenses incurred by and satisfy any judgment or fine rendered or levied against, a present or former Director, officer, or employee of the Club in action brought by a third party against such person (whether or not the Club is joined as a party defendant) to impose a liability or penalty on such person for an act alleged to have been committed by such person while engaged as a Director, officer, or employee, or by the Club or by both, provided, the Board of Directors determines in good faith that such Director, officer, or employee was acting in good faith within what he reasonably believed to be the scope of his employment or authority and for a purpose which he reasonably believed to be in the best interests of the Club or its members. Payments authorized hereunder include amounts paid and expenses incurred in settling any such action or threatened action.

Figure 7: Case Study 2 — *Fixing a Problem*

The bylaws committee of a yacht club has drawn up a bylaw governing when a club member can resign. A recent member had resigned while still owing the club the dues for the month in which he resigned. He refused to pay those dues on the grounds that he did not use the club for the full month. As the bylaws did not address resignations, the club was unable to collect the final month of dues.

The committee is concerned about making sure that all dues can be collected from all future resigning members and about trying to clarify for which dues a resigning member is responsible. This is the proposed bylaw:

A member may resign by giving written notice to the Club's business office at least thirty (30) days before the resignation is to become effective. All of the resigning member's indebtedness to the Club becomes due and payable upon the effective date of the resignation.

For the most part, the GM/COOs who reviewed this bylaw approved of it and said that it spelled out what it intended to do. However, one GM/COO would change the wording "and payable upon" to "prior to." This would make certain that a member is paid in full before the resignation is accepted.

Response to Specific Situations

No club board can foresee every situation that must be addressed in its bylaws. Each organization will have its unique problems and challenges. When solutions to new problems are found, many clubs wish to codify the solution to make things flow more efficiently in the future.

Figure 7: Case Study 2 — *Fixing a Problem* discusses a bylaw that board members had drafted in response to a specific situation.

More common changes that arise in response to specific situations include:

- Annual meeting time and procedures
- Resignations
- Non-payments of accounts
- Suspension or expulsion

Also, some clubs find themselves with bylaws that over the decades have become outdated. One club underwent a revision because it was no longer feasible to enforce the bylaws as written. There were references to member use of machines that no longer existed and procedures that were no longer relevant.

Many clubs have found that rather than addressing a specific situation in the bylaws, it is more efficient to set up a grievance procedure. The grievance procedure is able to address a wide variety of individual concerns without codifying the solution to each problem. Clubs that do establish grievance procedures need to carefully document them so that club members are ensured fair and equal treatment.

Practices That Need Documenting

Every organization constantly searches for better ways to accomplish its tasks. The organization may grow and subsequently change the way it operates. Clubs might also find that they have adopted certain processes and practices or have formed long-standing committees that have never been documented. Any time a process, committee, or practice has lasted for many years, clubs may decide to document it by adding it to the bylaws.

A club may also find that the bylaws provide insufficient procedures for the board to operate effectively. Figure 8: Case Study 3 — *Regular Meeting Dates* examines a bylaw that was proposed in response to the lack of procedure.

Change in Social or Legal Environment

While clubs are primarily private, social organizations, they are unable to completely isolate themselves from the political and legal maelstroms that swirl outside the security of the clubhouse gates.

More clubs find themselves caught up in the storms of controversy surrounding such issues as public accommodation, worker rights and the environment. At best, clubs are able to weather those storms with little change. Others find themselves forced to painfully rebuild after negative publicity. Still more clubs are being proactive and setting up storm walls and shuttering their windows before a hurricane strikes. These proactive clubs establish procedures and policies to deal with the media or other outside influences.

Several common changes in society and the legal environment that can cause changes in a club's bylaws are examined below.

Free Association Versus Discrimination

Traditionally, clubs in the United States have relied on the First Amendment right of free assembly or free association to defend discrimination based on race, national origin, or religion. However, courts have increasingly been reinterpreting that amendment and demanding that clubs remove discrimination policies in their membership admission and provide equal access to club facilities.

In 1988, the Supreme Court upheld New York City's laws which say a club with more than 400 members is a public accommodation and is subject to national civil rights laws. Since that ruling, at least six other states have pushed for laws to end discriminatory membership policies. In Kentucky, a bill under consideration would prohibit a club from excluding anyone based on race, color, religion, national origin, or gender if the club has 100 or more members, receives dues or payments, or receives government tax benefits. It also says that a club cannot, at risk of losing its liquor license, deny "full and equal enjoyment" of club facilities to members based on race, color, religion, national origin, or gender.

Some clubs have responded to these new laws by re-enforcing their image as strictly social organizations and banning any mention of business or showing of business cards or papers while on the club grounds. In New Orleans, private clubs were found to be strictly social because the clubs prohibited transacting or discussing business on the premises. Other clubs have changed their membership processes to end discriminatory practices based on race, gender, national origin, or religion.

Figure 8: Case Study 3 — *Requiring Meeting Dates*

The current board of a golf and tennis club has met only once in the past eight months, though committees have been meeting on a regular basis. Several of the committee chairs are unhappy that their proposals have been idling because of the lack of board meetings. They have proposed a bylaw to mandate regular meetings. The proposed bylaw reads:

The Board of Directors shall meet each year on the day following the annual election and meeting of the Club for the purpose of organization, election of officers and the consideration of any business that may be brought before the meeting.

The Board shall hold regular meetings for the transaction of business on the third day of each alternate month and shall hold special meetings whenever called by the President or by three or more Directors on written notice thereof given to each member of the Board at least one (1) day before the time appointed for such meeting.

The GM/COOs were split on this bylaw with half supporting the new bylaw and half opposed to it. One of the opposing GM/COOs said that the bylaw was too burdensome. The following changes were suggested by both supporters and non-supporters:

1. One-day meeting notice for special meetings is unrealistic.

2. Do not give specific days to hold meetings; instead, just establish the frequency of meetings.

One GM/COO suggested the bylaw be rewritten into two bylaws that read as follows:

Regular Meetings of the Board
An organization meeting of the Board of Directors shall be held each year on the day of the annual meeting of Regular Members immediately after the poll is closed and the Judges of Election have completed their tally of votes cast and delivered their report to the Secretary. Thereafter, regular meetings of the Board shall be held on such dates and at such time as may be fixed by the Board. No notice need be given of any regular meeting of the Board unless the same is to be held at a place other than the Clubhouse, in which event the Secretary shall give to each Director at least a 10-day advance written notice of the time and place of the meeting.

Special Meetings
Special meetings of the Board of Directors may be called at any time by the President or by any five Directors. The Secretary shall give to each Director, by mail or telegram, at least a 12-hour advance written notice of the time, place and purpose of each such special meeting.

Legal Operational Issues

The tentacles of U.S. bureaucracy have managed to pull even private clubs into their lair. Laws regulating worker rights, safety issues and smoke-free environments are affecting the members of private clubs and their ability to enjoy full social access to the organization.

Employment laws: The responsibility for enforcing the vast majority of employment regulations lies with the GM/COO, not the bylaws. However, recent rules such as the Americans with Disabilities Act affect governing as well as managing issues. Club bylaws may need to be revised to provide for better access or to educate members in harassment issues.

Safety issues: OSHA, state alcohol agencies and the Environmental Protection Agency all have strict policies that affect most clubs. Many clubs have found that codifying compliance statutes into their bylaws provides them additional defense against fines or other penalties.

Smoke-free environments: While the demand for non-smoking workplaces has grown in recent years, clubs first confronted this issue centuries ago. In the mid-1800s, White's, a prestigious club in London dating back to the 17th century, had divided its club into smoking and non-smoking areas. The Prince of Wales, a very heavy smoker, joined the club and refused to follow the smoking rules. After members voted at a general membership meeting to retain the smoking rules, the Prince, annoyed at not being able to smoke, left the club and started a rival organization.

Today, the decision to allow or disallow smoking is much more likely to be dictated by local, state and federal governments. As mandates to provide smoke-free workplaces to club employees are being handed down, clubs are being forced to revise their bylaws. In 1995, New York City proposed smoke-free air acts that ban smoking in workplaces, including clubs. In Maryland, a similar law passed, but the governor exempted clubs from the ban, allowing them to have smoking in club dining areas in 40 percent of the dining space as long as that space is enclosed.

Equal access and starting times: In response to lawsuits, more states are ruling that clubs may not deny equal access to members based on race, gender, religion, or national origin. In most clubs, this has affected golf tee-off times. On April 11, 1994, the Florida attorney general's office found that Cheval Country Club in Tampa was in violation of state law by restricting access to Saturday morning start times on the basis of gender and by having a Men's Grill and Card Room. This issue has also had the attention of courts and lawmakers in California, Colorado, Michigan, Minnesota, New York, Texas and Washington. Many clubs are now choosing to voluntarily eliminate gender-based restrictions to head off lawsuits. Clubs in some states are using a primary/secondary member category to allocate golf starting times. The primary member, whether man or woman, can choose on which day he or she wants to golf and the secondary member gets the alternate time.

Cycle of Change

There is little consensus in the club industry on how frequently bylaws should be reviewed; opinions range from almost never to a regular, predictable cycle. Because of the great variety of club types and needs, there will probably never be a consensus.

One GM/COO stated that once bylaws are put into effect, they are rarely changed: "A private club is a gathering of like people for social and recreational purposes provided at their expense. ...Because of this, bylaws rarely change. ... What does change, however, are club rules."

Clubs with bylaws that address only the purpose of the club probably have little reason to change. All of the catalysts of change discussed above would affect the club rules, but not the bylaws themselves. It is also important that when clubs do change their bylaws, they resist changing only for the sake of change. And that they change only what needs to be changed.

Some clubs review their bylaws annually. Others do so whenever board issues are discussed. At one club, the regular bylaw revision is done to make certain that the bylaws are still enforceable and that they remain relevant.

The pie chart in Figure 9 is based on a representative sampling of 52 GM/COOs.

Figure 9: Frequency of Bylaw Amendments

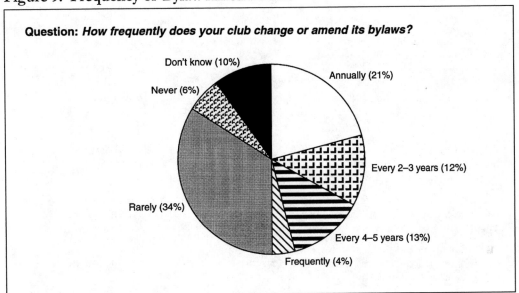

Question: *How frequently does your club change or amend its bylaws?*

Don't know (10%)

Never (6%)

Annually (21%)

Every 2–3 years (12%)

Rarely (34%)

Every 4–5 years (13%)

Frequently (4%)

Concerns About Bylaws

Once the need for a change has been identified, boards and bylaw committees must make sure they understand the issues surrounding the revision. Gone are the days when a bylaw committee need consider only the desires of the membership. While the members' needs and desires are still the driving force behind all bylaws, those doing the writing have several additional concerns to address.

Boards and bylaw committees have four major issues they must address when evaluating each bylaw revision:

- Membership concerns
- Legal compliance concerns
- Community awareness concerns
- Vocabulary and clarity concerns

Membership Concerns

As stated earlier, a club's foremost duty is to serve its members. The bylaws must remain responsive to the changing needs of the club's membership. When membership demand precipitates a change in bylaws, the bylaws committee needs to make certain that what it has written reflects the best interests of the membership.

Even if the membership did not demand a change that is before the bylaws committee, the committee should carefully analyze the written law to determine whether it will be accepted by the vast majority of their members.

Figure 10: Case Study 4 — *Rejecting a Nominee*

Some of the members of a swim club were upset about the rejection of a membership nominee that they thought had wide support. The nominee was rejected by the board and never came up for a membership vote.

The upset members proposed the following new bylaw:

Upon rejection of an applicant for membership, the Membership Committee shall provide that applicant with a written explanation within 30 days of the vote. The explanation will include information on when a candidate can reapply and how to reapply.

The GM/COOs unanimously rejected this bylaw. One GM/COO explained that the club was "setting itself up for a discrimination suit. Never ask a membership committee to justify — especially not in writing."

Another GM/COO suggested that the board may want to state a time before such a candidate can stand for re-election, as well as provide information on reapplication, but that "an explanation for rejection has all kinds of liability problems."

It was also suggested that a club not use the word "applicant" to refer to someone seeking membership. Words such as "nominee" or "candidate" are more exact and lead to fewer problems or misunderstandings.

Not all changes proposed by members should necessarily be adopted. It may be that the members' concerns can be addressed in another fashion. Figure 10: "Case Study 4 — *Rejecting a Nominee*" examines a situation in one hypothetical club and the bylaw the members proposed. In this case study, the board needs to find an alternative method to address the concerns of members.

Legal Compliance Concerns

Boards and bylaw committees must carefully consider the legal ramifications of a proposed bylaw. Private clubs with non-profit status must be careful to safeguard that status by lawsuits. Clubs should carefully evaluate each making sure the bylaws are clean and don't violate federal, state, or local regulations. Laws on issues such as drinking age, air purity and even wetlands can dictate the content of new bylaws. For example, as states raised the legal drinking age to 21 in every state, many clubs found that it made sense to raise the minimum membership age to 21 as well.

Likewise, bylaws must be carefully worded to minimize liability. Courts will expect clubs to live up to the standards of their bylaws. Clubs that do not do this open themselves to civil lawsuits. Clubs should carefully evaluate each bylaw to make sure it is realistic and enforceable. If the courts can interpret the bylaw as a commitment on the part of the club to provide a particular protection or service, the club can be held to that "promise."

Figure 11: "Recent Bills and Laws" lists some of the current legal issues affecting clubs.

Community Awareness Concerns

If clubs needed to worry only about preventing lawsuits, the job of writing bylaws would be handed over to those members who are business lawyers. However, clubs must often

Figure 11: Recent Bills and Laws

Some of the following laws affecting clubs have been proposed throughout the United States:

- The Texas legislature defeated a bill saying that a club with 50 or more members that receives $100,000 or more in dues, payments, etc. cannot discriminate based on race, color, religion, creed, national origin, or sex.

- The federal government has disallowed non-profit clubs from providing the following nontraditional business activities: gas station service, sale of liquor for off-premises consumption, barber shop service, or sale of food or goods to be taken off the premises.

- Pennsylvania courts said that club members who pay monthly food minimums must also pay sales tax, even if they don't actually buy the food.

- Texas defeated a bill that would have required private clubs applying for liquor license permits to give written notice to each resident and property owner within 1,000 feet of the premises. The bill would have also allowed the chief of police or sheriff to submit a sworn statement that the club endangers general welfare, health, peace, morals, or safety of the community. If such a statement were submitted, the permit would be canceled.

- A California bill prohibits smoking in the workplace, including club dining rooms.

look beyond the lawbooks and even beyond their own membership. They must have an appreciation of their community's needs and expectations.

Even an organization as private and reclusive as most clubs are, must have an understanding of the community in which it resides. A club that was built at the turn of the century in an exclusive downtown area may now find that the neighborhood has fallen victim to urban blight and that its members have new challenges in using the club facilities.

Likewise, a club that was once the only facility for miles around may find that, as new neighbors move in, there are greater restrictions on liquor licenses, entertainment licenses and development permits.

Vocabulary and Clarity Concerns

A bylaws committee may frequently find itself spending hours belaboring phrases or even words to make sure each one is right. It is an effort well-spent. If a bylaw cannot be clearly understood by the membership, it won't be upheld.

Although it is not uncommon for bylaws to be written in "legalese," such language frequently obfuscates the meaning of the bylaw. The bylaw committee needs to delete all ambiguities that might cloud the board's intent.

E.B. White's oft-quoted statement "It is easier for a man to be loyal to his club than to his planet; the bylaws are shorter and he is personally acquainted with the members" might

Figure 12: Case Study 5 — *Confusing Bylaw*

At a city club of 100 members, the board of governors has decided to let the general membership elect new board members. In the past, governors were chosen by a committee of past presidents. The following bylaw was adapted from the current bylaws and submitted to the bylaws committee:

> *The nominating committee shall consist of three men. The committee members shall be appointed as needed and serve for a year. The committee shall present to the board of governors nominations for governors to be elected by the board and for any office held on the board.*

The GM/COOs who reviewed this bylaw identified several problems:

1. The bylaw is not specific enough. It is missing:

    - Whether the members of the committee need to be club members

    - Who the members of the committee are

    - In what class of membership the nominees should be

    - An exact timeframe in which to operate

2. The wording is not gender-neutral. It is better to say "shall consist of three individuals" or "three active members."

3. It does not accomplish its purpose in that it still has the board, not the general membership, electing governors.

It was advised that in this instance the club would have been better off writing a bylaw from scratch, adapting a model bylaw, or adapting a bylaw from another club. Because they tried to adapt their old bylaw, too much of the old wording got left in and it is confusing and too general.

be taken as an admonition. The shorter and easier to understand the bylaws are, the more loyalty and obedience the club is likely to engender.

Some writing tips:

- Write in active voice.
- State clearly the objective of the bylaw.
- Keep the bylaws general so they do not become overly restrictive.
- Make sure the language is gender-neutral.

Figure 12: Case Study 5 — *Confusing Bylaw* examines a proposed bylaw with several wording problems.

Analyzing Bylaws

Once the above concerns have been addressed, it is time to start writing the bylaws. Every proposed bylaw should be subjected to rigorous analysis by the board, its members and its legal advisors. Club management can be very useful during this process because of their responsibility for and knowledge of club operations.

When making changes, it is suggested that six tests be applied to the bylaws. Each change should be:

- Consistent with federal, state and local laws
- Consistent with the club charter
- Consistent with reason; the bylaw should make sense
- Capable of being complied with
- Consistent with ownership or contractual rights
- Consistent with the club's tax status

In order to be consistent with ownership or contractual rights, the bylaws should not contradict the legal rights of the owners or violate any contracts the club has. For example, if the club has signed a contract with a vendor granting that vendor exclusive rights to provide a particular service, new bylaws may not then mandate that that service be provided by several vendors. Likewise, bylaws may not forbid the owners from examining the financial assets of the club.

Clubs that are tax exempt under 501(c)(7) should always make sure that they don't endanger their exempt status. Even adding a membership category such as "corporate" might put a club's tax-exempt status at risk.

It is also important that the approach to changing bylaws be systematic. Bylaws provide the club with continuity. They are what determine how the club will operate and what authority it has. Because of this, every bylaw should be submitted to the same evaluations, the same approval process and the same examination.

In order to revise bylaws most effectively, club boards and bylaw committees must identify the process by which bylaws are changed, the criteria used for evaluating and writing bylaws and sample bylaws that can be used as models.

Process of Change

Most clubs develop a process for changing bylaws when they ratify their original articles of incorporation. Usually, the bylaws themselves dictate the process for amendments, additions, or deletions.

Depending on the club, the process may be detailed down to the number of votes, the place and manner of posting and the number of days which a bylaw change must be considered. Other clubs may only codify the general requirements of bylaw amendments and leave it to the individual boards to set up a more formal process.

Different clubs have found different processes to be effective. Figure 13: Approval Processes illustrates some of the procedures clubs use to approve amendments to the bylaws.

A crucial step in an amendment process is the legal review. The club should submit each bylaw to the club's legal counsel. The legal counsel can evaluate bylaws to make certain they neither add liability to the club nor in any way jeopardize the non-profit standing of the club. Some clubs will submit their proposed bylaws to two or more individuals or law firms for review.

But whatever process is used to amend bylaws, the following four questions must be answered:

Who can propose a change? In many clubs, the board alone can make changes in the bylaws, usually with a four-fifths vote of the whole board (not a quorum). Others vest in boards the power to make changes, but they must give notice to the membership; and if a specified number of members object, then the bylaw cannot come to a vote. Other clubs allow the membership to propose changes on a petition basis. These clubs usually establish a certain number of full, senior, or junior members who must sign a petition before it will be considered by the board.

Who works on bylaws? Most clubs have a bylaw committee as either a standing or ad-hoc committee with a board officer as chair. It is recommended that this committee also have a lawyer as one of its members. Other clubs form special task forces appointed by the president to address bylaw issues. Still other clubs rely on the full board to work on proposed bylaw amendments.

How is a change voted in? There are three main methods of voting in bylaw amendments: the board alone votes, the board votes and then submits the amendment to the membership for approval, or the full membership votes on an amendment. The method a club uses will almost always be found in the bylaws. It is recommended that if the membership participates in the voting, that privilege be restricted to full, senior and junior (voting) members. Only those who have the right to vote for board members should be allowed to vote on membership changes. State laws may also dictate some of the procedure for voting on a change. Some states may govern how many days prior notice must be given to those entitled to vote and how to handle proxy votes.

How are members notified of the change? The importance of notifying members of changes in the bylaws is addressed below. However, a club needs to make sure that notification is a part of its bylaw process and is always included when planning changes.

Establishing Criteria

Any person or committee that undertakes a bylaw revision should carefully establish criteria by which to judge each proposal. It is most useful if these criteria are developed and published long before any amendment is proposed.

In addition to establishing general guidelines for bylaw amendments, it is a important to establish, even if on an informal, unwritten basis, what issues will *not* be addressed in the bylaws. Bylaws that are too confining may restrict the growth of the club.

General Guidelines

Of all the guidelines that those who develop bylaws should follow, one of the most important can be found in the words of a GM/COO who advises that committees "develop bylaws that are specific enough to guide the club but generic enough to allow flexibility to operate."

Club bylaws should state how frequently, for example, club boards should meet, but should refrain from giving a time, date and place. The bylaws are intended to provide a general direction and make known the intent of the law. They should not be so rigidly detailed that they eliminate all flexibility and creativity.

Other guidelines that GM/COOs have given for writing bylaws are:

- Research the topic thoroughly.

Figure 13: Approval Processes

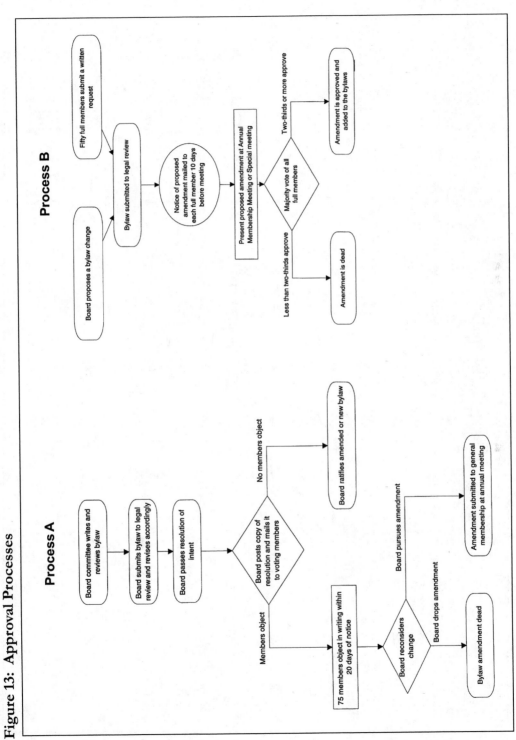

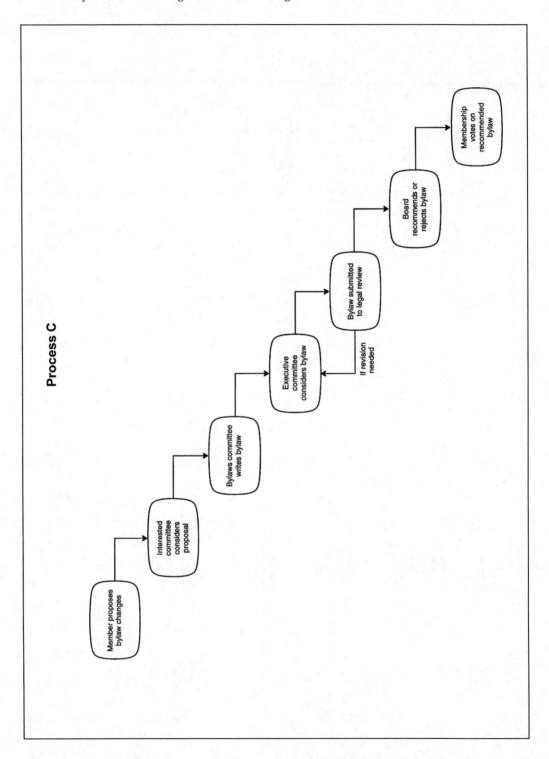

Process C

Member proposes bylaw changes

Interested committee considers proposal

Bylaws committee writes bylaw

Executive committee considers bylaw

Bylaw submitted to legal review

If revision needed

Board recommends or rejects bylaw

Membership votes on recommended bylaw

- Do not tie the hands of the board.
- Talk to members about how a bylaw may affect them.
- Make sure the proposed change fits the spirit of the charter.
- Don't change for the sake of change.
- Keep bylaws as simple as possible.
- Get all the input you can. Talk to anyone who has to work with bylaws.
- Discuss procedures with other members who have worked on bylaws.

The bylaw committee should establish guidelines for how it can make changes to the bylaws, beyond what the bylaws spell out. For example, the bylaws may establish the actual voting procedures and then the committee can establish who writes the amendment and how to review it before the vote. Turning these guidelines into a policy can help to ensure continuity as members change.

Issues to Avoid

As important as identifying which bylaws need to be changed or added is identifying which bylaws should remain the same and what issues should not be addressed. Clubs should develop a sense of which issues require documentation as a bylaw and which issues should remain unwritten.

Some commonly cited issues that GM/COOs say should not be added to bylaws are:

- Membership approval for raising dues
- Membership approval for spending money or incurring debt
- Membership approval for assessments
- Exact criteria for evaluating membership nominees
- Specific days and months to hold meetings
- Drinking age of members

Tools for Bylaw Revisions

Many GM/COOs say the most useful tool clubs can have when revising bylaws is a model from which to work. This model may be drawn from published sources, other clubs, or even from their own bylaws.

The time and effort of writing bylaws is compounded when members try to write from scratch. Frequently it triples the number of times a bylaw has to be rewritten and revised before being submitted for a final vote.

However, no bylaw should be taken verbatim from another source. Each club has its own unique style. The bylaw should reflect the individual concerns of the club for which it is written.

Another commonly cited tool is a working version of the bylaw under review. One GM/ COO said the most valuable tool his club has is a computer with the bylaws on it and a person familiar with current membership requests. The bylaws are taken section by section and revised with strikeouts so that members can see what the new bylaws will be. Refer to Figure 2: Simplified Membership Admission for an example of this method. Another club uses a combination of underlining and brackets on the old laws. The underlines indicate what will be added and the brackets surround material that will be deleted.

Model Bylaws

Publishers and the associations that work with clubs have long recognized the usefulness of model club bylaws. A club that is revising its bylaws can find model bylaws from a number of sources.

A few sources include:

- Club management textbooks, including *Private Club Administration*
- *Club Management Update: Club Bylaws* available from the Club Managers Association of America (CMAA)
- National Golf Foundation (NGF) has model bylaws available for its members
- Legal services such as Premier Club Services' vendor resources, including Page & Addison, a law firm specializing in the private club and resort industry

Model club bylaws are typically researched and address important issues facing club governance. The bylaws frequently need very little adaptation and can be easily customized to meet the needs of a particular club.

Sample Bylaws

Many committees find it more effective to adapt bylaws from nearby clubs or from clubs with a similar charter than to write bylaws from scratch or even to use model bylaws. The sample bylaws they collect are frequently more specific and more relevant to their situations than those produced by national organizations. City clubs should exchange bylaws with other city clubs, corporate clubs with other corporate clubs, golf clubs with other golf clubs, etc.

Another source for sample bylaws are the round tables at annual CMAA conferences. The round tables can provide an opportunity for GM/COOs and board officers to discuss bylaw changes and share their club's bylaws.

Clubs may also seek bylaws from clubs that have recently undergone revisions for similar reasons or who have updated similar bylaws. Clubs often find it much easier to learn from the mistakes and experiences of colleagues than to repeat the mistakes or experiences. Through networking with peers, GM/COOs are able to obtain information about other clubs' bylaws.

Bylaw Introduction

Once a bylaw has been ratified, clubs must make certain each member is notified of the change. If bylaws are ratified by the general membership, this task is made somewhat easier.

If a bylaw only affects the board, should membership still be informed? Yes. Since the board is merely a representation of membership, commissioned to act in the best interests of membership, even procedural changes should be explained to members. It may demonstrate that the board is responsive and is working to serve the membership.

Notification involves both informing members of the change in bylaws and thoroughly explaining them. Aside from the practical reasons for notification — members can't follow bylaws they don't know about — there are two other reasons for notification. One, clubs have a legal obligation to inform members. Two, the bylaws will be much more effective and future changes will have much more support if members understand the current change.

Legal Obligation

Clubs have an obligation to provide "actual notice" to the members of any change in bylaws. Without actual notice, the bylaws are not legally binding.

The law assumes notice has been provided if a club distributes the bylaws to each member's last known address. This is especially true if club members are required to file an address change for club records. Many clubs will also provide notification by posting the bylaw changes at appropriate places throughout the club.

It is also important to provide copies of relevant bylaws to any outside person dealing with the club if a bylaw affects that person. Bylaws that might affect vendors include those requiring board approval for capital purchases, certain procedures for obtaining quotes, or certain preferences given to members who provide particular services. If the vendor is not given a copy of a bylaw, then the vendor is not responsible for upholding it. Some states may require certain bylaws to be posted or provided to vendors.

Board and committee members are expected to be given "constructive notice" of bylaw changes. Under constructive notice, board and committee members are presumed to have knowledge of the bylaws because it is part of their duty as club officials.

Service Obligation

Since all bylaws are written for the benefit of the members, prompt notification is in the best interest of the club and its members. There is little sense in ratifying a bylaw and then letting it grow dusty and useless on the books because no one knows about it. Failing to notify the membership wastes the time of everyone who worked on the bylaw.

Boards should present members with a clear explanation of each new rule or change. The letters to members should give simple explanations that clearly state the benefits of a new or revised bylaw. By letting members know how the bylaw benefits them and improves their club, the board generates support for the change and for future changes.

On the other hand, members who learn about a change secondhand may be suspicious or may receive inaccurate information. This grapevine approach can be damaging to the club and its governance.

Figure 14: Bylaw Memo is a sample letter one club used to explain an amendment of the bylaws on which members were about to vote.

Figure 14: Bylaw Memo

To the Members of The XXXX Club

Enclosed is a Ballot regarding some proposed amendment to the XXXX bylaws. Please note that the right to vote is vested with the Regular Members of the Club and a Ballot is enclosed for their consideration. However, we are also sending this letter to the Non-Resident Members so that they are kept informed.

These amendments are recommended by both the Board of Directors and the Admissions Committee in order to remove what we believe to be unnecessary restrictions that are encumbering our admissions process. We addressed this matter in our April XX, 19XX letter to you (Item #7).

For your convenience, we have summarized these proposed amendments as follows:

1. Permit Members of the Board to propose or second candidates

2. Reduce the number of required references from six to four

3. Permit Non-Resident Members who have been Regular Members to act as references

4. Permit Non-Resident Members to act as references for other Non-Resident candidates

The Board and the Admissions Committee would appreciate your approval of these amendments.

Sincerely,

Board President

Prudent Bylaw Review

One GM/COO warned clubs against the impulse to change bylaws to meet only current needs, while ignoring long-term needs. He said that bylaws should be changed "as infrequently as humanly possible. Bylaws are the backbone of the club. ...If you get someone in with a personal agenda, the club could lose its rudder."

In the 125 years since his club was incorporated, he said, it has made no major revisions. He said the only "tinkering" that has been done has been to make the bylaws gender-neutral and to change the membership limits. This particular GM/COO said that the bylaws govern overall responsibility and establish the authority and responsibility of the rules and that club rules are able to aptly reflect the then-current wishes of the membership.

A club that rashly makes changes without careful analysis and a deep understanding of the club's mission may find that the bylaws no longer provide the stability or direction that they once did. However, a club that has recognized the need for change, addressed all of the legal and social concerns, carefully followed established procedures and properly notified everyone involved, will find that the bylaw changes benefit the club and its membership.

Proper review of bylaws can ensure the robustness of the club in the years to come and keep the club solidly grounded in its history. Ideally, careful analysis and proper notification will ensure that the club bylaws reflect the needs of the current and future membership while defending against change for the sake of change.

ACKNOWLEDGEMENTS

The following individuals generously donated their expertise and time to make this issue possible:

Mr. A. Christopher Borders, CCM
Mr. James Brewer, MCM
Mr. John Jordan, CCM
Mr. Willmoore "Bill" Kendall CCM
Mr. Jonathon McCabe, CCM
Mr. Murry E. Page, P.C.
Mr. Harry Richter, CCM
Mr. William Schulz, CCM

Additional Resources

Barbour, Henry Ogden, CCM, *Private Club Administration*, Maryland: CMAA, 1968.

CMAA, *Club Management Update: Club Bylaws*, Dubuque, Iowa: Kendall/Hunt Publishing Company, 1989.

Hopkins, Bruse R., *Starting & Managing a Nonprofit Organization: A Legal Guide*, New York, NY: John Wiley & Sons, 1989.

Houle, Cyril O., *Governing Boards: Their Nature and Nurture*, San Francisco, CA: Jossey-Bass Publishers, 1990.

Leifer, Jacqueline Covey and Glomb, Michael B., *The Legal Obligations of Nonprofit Boards: A Guidebook for Board Members*, National Center for Nonprofit Boards, Washington D.C., 1992.

Oleck, Howard L., *Nonprofit Corporations, Organizations and Associations*, Englewood Cliffs, NJ: Prentice Hall, Inc. 1980.

Webster, George D., *The Law of Associations: An Operating Manual for Executives and Counsel*, New York, NY: Matthew Bender, 1990.

White, Ted E. and Gerstner, Larry C., *Club Operations and Management*, 2nd edition, New York: Van Nostrand Reinhold, 1991.

Discussion Questions

1. How can a club determine when to review its bylaws?
2. What type of changes in a club might initiate a bylaw revision?
3. What are some of the major issues a bylaw committee needs to address during a bylaw revision?
4. What are some general guidelines for developing bylaws?

Additional Activities

1. Form a group of three to five people. Draft a bylaw addressing one of the following issues:

   - Divorces — who gets the membership?
   - Smoking
   - Use of club by significant others

2. Analyze a set of club bylaws. Identify whether any bylaws might be outdated or in need of review. Determine how to make a case to the membership to change the bylaws.

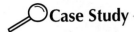 Case Study

Bothered by Bylaws

As was its annual custom, it was time for the Bylaws Committee of the Sunnyvale Golf and Racquet Club to review the club's bylaws. George Reynolds, the club's general manager, had presented a list of important club concerns to the committee members about a week before the chosen date. In this list, George suggested that the most urgent business concerned bylaws pertaining to membership. Several situations had arisen over the past year and the club had not yet established guidelines to deal with them. Some of these issues had important legal ramifications if not examined.

In the first situation, several members of the club had voiced their displeasure at the rejection of a membership nominee, a popular local businessman, who presumably had wide support. After these members had informed him he was a "shoo-in" for membership, his nomination was rejected by the deciding body. These unhappy members proposed the following new bylaw to the Bylaws Committee:

> *Upon rejection of an applicant for membership, the Membership Committee shall provide that applicant with a written explanation within 30 days of the vote. The explanation will include information on when a candidate can reapply and how to reapply.*

In the second case, two members of the club, Mr. and Mrs. Witherspoon, were divorcing. Mrs. Witherspoon's family has a long history with the club, but her husband joined after their marriage only because of his new ties to her family. Most people believe that Mr. Witherspoon's father-in-law paid the initiation fee so his daughter would have continued access to the club. Mr. Witherspoon is, however, the golfer of the family and uses the club's facilities with far greater frequency than his wife. The membership is also in his name. Now that the courts were proceeding to divide the Witherspoons's mammoth estate, the future of the club membership, which could not be divided between them, was in question. The club had never before addressed the issue of divorcing members and now had to establish pertinent bylaws.

In addition, the general manager pointed out, the Bylaws Committee should also use this opportunity to consider how the club should address the membership rights of significant others—an issue which he had observed becoming increasingly important among competing clubs. George raised some of the thornier questions. "Should the club extend membership privileges to a member's girlfriend or boyfriend, for example? How should a club determine if someone is a significant other? What happens to these privileges if the relationship ends?"

When the Bylaws Committee met, these issues understandably generated a great deal of discussion. The committee decided to table the issues for 30 days and then vote upon them.

Discussion Questions

1. Should the Bylaws Committee accept the first proposed bylaw? Why or why not?

2. How should a club address the issue of membership rights in the case of divorce?

3. What are some of the membership issues raised by significant others?

The following industry experts helped generate and develop this case: Cathy Gustafson, CCM, University of South Carolina; Kurt D. Kuebler, CCM, Vice President, General Manager, The Desert Highlands Association; and William A. Schulz, MCM, General Manager, Houston Country Club.

Club Rules

Societies through the ages have written rules on every conceivable topic. Those writing the rules hoped that they would result in a more orderly, civilized and secure environment. Sometimes they did. Other times they failed abysmally.

Private clubs, often seen as the microcosm of society's most upstanding people, have always had rules to cement the expectations of the majority of the members. These rules were written so that a standard of behavior can be set and so that the club can fulfill member desires. But that does not mean that rules have always been observed. A general manager/ chief operating officer (GM/COO) doesn't have to be at a club for very many years before he or she has stories to tell about rules that were broken, bent, or turned inside-out. While these stories can be humorous, they also identify one of the many challenges club professionals face: enforcing the rules. At best, professionals must deal with members seeking exceptions to the rules. At worst, professionals must confront members who purposely defy the rules.

One GM/COO said that the ideal situation for a club is to run without rules: "If everybody followed the Golden Rule, we wouldn't need rules. However, we don't live in a perfect world, so they are necessary." This issue of the Topical Reference Series addresses the purpose of club rules, some of the challenges involved with enforcing rules and a brief examination of their origins and evolution. In the preparation of this document, 26 sets of club rules were examined and analyzed and more than seven experienced GM/COOs from a variety of club types and locales were interviewed. *It is important to note that what works for one club may not work at another.*

Purpose of Club Rules

Without rules, club members would be adrift in a sea of undefined expectations. Rules establish what club members can expect from the board, each other and the employees. One GM/COO prefers the term "guidelines" to "rules," because it more aptly describes their purpose. The rules are meant to establish the expected behavior — not to limit or restrict the members' enjoyment of the club. Ideally, the adherence to club rules results in greater enjoyment for all.

Few members consciously choose to engage in behavior they know causes discomfort or unhappiness to fellow members. Good rules can identify correct behavior and resolve conflicts arising out of the use of the club. By establishing rules, clubs can set the parameters of behavior to bring about the greatest amount of enjoyment for the greatest number of members. The club's rules answer the members' questions about how they should dress, how they should use the club's facilities, when they can go to the club and who has access to which services.

Several purposes for club rules are found in their rule books as shown in Figure 1: Rules Introductions.

Defining Rules

Club rules are written to remove ambiguities in club bylaws and to address the multiple issues involved in everyday club use. In *Webster's New Universal Unabridged Dictionary*, the definition for "rule" is four and one-half inches long. But although its meanings are many, its application is much more narrow. For the purpose of club rules, the first entry states the definition very succinctly: "a principle or regulation governing conduct, action, procedure, arrangement, etc."

Club rules are what govern the day-to-day operation and use of club facilities and services. They spell out the allocation of services offered by the club such as tee times, court reservations and private room rentals. Club rules can resolve complex issues and set member expectations for conduct at the club.

The basic club rule answers the following questions:

- What is the rule governing?
- To whom does it apply?
- When does it apply?
- What are the exceptions?
- What are the penalties for noncompliance?

Bylaws vs. Rules

Bylaws empower clubs to create rules. The bylaws make up the club's consistent standard. The rules are subject to change based on the needs and desires of the membership, facilities, employees and owners.

A purist's comparison of "bylaws" and "rules" is that bylaws affect only the governing boards, while rules are the regulations that affect everyone else. However, this comparison is overly simplistic for most clubs. See Figure 2: Bylaws vs. Rules for a more detailed comparison.

A better definition of these two words was proposed by a GM/COO who said that clubs don't usually have to seek membership permission to get rules changed, but with bylaws they do. "To use a house metaphor, the bylaws make up the structure of the house, the walls, the floors and ceiling," he said. "The rules are the color of the sofa, the chairs, or the carpet and are subject to change." Clubs are able to change their rules without consulting members. Bylaws, on the other hand, usually require membership input or approval before being amended, deleted, or added.

Another GM/COO pointed out that bylaws and rules are different forms of governance. Bylaws set up a corporate entity while rules govern the day-to-day workings of the club. Most clubs cannot exist as corporations unless they have bylaws. The rules provide the practical guidelines for how the corporate entity established in the bylaws operates. Generally speaking, bylaws create policy and rules are operational.

A final difference between rules and bylaws is that bylaws are usually changed in response to membership demand, whereas rule changes typically originate in committees.

Figure 1: Rules Introductions

Why Have Rules?

The most articulate statements about the purposes of club rules can be found in the introductory paragraphs from several club rule books. The following introductions sum up several reasons why rules are important:

- Efficient operation of the club

  The following Standing Rules have been adopted by the Board of Directors for the purpose of efficient operation and assurance to each member of the fullest enjoyment of the Club facilities consistent with the interest of the membership as a whole.

- Maximum enjoyment of the club

  Rules of usage have been established to assure the maximum enjoyment of the <club's name> by all of its members. Membership in the Club involves a cheerful and willing obligation to observe its Rules.

- Better member relations

  Rules are important in our society if we are to live together harmoniously. ... If all members and their families are familiar with the rules and follow them, it will make our Club more enjoyable, the statement "always have consideration for others" being our guiding philosophy.

- Resolve problems

  These rules are established for the purpose of providing maximum enjoyment of <club's name> by all members, their families and guests. They are intended to resolve many of the complex and difficult issues that arise within a membership community as large as <club name>; but specific rules cannot be provided to resolve each possible situation. As a general rule, members are urged to conduct themselves in their dealings with others under the rules of reasonableness, courtesy and common sense that have guided the conduct of ladies and gentlemen over the years. <Club name> is our Club and the manner in which we treat the facilities and our fellow members is the key to full enjoyment of the Club by all of us.

- Provide equitable access to facilities

  *These **Rules and Regulations** have been carefully developed over the years to provide the maximum use and enjoyment of <club name> facilities by the membership, their families and guests. We believe they constitute the best solution to the many complex and difficult problems associated with an operation as large and active as our Club. ... Treat these **Rules and Regulations** with respect, for they help each member of our Club to share equitably in our facilities and should make the time spent here more enjoyable.*

- Provide the best service

  This is your Club. To provide the best possible service by the staff and in order that all members and their guests shall obtain the greatest enjoyment at the Club, certain rules have been established. If everyone will carefully observe these rules and be considerate of others, this will add to the pleasure of all.

Figure 2: Bylaws vs. Rules

	Bylaw	Rule
Definition:	A standing rule governing the regulation of a society's internal affairs.	A principle or regulation governing conduct, action, procedure, arrangement, etc.
Example:	Membership on the Board of Directors or on the Committee on Admissions of a person who fails to attend four successive meetings of the Board or such Committee, as the case may be, may be forfeited at a meeting of the Board of Directors by the vote of a majority of the Directors present.	Persons who stay in the Clubhouse overnight are not required to conform to the Dress Code at the time of checking in and checking out.
Whom example affects:	Board and committee members	Overnight guests

Types of Rules

Rules can be classified into general categories, though not every club will write rules to cover every category. For example, a city club may have rules in only a few of the categories listed below, while a country club may have rules in many more categories than those outlined here.

Generally, rules are sorted into the following six categories:

- Operation
- Conduct
- Sports
- Dress code
- Facilities
- Special event

Other categories might include spouse privileges, children's privileges, guests, reciprocal clubs, membership and discipline.

Operation rules govern the club's hours, fees, how charges are paid, what services are offered and other related topics.

Operation rules can be very complex. A partial rule on club statements and payment is used as an example below:

Pursuant to the bylaws, a member's statement of account will be due and payable as set forth in this rule:

(a)   The member's statement of account will be closed on the last day of each month.

(b)   The member's statement of account will be due upon receipt and will be deemed delinquent if payment in full is not received on or before the last day of the month in which the statement is received.

(c)   Upon a member's statement of account becoming delinquent, the member will be assessed a late fee of $50.00, which will appear on the member's next statement of account.

This rule continues for ten sections.

Club Rules Past and Present

Social organizations originally developed rules for many reasons and some of the most unusual rules can be made clear when one learns the circumstances that originally dictated them. Clubs establish traditions that help define what the club is — and rules are a part of this definition. Frequently these rules reflect the social environment of the period in which they are written.

Origin and Evolution of Club Rules

The first glimmerings of today's social clubs are sometimes traced to the baths of the ancient Romans. The baths at Caracalla included courts, athletic rooms and recreational facilities in addition to the three bath rooms. Though the rules were strictly enforced, they didn't prevent the scandals that came out of the baths.

Centuries later, the imported coffee bean would give people an excuse to gather in coffee houses in England and Scotland. These coffee houses soon became clubs that encouraged drinking, eating and gambling. In Scotland, the Spendthrift Club was attributed with creating the first minimum charge — members had to spend 41 shillings and 2 pence on each visit. (White, Ted E. and Gerstner, Larry C., *Club Operations and Management*, New York: Van Nostrand Reinhold, 1991, p. 7).

The Royal and Ancient Golf Club of St. Andrews in Edinburgh, Scotland, formed the rules of golf that were used in the Open and Amateur tournaments. These rules soon became the standard for all clubs with golf courses.

In the United States, most club rules can be traced back to only the late 1800s. Many GM/COOs say that the rules of their club have undergone few changes — regardless of how many years they've been in business. According to one GM/COO, a club in Louisiana has never changed its bylaws and has made very few changes to its rules. One of the rules states that the club will serve vegetable soup every Wednesday and, says the GM/COO, "there's never been a Wednesday in the last 120 years that that club has not served vegetable soup."

However, the wordings of rules do sometimes change. The figure on page 5 shows two sets of rules from the same club. The first lists rules that were in effect in 1899. The second lists the equivalent rules from 1994.

Conduct rules cover the spectrum of member and guest behavior in terms of smoking, drinking, language and conduct toward employees.

An example of a conduct rule is:

Any conduct unbecoming a lady or gentleman will be met with prompt and decisive action by the appropriate Standing Committee. Unbecoming conduct includes, but is not limited to, the use of loud, boisterous and obscene language and the attempt to reprimand Club employees, as well as any conduct which is likely to endanger the best interest or character of the Club.

From 1899 Rules:

Superintendent

6. The Superintendent must remain constantly on the Club premises, hours for meals and unavoidable absence alone excepted and have custody of the property of the Club.

7. He shall have general control and superintendence of all servants and be responsible for their conduct and cleanly appearance. He shall see that they carry out the different duties assigned them and, in case of misconduct, shall report the same to the President.

8. He must report to the President every violation of the bylaws and rules that comes to his knowledge and notify members of violations by them of any law of the Club.

9. He must account to the Secretary and Treasurer for all moneys and supplies received by him and belonging to the Club.

10. He shall give bond, with security, to be approved by the Board, in a sum not less than $1,000.

Strangers

11. Any member of the Club may introduce any visitor who does not reside in the county of <club's county name>, by inscribing his name in a book kept for that purpose and adding his own name and date of such introduction. The limit of such introduction shall be for fifteen days and such introduction shall not be renewed by any member until at least thirty days after the expiration of the previous invitation, unless authorized by the Board of Directors.

Same Rules from 1994

General Manager

3.1 *General Responsibilities.* The General Manager of the Club will report to and be responsible to the President and will have general control of the properties and all employees of the Club and will be responsible for the conduct and appearance of the employees. The General Manager will see that the employees carry out the duties assigned to them. Serious infractions will be reported to the President.

3.2 *Violations of Rules and Bylaws.* The General Manager will report to the President every violation of the bylaws or rules that comes to the General Manager's attention.

3.3 *Monies and Supplies.* The General Manager will account to the Board of Directors for all monies and supplies belonging to the Club.

3.4 *Bond.* The General Manager will give bond, in such amount and with such security, as approved by the Board of Directors.

Privileges

4.3 *Other Non-Members.* Non-members are not permitted to use the Club except under the following conditions:

(a) A non-member may use the Club if accompanied by a person entitled to use the club (as a member or family of member). A guest card may be issued to a non-member resident of <name of city> for the purpose of hosting a wedding party, provided that such party is honoring the marriage of a member, or the marriage of a member's child.

(b) Resident members may from time to time, submit a request for guest card privileges to be extended to close personal friends or relatives wishing to use the facilities of the club.

Sports rules, frequently the largest portion of a club's rules, include how and when sports facilities may be used.

An example of a sports rule is:

> *There shall be at least one Caddy or Forecaddy in each group of golfers, regardless of the size of the group. The Caddymaster shall have discretion to waive this rule only in the case of non-availability of caddies. Forecaddies not carrying a bag shall be paid by each golfer utilizing a cart.*

Dress code rules detail what members and guests should wear or not wear while visiting each of the facilities.

An example of a dress code rule is:

> *No cutoffs, shorts, jeans, short shorts, halters or tube tops, sweat suits, or swimsuits will be allowed in the dining room.*

Facilities rules let members and guests know how they should treat the club's property and equipment.

An example of a facilities rule is:

> *Park only in lined spaces. The front of each building should be used for pickup and drop-off of members. Handicapped spaces are provided for those displaying a handicapped sticker. A $10.00 fine will be assessed for illegal parking. Repeat violators will be subject to disciplinary action.*

Special event rules spell out fees, times and other information to members who plan to hold weddings, reunions, or other events at the club.

An example of a special event rule is:

> *Party facilities — Certain rooms in the Club are available for private parties.*
>
> *Arrangements for private parties should be made in advance through the Club Manager's office.*
>
> *Meal reservations should be made in advance whenever possible. If a party includes an unusual number of people or if special menus or service is desired, the Club Manager's office must be given adequate advance notice.*
>
> *The sponsoring member must attend all member-sponsored functions.*

Publication of Rules

Because club rules change frequently and because members need to be intimately familiar with them, the rules should be published in an accessible format. This poses a challenge to many clubs that struggle to determine which format will most closely meet their members' needs and still be cost-effective.

There are several formats in which club rules are distributed:

- Staple-bound booklets of bylaws and rules
- Spiral-bound or perfect-bound booklets of bylaws, rules and membership lists
- Full-size yearbooks which include articles of incorporation, bylaws, rules, schedules, calendars, membership lists, officer lists and lists of reciprocal clubs
- Three-ring binder notebooks with the rules printed on high-quality stationery

- Folders embossed with the club emblem and the rules printed on full-sized sheets and inserted in the folders
- Postings in locker rooms, pool areas and the clubhouse

It is suggested that however the rules are bound or displayed, they should be clear, readable, easy to follow and easy to understand. One GM/COO said it's very important that members are able to find the rule that they need without having to search through an entire booklet. Logical organization that divides rules into categories can help members find the rules they need. Some clubs alphabetize their rules or include an index or table of contents in the booklet.

When choosing a format, some clubs undertake a cost-benefit analysis that addresses several concerns:

Distribution. The method of distribution will dictate several costs — postage, number of copies printed, durability of paper and type of packaging. Many clubs issue new rule books every year and mail them to all members. This method is especially common if the rule book includes sports schedules and membership lists. One club recently stopped sending out the new books to all members. Instead, it substantially cut its production run and gave the revised rule books only to new members. The remaining books were made available at the front desk for other members.

Frequency. As mentioned above, some clubs choose to publish rule books annually. Another club said it sends out its books to all members every other year, but publishes an addendum in the off-year which includes all rules and membership changes. Still other clubs publish rule books only when there has been a major change.

Updates. Most clubs do not wish to delay the start date of a rule until the books are reprinted. For clubs that choose spiral-bound notebooks, it is easy to publish one new page or an addenda to send out to members. At one club, they added to the back page of the rules booklet a pocket in which members could put any subsequent additions or alterations.

Cost. Club management and boards need to carefully analyze all of the costs involved before picking a format. There is the expense of the original publication and then the expense of making changes. Publishing a customized three-ring binder can have expensive initial costs, but money is saved when changes can be issued on three-hole punched sheets. A perfect- or staple-bound booklet may have to be reprinted every time there is a change.

Changing a Rule

Board or committee members usually change rules, but some club members will even go to court to change rules they don't like. One GM/COO said that it was the most counter-productive thing he's ever heard of for members to sue their clubs over rules they didn't like. "They should either live with the rules, get out of the club, or try to change the rules internally in a constructive manner."

Club rules are designed to provide the best possible atmosphere for the greatest number of members, so they need to be sensitive to the wishes of those members. Because of this, the process for changing a club rule tends to be straightforward. Although the procedure may vary from club to club, the manner of amending, deleting, or adding a club rule is usually spelled out in the bylaws or in other club rules. Usually, the task falls to the Executive Committee of the club and rule changes rarely need to be approved by the membership. See Figure 3: How Rules Are Changed.

Figure 3: How Rules Are Changed

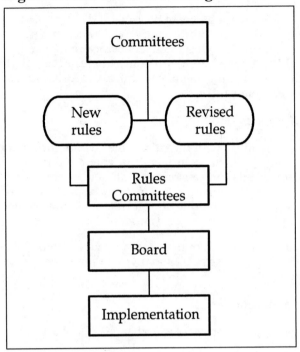

The following procedures for changing club rules are taken from several club rule books:

- *The House Committee has full power to make, suspend, amend, or otherwise modify the House Rules at any time without notice.*

- *These Rules may be changed, amended, or repealed by the Board at any regular or special meeting and members will be informed. Notice of any amendment or repeal of these rules adopted by the Board will be promptly given to the members.*

- (At a management-operated club) *Management shall issue Rules and Regulations and members of the club agree to be bound by said Rules and Regulations. Management reserves the right to change the Rules and Regulations when deemed necessary.*

- *The rules may be repealed, amended, or new rules may be adopted by a vote of two-thirds of the directors present at any meeting of the Board of Directors. These rules will be interpreted by the Board of Directors.*

- *These rules may be amended or supplemented from time to time as may be deemed necessary by the House Committee.*

- *The Rules Committee shall coordinate and enforce current rules and shall recommend new or revised rules of general application. Each standing committee shall propose such rules as it may deem fit governing the matters within its province and submit the same for discussion and coordination to the Rules Committee, which shall submit the final proposals to the Board; such final proposals shall become effective immediately after the Board meeting following their submission to the Board, unless the Board has taken contrary action thereon.*

Communicating Changes to Members

All new members should be made aware of the rules and the importance of obeying them. Likewise, *all* members need to be informed of any changes in club rules. While it is not necessary to seek the approval of club members before changing a rule, one GM/COO strongly recommends that members be informed before the rule takes effect. Good communication will avoid having members embarrassed because they inadvertently violated a rule they were unaware of.

Informing New Members

New members who are familiar with the rules either before they join or soon afterward are more willing to abide by them than members who are not formally exposed to the rules. Some clubs hold orientation sessions that all new members must attend. Parts of these orientation sessions cover club rules and member responsibility for those rules. Other clubs have a welcoming packet that includes a rule book and members are specifically asked to read the book before coming to the club.

A few clubs highlight a rule in each of their monthly newsletters. By doing this, the club reinforces its commitment to these rules and gives all members a reminder of rules they might have forgotten.

Informing Current Members

Current members need to keep abreast of rule changes. Clubs accomplish this in a number of ways:

- Sending out newsletters
- Updating the rules book
- Sending out individual letters
- Including a stuffer in the monthly statements
- Posting changes throughout the club for several weeks

One member of a club management staff said that the club combines several of the above methods. It will first post changes everywhere — in the locker rooms, starter desks and lounges. The change will often be posted for six to twelve weeks depending on how broad the change is. Then the club will publish the change in the monthly newsletter and include a stuffer in the monthly statements. Depending on the importance of the change, the club will sometimes put a tagline on the statements requesting that members read the stuffer.

Some club rules dictate which communication channels will be used whenever changes are made. Here's what two clubs do:

> *Rule changes and other official Club notices will be communicated in the monthly newsletter or by separate mailing. It is the responsibility of each member to be acquainted with the correct House Rules.*

> *Any changes or additions to these rules, subsequent to publishing, will appear in the minutes of the Board of Governors and will be published in the Club newsletter.*

Enforcement

In some organizations, rules are merely a formality, rarely enforced and sporadically obeyed. Non-enforcement leads to rule obsolescence. Everyone has heard of bizarre state laws such as one in Idaho that says it is illegal for a man to give his sweetheart a box of candy weighing less than 50 pounds. Or a Vermont law that says a woman is forbidden to walk down the street on a Sunday unless her husband walks 20 paces behind her with a musket on his shoulder. It is likely that if someone did try to enforce absurd rules like these, the rules would soon be stricken from the book.

Non-enforcement is a concern of very few clubs. Most clubs are concerned about enforcing rules in a proper way. GM/COOs consistently identify enforcement as one of the most difficult issues involving club rules. One GM/COO said, "The manner in which we enforce club rules is the biggest issue. Many times clubs create unenforceable rules or put the staff in a tough position."

Rare is the club in which rule violations are rampant. At city clubs, violations usually involve only the occasional dress code problems or the improper display of business papers. One city club GM/COO reported very few problems with enforcement: "We have very responsible members who are honorable gentlemen and ladies. They show a lot of decorum and very rarely violate any rules."

It is the very presumption that all members are ladies and gentlemen that can make enforcement a delicate issue. No one on the staff or board wants to offend or embarrass a member. The dining club that loaned bright-colored jackets to men who showed up without a coat found their members and guests embarrassed at being singled out. But clubs do not want to allow fair and just rules to become obsolete because they were too timid to enforce them.

It can be especially difficult to avoid embarrassing a member when other members are demanding that the rules be enforced against the violator. At one club, the staff has been trained to respond to members, "Thank you for pointing out the violation. We will be contacting that member, but we do not wish to embarrass him/her in the presence of guests, just as we would not want to embarrass you."

"The finest clubs in the country live by the rules and enforce the rules," said one GM/COO.

Necessity of Enforcement

A common theme among club managers is that boards should only enact rules that they are going to enforce. "If you have rules, enforce them. If you're not going to enforce them, take them out," suggested one GM/COO.

Another manager concurred, saying, "If you don't intend on enforcing a rule, don't make it in the first place. It tells people they can do whatever they want and they won't be penalized."

A few GM/COOs spoke of the necessity of enforcing even the bizarre rules. They said that the rules may be maintaining a tradition that was part of the club's character, or that it was a bad rule that would languish on the books unless consistently enforced. By consistently enforcing a bad rule, GM/COOs give club boards and committees the impetus to change or remove it.

Failing to enforce a rule compromises the credibility of the staff who must enforce it and compromises the authority of the remaining rules.

One GM/COO described a rule that put his staff members in an awkward position: Several members felt very strongly that smoking should not be allowed on the premises. Other members didn't care for the smoking, but didn't want to make the entire facility smoke-free. As a compromise, the board decided to make the dining room a non-smoking area — but chose not to enforce the no-smoking rule. The dining room staff was then faced with the unpleasant task of informing members that they shouldn't smoke but had no authority to ask diners to extinguish the smoke or leave the dining room. The GM/COO said the club ended up easing into the rule. The club gave members a grace period and then the professional staff ended up enforcing it — even though they knew that there could be no penalties for those who persisted.

There are two tenets that can help make sure the rules are enforceable:

1. Be practical and precise.
2. Identify exceptions in writing.

Be Practical and Precise

When members understand the rules, they are more likely to follow them. When staff members understand the rules, they'll know how to enforce them. It is important to remove all ambiguities from rules to prevent misunderstandings. One GM/COO encourages rule writers to: "Be precise! Eliminate the possibility of misinterpretations."

The following rule, for example, could be written in a clearer fashion:

> Men and ladies who are employed on a full-time basis will have priority for tee times from 9 a.m. to 3 p.m. on weekdays and weekends and may make such reservations two days in advance. Tee times not reserved for such hours by men and working ladies by 7 p.m. on the day before play then may be reserved by ladies. Mixed groups are considered the same as working men or ladies play.

It can be difficult to determine whether the people with tee time priority are both men and women who work full-time, or whether it is women who work full-time and all men. The rule fails to clarify itself when it later mentions working ladies in one sentence and working men in the next.

Identify Exceptions in Writing

There are exceptions to some rules. Some GM/COOs say they make exceptions on an individual basis, keeping it between themselves and the member involved. One GM/COO who uses this method warns that there are some rules you never deviate from, even though others require a little more laxity. Nonetheless, he says, "If you have a rule you're constantly breaking, it's not a good rule."

When handling accounts or private matters, it is easier to make exceptions on a case-by-case basis. For exceptions that are more public, other members could resent what they see as unequal treatment. One way to maintain a sense of fairness among members is to identify in writing what the exceptions to the rules are.

"You need to have predetermined exceptions," said one GM/COO. "How do you handle disabled golfers at a club that doesn't allow motorized carts on the golf course? Do they need to get a medical note? Who makes the decisions? You need to spell these things out in some formal method. If there are exceptions, print them up."

Two examples of rules with stated exceptions are:

> *In no event will a guest be permitted to play the course more than ten times (not 10 times with each member — this means a total of 10 times) during a calendar year, except that rounds played in the Member/Guest Tournaments, outings and similar events will not be counted. Included in the ten (10) times permission will be a restriction that guests cannot play more than five (5) of the ten (10) times on weekends or holidays.*

> *Business dress attire. Business dress attire is required in all dining rooms, meeting rooms, lounges and the library Monday through Friday and after 5:00 p.m. on Saturday; and in the 4th Floor Rendezvous Room before 1:30 p.m. Monday through Friday.*

> > *The code will not apply to overnight guests or members attired in neat casual or travel clothes who are transiting lobby and elevators directly to or from their sleeping rooms, or between their rooms and the Athletic Department. Members of a uniformed organization such as military, police and similar organizations may be attired in the dress uniform of the day. Members of the clergy may be attired in customary clerical garb.*

Painful Process

Enforcing the rules sometimes can be an uncomfortable and painful process for a club. A GM/COO can find himself or herself in a precarious position when enforcing rules. However, because rules reflect what the majority of the members want, most club managers believe it's important that rules be applied fairly and consistently.

Some rules require GM/COOs to possess a great deal of courage to confront a member and much tact in deflecting hostility. Some of the most difficult situations arise when rules must be enforced against:

- Celebrities
- Uncooperative members
- Officers and board members

Celebrities

Doing the right thing can land a club in hot water. Clubs know that they have to enforce their rules equally. However, it can be tempting to make exceptions for a celebrity who can make waves:

> In the 1980s, a well-known personality attended a private function at a club as a guest. She approached the club wearing an expensive pantsuit. The dress code — which members were responsible for communicating to all guests — was that women had to wear a dress or a skirt. A club employee approached the guest and offered her a skirt that the club made available. The guest refused the skirt and was turned away. The employee who enforced

the club's rules found himself approached by national media who wanted to publicize what they perceived as an injustice.

There is a fine line between upholding the high standards of a club and exposing the club to public scorn. However, if a club can show that its rules are supported by the membership, are consistent with the standards of the club and are equally enforced, it can often deflect criticism. A greater concern for clubs would be if the members resented an unequal application of the rules.

Nonetheless, there may be occasions when a club will have to bend a rule in order to preserve its image. If it does become necessary, the club may need to evaluate the rule in question and decide whether it should be changed for everyone.

Uncooperative Members

It is not just celebrities who cause discomfort to those enforcing the rules. At another club, a board officer approached a golfing member who consistently parked his golf cart too close to the greens. On being told of his infraction, the member (a relatively new one) told the board officer to mind his own business. After the incident was reported, the board asked the GM/COO to write a letter from the golf committee and suspend the member's golfing privileges for a week. The member responded angrily and by the end of the golf season had resigned from the club.

No club wants to lose members because of an altercation over rules. One GM/COO said that at some clubs members feel they are exempt from the rules and that the rules are only for other people. In these situations, enforcing the rules can be very difficult. It becomes necessary to first communicate to the member why the rule applies to him or her and to remind the member that he or she agreed to the rules when joining the club.

Alcohol can also occasionally cause problems for clubs. Members who might otherwise be very reasonable become belligerent when intoxicated. At one club, a new manager asked the son of a member to put a coat on to comply with the dress code. While the son agreed in a friendly manner, a few drinks later his father approached the GM/COO and began yelling at him for telling his son how to dress. The GM/COO tried to calmly explain the dress code while the father threatened to have him fired.

Few members respond to reminders with antagonistic behavior. But when they do, a club must handle the matter delicately. The club does not want the member to be hostile toward the club or to tarnish other people's image of the club. If the member is intoxicated, the club must take several steps to ensure the safety of the member while not allowing him or her to interfere with the enjoyment of others.

Officers and Board Members

Board members are usually the ones charged with creating and enforcing rules. But when they set themselves above the rules, it fosters an unhealthy environment for members, staff and other board members.

Some of the most volatile situations described by GM/COOs occurred when they had to enforce rules against a board member. Allusions were made to altercations that few managers wanted to recount on the record. Those altercations are ones that few managers can hope to win. After all, the board is boss. In most cases, because board members make the rules, they understand their necessity and importance. They also have the power to change rules that they think are unfair or onerous. However, these factors do not eliminate all problems.

In most cases the board itself handles a rule violation by a board officer because enforcing a rule against a board member is a delicate situation for a staff member. The board on which this person is a member has the power to fire or make contract stipulations with the GM/COO. However, in at least one area, delinquent accounts, GM/COOs are typically given complete control to enforce and penalize. One GM/COO said he would never post the name of a board member on a delinquent list without first informing the member. He said the person never fails to pay before the name is posted.

GM/COOs that do have to deal with this situation need to make sure that they can count on the support of the other board members and the membership. Careful documentation and a history of consistent enforcement can profit the GM/COO who must enforce rules against board members.

Enforcement Challenges

There are some rules that have never been violated and are put into writing merely as a formality. Other rules are frequently broken. However, there are rules that are generally obeyed, but retain challenges to those charged with enforcing them.

GM/COOs have identified some of the following rules as the most difficult to enforce:

Dress code. As society becomes more casual in its dress, more people violate dress code rules. Many clubs that choose to retain their formal dress code offer loaner coats, ties and skirts. Several clubs have instituted casual dining on Fridays because so many businesses have gone to casual dress on Fridays. One GM/COO cited a colleague of his in another state whose dining room patronage was down to 20 percent at lunch on Fridays because members didn't want to have to dress up to come to lunch when they were wearing casual clothes at work.

Business papers. Most clubs insist that business papers not be displayed in the public areas of the club. It is a rule that must be strictly enforced by clubs that want to retain their status as non-profit social institutions. Many clubs will offer private dining rooms to guests who insist on conducting business at the club. In addition to papers, non-profit club members cannot display any cellular phones or laptop computers, either.

Delinquent accounts. "Collections is the most difficult subject to deal with," said one GM/COO. "It's our number-one priority. We have some members who play us like a Stradivarius. They only pay the delinquent amount and hang on to their money until the last possible moment." Some GM/COOs choose to make exceptions under extenuating circumstances, but realize that the fees are intended to prevent late payments and, therefore, cannot be casually set aside. Members sometimes complain that the late fees are usurious. At least one GM/COO answers charges of usury with, "If you would have paid your bill, we wouldn't be having this conversation."

Tipping. Many clubs prohibit tipping because they feel it will compromise the consistency of service. If a server knows that one member is a good tipper and the other is not, the first member will get better service. One club employee said that allowing tipping "takes the focus off of the member and on to 'what can I get?' " At some clubs tipping is allowed only in certain areas. One club in particular ruled: "Tipping is allowed in the locker room area only." The GM/COO reported that the club had wait staff going into the locker rooms to pick up tips. Another club manager said that the solution is to have either no tipping at all

— and to fine the members that are caught slipping gratuities to employees — or change the rule to allow tipping everywhere.

Guest access to the club. Most clubs restrict the number of times any guest can visit the club. Yet the rule remains ambiguous at some sports clubs. Does visiting the dining room or spa carry the same weight as visiting the golf course? Should visits be equally enforced when one activity makes more money for the club? Clubs that have automated guest registrations can track how frequently a guest has been at the club. If the club is not computerized, the staff needs to automatically know what to do when they see a guest and how to tell how many times that guest has used the club.

Divorces/separations. Club professionals report being challenged by how to enforce rules affecting a member who is going through a divorce or separation. The situation becomes especially vexatious in clubs with single memberships. A member may come in and say that he or she is undergoing a separation and doesn't want the spouse to use the club. Small clubs may try to monitor the spouse's use of the club and absorb any charges or guest checks made by the spouse. Many larger clubs say that they won't get involved until the divorce is final. As one manager explained, "We don't want to get involved in marital disputes. A divorce is a legal severance; a separation is not. It's a sticky, unpleasant situation."

Who Enforces?

Clubs bear a duty to enforce the rules that the membership adopts. As one GM/COO put it, "At the best clubs in the country, members and management enforce the rules alike and equally. Members need to give 100 percent backing to their professional staff and support the rules the members made."

The ideal situation is that everyone at the club enforces the rules equally. However, enforcement is most frequently a task that must be delegated to individuals. Typically the rules themselves define who the enforcers are. Depending upon the club and the type of rule, there may be several different enforcers. Clubs may establish:

- Self-enforcement
- Member enforcement
- Officer enforcement
- Staff enforcement

Self-Enforcement

Many clubs rely on the integrity of their members to obey the rules. After all, each member is screened before admittance. As one GM/COO said, "One thing we have today that we've always had is exclusivity. It's a feature that has not changed. You have to be voted in to belong." Most clubs rely on their screening process to keep out people who cannot discipline themselves.

However, another GM/COO warns that no matter how thorough the screening process, there is no litmus test for integrity. "Not all of our members possess integrity. We need to be sure we accept that fact when writing rules. A good example is a member cheating on the golf scorecard to bring the handicap up." He also points out that alcohol can cause a person to cease acting as a lady or gentleman.

The rules establish the code of conduct that the majority of members believe will endow their club with the character they desire. Rules are guidelines that the members who wish to maintain a harmonious environment will follow. Those clubs that rely on self-enforcement also rely on the members' ability to see that adherence to the rules is in their best interest.

Many clubs spell out the expectations for self-enforcement in their rule books:

- *It is anticipated that these rules will be self-enforcing by a membership wholly aware of their necessity. Otherwise, enforcement will be handled by the appropriate committee of the Board of Directors through warning, fine of $5.00 or more, or other disciplinary action including expulsion. The General Manager, Golf, Tennis and Swimming Professionals and other supervisory employees are charged with enforcing these rules and the membership will respect their positions in this regard.*

- *All members and other persons using the Club will be held to the standards of a "gentleman" or a "lady" as the case may be and failure to conform to that standard may result in termination of membership, fine, suspension, or expulsion from the Club.*

- *Membership in the Club involves a cheerful and willing obligation to observe its Rules. It is the duty of the membership of the Club to know its Bylaws and Rules and to actively cooperate with the Officers and Directors in the enforcement thereof.*

- *Treat these Rules and Regulations with respect, for they help each member of our Club to share equitably in our facilities and should make the time spent here more enjoyable.*

- *Rules are important in our society if we are to live together harmoniously. At <this club> the honor system has been the method by which the rules have been observed over the years. If all members and their families are familiar with the rules and follow them, it will make our Club more enjoyable, the statement 'always have consideration for others' being our guiding philosophy.*

Member Enforcement

Clubs also encourage members to monitor each other. Often a disapproving word from a fellow member can be more effective than any action taken by a club employee or officer. Ultimately, the membership must monitor itself or the club rules are rendered ineffective.

Clubs that expect members to help with enforcement include such rules as these two:

All members and employees of the Club are requested to report any violation of these House Rules. Members violating same will be subject to action as deemed necessary in accordance with the Club Rules and Regulations.

Any infraction of the Rules and Regulations should be reported immediately to the General Manager, the appropriate Committee Chairperson, or a member of the Rules Enforcement Committee.

Many GM/COOs suggest that while "the strongest pressure in the world can be friendly pressure," clubs should not foster a contentious environment among club members. There have been cases, especially concerning dress code issues, where member enforcement has led to bickering and uncomfortable confrontations. If members enforce the rules, some managers said, it needs to be done in a helpful manner with equal respect for their fellow members.

A GM/COO told about a member who was fanatical about enforcing the club's rule that hats may not be worn in the dining room. The member — who ate at the club four or five nights a week — became incensed whenever anyone wore a hat and would explode at the dining room managers. The scene would make everyone around him uncomfortable, but he claimed to be enforcing the rule. Eventually, club members who were irritated by this behavior began wearing hats just to anger him. The GM/COO finally had to ask him to stop enforcing the rule because he was creating a larger problem.

Officer Enforcement

When self-enforcement or member enforce-ment is neither practical nor effective, the board may resort to appointing a committee member or one of its own officers.

> *Committees.* In clubs where the committees write the rules, monitoring for compliance falls on the committee's shoulders.

> *The House Committee is charged by the Board of Directors with the duty and responsibility of calling attention of a member, when necessary, to violations of the Bylaws or of these Rules.*

> *Club board member.* Monitoring members for rule compliance may be a duty assumed by the entire club board. One GM/COO said that management typically enforces the rules, it involves the board on sensitive issues. "Our health club closes at 9:30 p.m. We had a member who would show up at 9:25 and take 45-minute showers. I had to go to the board on that one."

> *The Board will have the right to call upon any member to make, on honor, a full statement, oral or written, in reference to any infraction of the Bylaws or Rules of the Club and the member will not be excused therefrom on the ground that any statement would be self-incriminatory.*

One former GM/COO recounted an incident that was resolved only by the board president coming in to deal with the member. The GM/COO said a waitress came into the kitchen in tears because a member had just "fired" her. The member had been drinking heavily and began to systematically fire the entire dining room staff. When the GM/COO tried to intervene, the member said, "I like you, but I'm just going to have to fire you too." As the member's behavior grew more rowdy, the GM/COO called the board president at home and asked him to come in and handle the situation. The board president put on his suit and walked into the dining room with the GM/COO. As soon as the offending member spotted the two of them standing near the entrance, he ran out another door and left the club for the night.

Staff Enforcement

The GM/COO is often charged with ensuring that members as well as employees follow the letter of the bylaws and rules for the good of the membership at large. Since the GM/COO is likely to spend more time at the club than the committee members or board members, this is often a practical choice. The majority of clubs rely on their professional staff to be guardians of the club and to enforce the rules as necessary.

> *The General Manager will report to the President every violation of the Bylaws or Rules that comes to the General Manager's attention.*

> *Members are requested to observe all rules of etiquette so Club facilities may be enjoyed by all. The Club Manager shall have full and complete charge of the clubhouse and grounds at all times.*

At other times, several people are involved in the enforcement of the club rules. It is also practical for staff members to be charged with enforcing such rules as conduct, sporting

Figure 4: Examples of Rules Staff Enforce

Rule infractions	Staff responsible
Guest plays course too often	Golf starter
Denying alcohol service to intoxicated member	Cocktail server
Dress code violation in dining room	Dining room manager
Smoking in non-smoking area	Manager in charge of area
Horseplay in the swimming pool	Aquatics director or lifeguard
Delinquent dues	General Manager/Chief Operating Officer

and dress. A cocktail server might tell a member that no more alcohol will be served because the member is nearing intoxication. Or a golf starter may turn away a guest who has visited too many times. See Figure 4: Examples of Rules Staff Enforce.

One GM/COO said he tries "to have several levels of enforcers when it comes to rule violations." He said it usually encourages a greater amount of compliance because this allows for a repeated reinforcement of the rule.

This GM/COO described an incident at his club in which a member entered the dining room and specifically asked to sit in the non-smoking section. The member then lit up a cigarette and refused to put it out. The server asked the member if he would like to be moved to the smoking section. The member refused. Then the maitre d' approached the member, reminded him that he was sitting in a non-smoking section and asked him to put out his cigarette. The member refused. Next, the assistant manager approached the member and also asked him to put out his cigarette. The member again refused. Finally, the GM/COO was brought in to talk to the member. The GM/COO asked the member what the problem was. The member objected to the new non-smoking rule and said he was trying to make a point. After a brief discussion, the member put out his cigarette, finished his dinner and left. The next morning he called the GM/COO and apologized. Had it not been for the apology, the GM/COO said the next step would have been to bring his name up before the board.

Many GM/COOs might choose to report the incident to the board anyway, depending upon the club, their relationship to the board and the number of people who witnessed the event. However, this particular GM/COO felt the enforcement was sufficient to prevent recurrence of the event.

How Do Clubs Enforce Rules?

Most GM/COOs concurred with their colleague who said "enforcement is handled by calling a rules infraction to the attention of the member. This can be done at the lowest possible staff level. More serious matters are taken to the department head and from there to the manager-on-duty or the GM. The GM ought to be able to resolve the problem. Repercussions go to the board."

In the majority of cases, simply telling members they are committing an infraction and reminding them of the rule is sufficient. In a club where the management staff enforces the rules, the staff members are usually trained to introduce themselves and explain the rule. Depending upon the violation, staff members might offer members alternative ways to obey the rule while still being able to conduct activities that are important to them. For example, private dining rooms are offered to members who insist on conducting business at the table. "We're very accommodating and apologetic," said the GM/COO of a city club.

Frequently clubs find that offering some form of reinforcement that communicates what the rules are can be helpful in avoiding future infractions. At one club, they are considering making embossed rule cards for club personnel to hand out to members who show business papers or use cellular phones or laptops in the dining room. Another club has developed a golf course brochure that is handed to any members violating a golf rule. The appropriate rule is pointed out and then the member or guest is invited to keep the brochure.

Penalties

If there is no penalty for breaking a rule, then there is no authority its enforcement. In the perfect world, a mere appeal to a sense of community would be sufficient to put an end to any infraction. However, there are those members — no matter how carefully a club screens — who will persist in breaking a rule even after the violation has been pointed out to them. In order to deal with these members, penalties that make it unprofitable to break the rule must be assessed. Penalties usually are designed to deter rule-breaking, not to punish violators.

This section examines what type of penalties clubs use to enforce their rules and who determines what those penalties are. Each explanation is supported with sample rules taken from various types of clubs.

What Are the Penalties?

The penalties for breaking the rules often depend on the severity, frequency and nature of the offense.

Penalties for rules infractions can be broken down into three main categories:

- Blanket penalties
- Progressive penalties
- Violation-specific penalties

Blanket Penalties

Some clubs have one blanket penalty spelled out for all rule infractions. Usually this penalty is broadly stated to allow fairness in enforcement. With minor exceptions, these penalties will apply to *all* rule infractions without respect to type. Likewise, these penalties are assessed whether the member is a first-time violator or a repeat offender.

Violation of the Rules or Bylaws of the Club may result in a reprimand or, following a review by the Board of Governors, suspension or expulsion.

If, after a hearing, the Board determines that the complaint is without merit, no further action shall be taken; but if the Board determines that the member should be disciplined, its action may include, but not be limited to, one or more of the following:

(a) Fine: The Board may levy a fine against a member.

(b) Suspension: The Board may suspend some or all of a member's privileges to use Club facilities for a period not in excess of two (2) years. Dues and other obligations of a suspended member shall accrue and be paid by such member during the suspension period, payable on the same schedule as by a non-suspended member.

c) Expulsion: Membership in the Club may be terminated and the member expelled by a two-thirds (2/3) vote of the members of the Board. Any member so expelled shall not thereafter be eligible for Club membership, may not use any facilities of the Club and may not be permitted on the Club's premises as a guest or otherwise.

Progressive Penalties

Frequently, a club establishes a policy of progressive penalties. The first offense may come in the form of a verbal or written warning. Continued offenses may result in a suspension of membership, a fine, or even expulsion from the club.

This progression of penalties gives the members plenty of opportunity to change their behavior or remove themselves from the club. However, all clubs reserve the right to immediately enact the most stringent penalty for flagrant or dangerous violations.

Examples of progressive penalties include:

Violation of the Rules or Bylaws of the club may result in a reprimand or, following a review by the Board of Governors, suspension or expulsion.

If the Chairman of the Activity Committee...decides that the conduct of the reported member is in violation of the Constitution, Bylaws, or House Rules of the Club, or that such conduct is prejudicial to the good order, character, or welfare of the Club, the Activity Committee Chairman...may censure such member or take other steps to ensure that the violation shall not reoccur as may be appropriate...In cases involving serious or repeated violations...the Activity Committee Chairman shall refer the matter to the Board of Governors and may include in its reference the recommendation that the member be suspended from all privileges of the Club pending final action of the Board.

Violation-Specific Penalties

When clubs incorporate penalties into individual rules, they are able to tailor the penalty to the offense. The specific penalties are growing increasingly common according to one long-time communications director: "The discipline has become more specific. The rules now state 'this is what we will do in this situation, this is the appeals process, this is the penalty.' There's no longer a single broad statement."

There are slight variations in the specific penalties based on the type of rule as in the following examples:

Operation rule. Many of the operation rules build penalties into the wording. Frequently a penalty involves a restriction of access or a fee.

Forty-eight (48) hours notice of cancellation of reservations for Club functions is required. At time of cancellation, a cancellation number must be obtained for record purposes. If a member cancels after the prescribed time, a full charge will be assessed.

Conduct rule. The club's immediate concern when a conduct rule is violated is usually to remove the offender from the club premises so that few members and guests will be offended. Depending upon the severity or frequency of the offense, additional action may be taken at a later date.

> *Decorum will be observed in all parts of the Clubhouse and premises at all times. Any member or guest conducting himself in an unbecoming manner shall be requested by the General Manager, or his designee, to leave the Clubhouse. The General Manager will notify the Board of such action.*

Sports rules. Penalties for violating sports rules often result in lost points, lost place, or a ban from future participation. See Figure 5: Penalties for Sporting Rule Violations for a sport-by-sport analysis.

Dress code rules. Dress code violations have the most clear-cut penalties. If dress code rules are violated, the member or guest is not be permitted to enter the area where the dress code is in effect.

> *The following Dress Code has been adopted by the Board of Directors and the staff has been advised that they are to politely decline service or disallow use of the Club facilities to any member or guest not in compliance with this code.*

Facility rules. Clubs must take great care to be sure that their facility rules meet all applicable codes for roadways and parking. Penalties range from warnings to towings. Clubs also must make certain that they protect the substantial investment in club facilities and property. Frequently, if damage is done to the property or the facilities, the club will demand reimbursement from the member who caused the damage. If a guest has caused damage, the club will demand reimbursement from the guest or from the member who sponsored the guest.

> *Cars shall be parked within the designated parking spaces. Cars shall not be parked in any restricted or reserved areas, including roads, lawn, golf course, driveway or entrance to Club property. Restrictions regarding parking in the ten-minute parking spaces, in the fire lane around the circle at the Clubhouse entrance and in any other no-parking zone must be strictly observed. Cars parked improperly will be subject to being ticketed and towed at the owner's expense.*

> *Property of the Club that is removed, damaged, or destroyed by a member or guest will be charged to such member or guest.*

Special event rules. The penalties associated with the violation of special event rules are typically financial ones.

> *Members are responsible at all times for the actions of their guests or any organization which they have sponsored for use of the Club facilities. Specifically, decoration plans for any occasion must be approved in advance by the club management; the use of nails or staples for decorations in any part of the Clubhouse is prohibited and furniture may not be removed or the furniture location changed, without the approval of either the Chairman or Vice Chairman of the House Committee or the President or Vice President of the Club. An appropriate monetary penalty shall be assessed the sponsoring member by the House Committee for any infraction of the foregoing. Members who injure or sponsor functions which result in injury to the property of the Club will be required to pay for the cost of repair or replacement thereof. All repair work resulting from injury to Club property shall be done by persons or firms selected and supervised by the Club Management.*

Who Determines Penalties?

Once a club has established what the penalties are for breaking a rule, it must choose who will determine the guilt of the member and assess the penalties. Typically this duty is

Figure 5: Penalties for Sporting Rule Violations

Sample Penalties

Golf rules:

"Any member who has signed up for a Tournament and is unable to play must notify the Pro Shop at least 48 hours in advance of the start of the Tournament. FAILURE TO NOTIFY THE PRO SHOP WILL RESULT IN THE MEMBER BEING PENALIZED FROM PLAYING THE NEXT TWO SCHEDULED TOURNAMENTS."

"When a starting time is to be canceled it must be done as early as possible. Arriving late will result in the loss of the starting time."

"Regulations covering the use of golf cars are posted on the golf bulletin boards. The Grounds and/or Golf Committees may prohibit the use of cars at any time if weather or course conditions warrant such action. The failure of any member to observe the regulations of car usage may result in the suspension, by the Golf Committee, of future usage by that member."

Tennis rules:

"Reservations for courts may be canceled without penalty by notifying the Pro Shop before 6 p.m. on the evening preceding the day of reservation. In the event that the court reservation is canceled after 6 p.m. of the preceding evening and the court is not used, a $5.00 charge will be levied. A $25.00 charge will be levied in the event a member holds a court reservation and does not appear."

"Tournament Rule: If a match cannot be played when scheduled, the team/player who cannot make the scheduled date may ask opponents for another date. If the team/player requesting cannot be accommodated before the next scheduled round of matches, the original match will be defaulted to the team/player who appears at the original date and time. ALL date changes must be cleared and approved by the Tennis Professional."

Swimming and beachfront rules:

"The Swim Professional may direct that such precautions be taken as he or she feels are essential for the safe use and enjoyment of the pools. Members and their guests are required to cooperate in order to ensure the proper and safe operation of the swimming activity. The Swim Professional has the authority to request members and guests violating the Rules to leave the pool area for the day."

"The Swimming Pool Committee reserves the right to cancel or suspend at any time the pool and snack bar privileges of any person who does not comply with these rules and regulations. The Pool Director has authority at all times to enforce the rules of the Swimming Pool Committee."

Card playing rules:

"Card games may be played in the Men's Grill and such other rooms as may be set aside for such purposes; however, the House Committee will exercise its authority to suppress any game of gambling or other game which may be considered to disturb others or be improper or prejudicial to the Club."

Fitness center and spa rules:

"Any members, spouses, children and guests not adhering to the above rules can and will be asked to leave the Wellness Center. Anyone exhibiting inappropriate behavior can and will be asked to leave the Wellness Center by the Director or the Assistant Director."

handled by board members, committees, or occasionally staff members. The designated person will also choose which penalty will be given if there is more than one type of penalty for a given offense.

Board Members

Since the board members are ultimately responsible for the creation of the rules, some clubs also make them responsible for determining penalties. It is also deemed more acceptable by most members to have penalties assessed by their peers rather than by employees of the club.

Rules that give board members the power to penalize include:

> *In accordance with the club bylaws, the Board has the right to discipline a member who violates Club rules.*

> *In no case will a resolution which would terminate the membership of, censure, fine, suspend, or expel from the Club a member be considered without notice in writing being sent by the Secretary to each member of the Board at least one week before the meeting at which action is contemplated.*

Most GM/COOs prefer that penalties come directly from the board. One GM/COO said he was having a problem with a member who kept violating a rule. He had already spoken with the member about the rule and was in the process of writing a reprimand letter. He shared his difficulty with a fellow manager who said, "Why are *you* writing the letter? The board should write the letter! What if that member gets on the board later and decides to fire you?" By requiring the board to give out penalties, there are not as many repercussions for the staff and members make less of a commotion.

Committees

Committees are specialists in particular club-related areas and are often seen as the ideal people to penalize infractions of rules in the committees' area of influence. They are frequently able to determine the exact nature of the infraction, its seriousness and the appropriate response.

Two ways that clubs invest committees with this power are:

> *Upon receipt of a signed, written complaint charging a member with a violation of the Club's House Rules, or with conduct injurious to the good order, character or welfare of the Club, the Activity the Activity Committee responsible for the area in which the alleged violation took place, shall appoint a subcommittee consisting of three or more members for the purpose of conducting an investigation and making a factual determination regarding the alleged violation. Additionally, upon initial receipt of the written complaint by the cognizant Activity Committee, the Chairman of said committee shall forward a copy of the complaint to the alleged violator, to the General Manager and to the Chairman of the House Committee for purposes of information, monitoring, control and follow-up of the complaint. The subcommittee so appointed shall review the facts and circumstances surrounding the alleged violation(s) and shall prepare and submit to the Chairman of the Activity Committee a written recommendation as to the corrective action to be taken.*

> *Any infraction of Club rules by a member or by one of his or her family or guests shall be reported to the Rules Committee which may give written notification thereof to the member. If necessary, such communication will include the member's rights and the grievance procedure.*

Staff Members

Because certain club employees are always on the premises and have responsibility for the day-to-day operations of the club, many organizations rely on the GM/COO, sports professionals and dining room managers to penalize members in their areas for any infraction of the rules of conduct and dress.

When a board gives the responsibility of penalizing rule infractions to the club staff members, it can place an uncomfortable burden on them, according to GM/COOs. After all, the person a staff member penalizes today could, in the future, become a board member seeking revenge. This makes staff members extremely reluctant to penalize members. Usually the clubs that require staff members to assess penalties are those that are corporate-owned. In corporate-owned clubs, the members do not own the club and therefore don't have the authority to determine penalties or make rules.

However, there are certain administrative areas where common sense dictates that the GM/COO assess at least the first stage of penalties. One area that fits this description is collecting delinquent dues. As mentioned earlier, boards frequently invest in the GM/COO the full responsibility for collecting delinquent dues — and in administering any appropriate penalties. These penalties may range from assessing late fees, to posting names, or suspending members.

Guests

A member of a club agrees to the rules upon admittance and eventually may have input on the formation of new rules. A guest, however, does not have the same knowledge of the club rules, nor does a guest usually have the incentive to become intimately familiar with the rules. Nonetheless, a club cannot exempt guests from rules and expect to maintain the same equitable atmosphere on the premises.

Each club must determine how guests will be informed about the rules and who will be responsible for any infractions committed by guests.

Role of the Club

Clubs that expect guests to obey the rules need to make sure that all guests are aware of and understand those rules. This can be a challenge since few guests will take the time to read the entire rule book just to have lunch in the dining room or to play a round of golf.

On the other hand, they may be willing to read a shorter version of the rules telling them specifically what they need to know.

With this in mind, some clubs, especially those with very strict rules, publish literature specifically for guests. Because they recognize that an entire rule book can be daunting to a visitor, they design condensed versions that address specific guest needs. One club gives members engraved cards to include in wedding or special event invitations. These cards let all guests know what the dress code is. Other clubs publish brochures that are available in the golf shop or club lobby. These brochures not only inform guests of the rules of the clubhouse and golf course, but also can be used for marketing purposes. They are especially common in clubs that allow non-members to use the club without a sponsoring member.

At some clubs the board charges the staff to review the rules with guests when the staff issues guest cards. These clubs see this contact as an extra opportunity to make sure all guests understand what is expected of them.

Members Responsible for Guests

Most clubs expect members to tell their guests what the club rules are. This way members can share with guests the specific rules that will affect their visit to the club. It is expected that members want their guests to have an enjoyable visit and will give their guests any additional information they need.

Since it is difficult to penalize a guest, most clubs hold the sponsoring member responsible for guest infractions. Members are most frequently assessed penalties for guest infractions when there is damage to the club facility, improper debts are incurred, or guests are brought to the facility an excessive number of times. Penalizing the member instead of the guest provides an added incentive for the member to make all the rules clear and to invite only guests who meet the standards of the club.

The following rules are examples of responsibilities given to members for their guests:

A member is fully responsible for all indebtedness to the Club incurred by any guests, or children registered as juniors under article VII, paragraph 5 of the bylaws. A member is generally responsible for the conformity of guests, a spouse and children to all the house rules and bylaws of the Club. In cases of resignation, expulsion, suspension, or withdrawal of credit of a member, the privileges extended at such member's request shall terminate.

The member shall be responsible for the conduct of and any indebtedness incurred by all members of his family or his guests.

Even at clubs that place on members the full responsibility for guests, it is rare for a member to be expelled or to have his or her membership suspended due to a guest's action. Typically penalties assessed are limited to fines, denied access, or restricted privileges. On some occasions, a member may lose the privilege of inviting guests to the club altogether.

Holding Guests Responsible

While it is most common for members to be penalized for any guest infractions of rules, in some instances guests may be held immediately accountable. Most clubs recognize that the member cannot fully predict or be held accountable for all rule violations.

The most common rule infraction by guests is dress code. When a guest shows up improperly dressed, the staff must enforce the dress code immediately. One GM/COO who works at a club requiring all golfers to wear shirts with sleeves and collars asked a colleague, "What do I do if President Clinton shows up with his brother — who always wears muscle shirts when he golfs?" His colleague answered, "It doesn't matter who it is — you enforce your rules." When a guest violates the dress code, it would be absurd to turn the member away. It is the guest who must be denied access until he or she is appropriately attired.

Most of the rules at sporting facilities are designed to protect the safety of the participants and to ensure the enjoyment of the game. Because of this, rules are usually enforced and penalties assessed directly against the guest, not the member. Likewise if guests are found on the premises without the sponsoring member or a guest pass, it is usually customary to escort the guests from the premises.

Changes in the Past Century

While most rule changes are instigated at the individual club level, there have been a few issues that have affected clubs nationwide. The issues most consistently cited by GM/COOs as the ones requiring the most updating of rules have been:

- Race and gender issues
- Dress code issues

Race and Gender

Several GM/COOs identified race and gender issues as those that have precipitated the most changes in rules. In the past, club rules dictated that only specific races, religions and genders could join the club, walk in the front door, or use particular areas of the club. Jim Crow laws were still common in several states and clubs often assimilated these laws into their rules. Clubs have since become much more inclusive in their rules. Without losing their inherent exclusivity, clubs now set the standard based on a person's accomplishments, behavior, or status in society.

The civil rights movement in the '60s led most clubs to do away with all references to race. For most clubs it was a quiet change with little fanfare. However, even after the race-specific language was stricken from rule books, some clubs persisted in keeping their membership as homogenous as possible. Two major factors were instrumental in changing this for many clubs: golf tournaments and adverse publicity.

Tournaments. In the late '80s, the PGA announced that it wouldn't hold tournaments at clubs that did not have integrated memberships. This announcement hit clubs in the pocketbook. Clubs that discriminated were forced to decide if they could afford to give up millions of dollars in tournament revenue. Most clubs said no. While public attention focused on one club, that club was merely the test case. There was a ripple effect throughout the industry that led many clubs to change their rules quietly.

Adverse publicity. Other clubs ended discriminatory policies to avoid negative publicity. Clubs that denied membership on the basis of race or religion risked losing prominent members and hampering future recruitment efforts. One club had a very prominent applicant withdraw his nomination because of perceived discrimination of that club against another applicant.

Many clubs still struggle with gender rules. There are many all-men's clubs and all-women's clubs that are being forced to re-evaluate their positions in the light of potentially poor publicity. Most clubs that decide to end single-gender memberships are able to do so quickly with few problems. Many of the problems that do exist involve remodeling the facilities that were intended to serve only one gender.

Because some states have passed laws forbidding private clubs to reserve starting times based on gender, many clubs have decided to give a primary member the top priority tee times on the golf course and precedence in reservations at other sports facilities. The spouse or junior member is given the alternate times. The priority starting time would go to the member regardless of gender. These rule changes have given club employees a new challenge in scheduling tee times and other sports reservations. At one club, the member has the right to bump the reservations of spouse or junior members, or guests on the tennis court. Staff members should also remember that the woman is not always the spouse, but may be the primary member.

Dress Code Standards

In the last decade, many clubs have found themselves with financial incentives to relax their dress code standards. Many members choose not to dine at the club if they have to put on formal or semi-formal attire. To a certain extent, club dining rooms compete with fine dining establishments in the area. The club member chooses between coming to the club to eat or going to a restaurant. If the club member feels he or she can get the same level of food and service at a restaurant — and he or she doesn't have to go home and change clothes first — the club may lose dining dollars.

Some clubs have responded to the pressure to relax the dress code by allowing casual clothes in some of the dining outlets but not in others. As these clubs add more dining rooms, they have a more informal dress code. This solution allows the clubs to continue to maintain their formal standards in at least one dining room.

However, it is not just in the dining room that dress codes are changing. One club manager pointed out that "the dress code on the golf course has become more lax. We're in a more casual swing right now."

Looking Ahead

Club rule books have grown through the years. Most GM/COOs say they rarely change the rules that are on the books, but they frequently add to them. As the rules continue to grow, clubs will continue to balance the need to enforce the rules with the need to provide a high level of service.

Lawmakers have a habit of springing new restraints upon the operation of a club. Continued societal changes will affect club memberships and relationships. All of these things will force GM/COOs and board members to be ever vigilant about their rules and how they are written, distributed and enforced.

Until the day that all club members are committed to following the letter and spirit of every rule, enforcement concerns will continue to plague club professionals. However, as professionals draw upon each other's experiences, they will find creative ways to resolve the challenges that they face.

ACKNOWLEDGEMENTS

The following individuals generously donated their expertise and time to make this issue possible:

Mr. Albert Armstrong, CCM
Mr. Warren Arseneaux, CCM
Mr. A. Christopher Borders, CCM
Ms. Leslie W. Boyette
Mr. David Chag, CCM
Mr. Jay DiPietro, CCM
Mr. Ian Fetigan, CCM
Mr. John Foster, CCM
Mr. Terry Gilmer, CCM

Mr. G. Mead Grady, CCM
Ms. Donna Hand
Mr. Michael Kaplan, CCM
Mr. Willmoore "Bill" Kendall, CCM
Mr. Brian Kroh, CCM
Mr. Robert E. Lee, CCM
Mr. Jonathan McCabe, CCM
Mr. J. Saal, CCM
Mr. Donald Schrotenboer, CCM
Mr. William Schulz, CCM
Mr. Paul Skelton, CCM
Mr. Paul Spellman, CCM
Mr. John Spidalette
Prof. John Tarras
Mr. Henry Waddington, CCM
Mr. Gordon F. Welch, CCM

Discussion Questions

1. How do rules differ from bylaws?

2. What are different ways to change rules?

3. Why is it important to enforce rules?

4. What sort of challenges do GMs/COOs face when trying to enforce rules? How can they respond to these challenges?

5. What type of penalties are used for rule infractions and who determines what the penalties are?

Additional Activities

1. Analyze a club rule book. Identify rules that may be difficult to enforce or may be in need of changing. Develop a scenario for what might happen if one of the rules was consistently ignored.

2. Form groups of four people. Assign the following roles to each group: member, board member, grill server, and general manager. Each person should role play the following scenario. The member enters the grill after a round of golf. He or she is wearing a golf hat. Hats are not allowed indoors. What can each of the other people do to enforce the rule. Discuss the differences in how a member responds to each person. What ramifications could occur for each person?

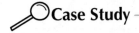

Case Study

Dressed to Play

Pierre, the bartender at the Windfield Country Club's men's grill, shifted nervously as he watched the Lepsog foursome come in off the course. All four brothers had been very vocal in their opposition to the new dress code and seemed determined to challenge it. They had a reputation for being querulous, but Pierre had always gotten along well with them. He hoped that wasn't about to change.

Last summer some of the older club members complained loudly that men and boys were wearing golfing hats inside the clubhouse and the club's formal dining rooms. Although hats were allowed in the men's grill, they were not supposed to be worn anywhere else in the club. To stop the problem, last winter the board passed a new rule which stated that hats could be worn only outside; they were not allowed in any interior space in the club. This summer some of the younger club members have been complaining about the new hat rule. Older members don't want the new rule relaxed, however, because they claim hat wearing in the men's grill was the reason hat wearing spilled over into other areas of the club. Although everyone agrees that this is a rather silly issue, no one seems willing to compromise and its causing bad feelings among club members.

"Hello! Did you all have a good round?" Pierre asked, placing bar napkins in front of each one of them.

"John did," Matthew answered, "I think I just doubled my handicap!"

The others laughed and began discussing their game. Pierre waited patiently, congratulating them as appropriate. After a moment, he asked, "Could I hang your hats for you?"

There was a moment of ornery silence as the young men scowled almost in unison. "Aw, Pierre, not you too!" Luke said.

"It's only the grill, we're not going to wear them in the dining room," Matthew protested.

"Look, Pierre, we've been out on the course in the hot sun for the past four hours." Mark lifted his golf hat briefly, "Do you really think anyone wants to look at that sweaty head while they're eating? For the sake of our stomachs, spare us!"

Pierre chuckled, "Hey, I don't make the rules. Take it up with your rules committee if you don't like it, but please don't put me on the line."

"We won't get anywhere with the rules committee," John laughed, "They're a bunch of stodgy old men who would have us wear ties and spats on the golf course if they could get away with it. But we wouldn't want you to get in trouble. Come on lads, let's remove our hats."

The foursome grudgingly doffed their caps and ordered their drinks. Pierre walked away as he heard Matthew suggest they get together with several of their buddies and protest the rule by wearing hats throughout the clubhouse.

Later that evening Aaron Forthwight, the general manager, stopped by the grill. "Hi, Pierre, how is everything going today?"

"Not bad on my end, but you're about to have a revolution on your hands over the dress code," Pierre said as he swabbed the bar top. He briefly filled Aaron in on the plans being made by the club's younger members. "Frankly, Mr. Forthwight,

I'm really uncomfortable asking people to remove their hats, or telling them they can't come in if their jeans are blue. The other day, a member complained that I was refusing to serve him in blue jeans that cost him $150, but that I'd serve him in a cheap pair of second-hand polyester pants. What am I supposed to say?"

Discussion Questions

1. How does Mr. Forthwight respond to Pierre?
2. Is there anything Mr. Forthwight can do to build consensus in the club about the dress code?

The following industry experts helped generate and develop this case: Cathy Gustafson, CCM, University of South Carolina; Kurt D. Kuebler, CCM, Vice President, General Manager, The Desert Highlands Association; and William A. Schulz, MCM, General Manager, Houston Country Club.

Roles and Responsibilities of Club Volunteer Leaders

A private club depends on its volunteer leaders for long-term guidance, leadership and policy-making. Each volunteer leader — whether a member of the board or a member of a committee — plays an integral role in ensuring that the club continues to thrive and to meet the needs of its members.

With such an important responsibility, it is important for incoming volunteer leaders to understand the role they are assuming. This issue of the *Topical Reference Series* provides guidelines for clubs attempting to define more precisely the roles and responsibilities of a club volunteer leader. This issue offers club volunteer leaders and General Managers/ Chief Operating Officers (GMs/COOs) suggestions for developing position descriptions — documents for unpaid volunteer leaders that are similar to job descriptions for the club staff — that will:

- Detail the duties a volunteer leader must perform
- Familiarize the incoming volunteer leader with budgets, policies and schedules
- Define the policies for which volunteer leaders are responsible
- Assist in recruiting and orientating new volunteer leaders

Because each club's operations and facilities are unique, this issue does not attempt to establish a single format or standard for a position description. Instead, this issue compiles practical advice from club industry professionals to help clubs develop position descriptions for their own volunteer leaders.

For the purpose of this issue, the term *volunteer leader* refers to both board members and committee members.

Position Descriptions

While few clubs could or would operate without job descriptions for their employees, many of these same clubs operate without position descriptions for their volunteers — the board and committee members. Just as employees need job descriptions to help them understand what is expected of them and how to work at top efficiency, board and committee members need a position description that tells them what they need to accomplish so that they can have a productive service term.

Most board and committee members are successful people in their own businesses and bring to the club a wealth of experience and knowledge. However, few business people, even within the hospitality industry, can really understand the concerns and needs of a private club without some additional information. One GM/COO stresses the importance of educating board members, saying that teaching volunteer leaders is a primary duty of GMs/COOs.

A position description can help begin the process of educating a volunteer leader. It spells out the roles and responsibilities a volunteer leader is expected to fulfill. The position description can help set the parameters of club volunteer leaders' influence. The appendix of this issue (starting on page 23) contains some sample position descriptions collected from private clubs or compiled from information supplied by clubs.

Richard P. Chait, in "How to Help Your Board Govern More and Manage Less" (National Center for Nonprofit Boards, Washington D.C., 1993, pp. 8–9), wrote that an annual work plan should be developed for each board and standing committee. This plan, given to every volunteer leader, would help create clear expectations for everyone by listing specific objectives. At a club that is committed to updating and revising its position descriptions on an annual basis, such descriptions could double as annual work plans. Otherwise, the description could serve as the basis for a work plan, with portions of the plan taken from each position or position description.

Nearly every volunteer position within the governing structure of the club can use a position description. Figure 1: "Sample Club Organization Chart" shows several of these positions.

Why Have Position Descriptions?

Developing position descriptions is a time-consuming task which may not always have a high priority on the to-do lists of busy club executives. However, GMs/COOs have cited the following reasons why creating position descriptions pays off for clubs that use them:

- Volunteer leaders are more effective
- Volunteer leaders have access to important information
- Clubs enjoy greater consistency among volunteer leaders

Volunteer leaders are more effective. A volunteer leader can be much more effective when provided with a clear definition of his or her duties through a position description. The position description can be the beginning of a volunteer leader's education and shorten the time it takes to learn the requirements of the position. A position description can also be used as a quick reference throughout a person's term of service and shorten the learning curve with which every volunteer leader grapples.

Volunteer leaders have access to important information. The most useful position descriptions are like roadmaps that show where a club is headed by outlining club goals, budgets, policies and duties. Position descriptions can also include information on how volunteer leaders should relate to other volunteer leaders, committees and staff members. These descriptions make sure that volunteer leaders have the most important reference material they need to perform their duties effectively.

Clubs enjoy greater consistency among volunteer leaders. Clubs that have developed strategic plans often struggle to keep up the momentum when volunteer leaders change on an annual basis. Comprehensive position descriptions can provide consistency by informing each volunteer leader what his or her role is in the strategic plan. Even without a strategic plan, some clubs struggle with making sure volunteer leaders are consistent in their policies and method of governing. Position descriptions promote consistency in club policies, areas of responsibility and each individual volunteer leader's duties.

Figure 1: Sample Club Organization Chart

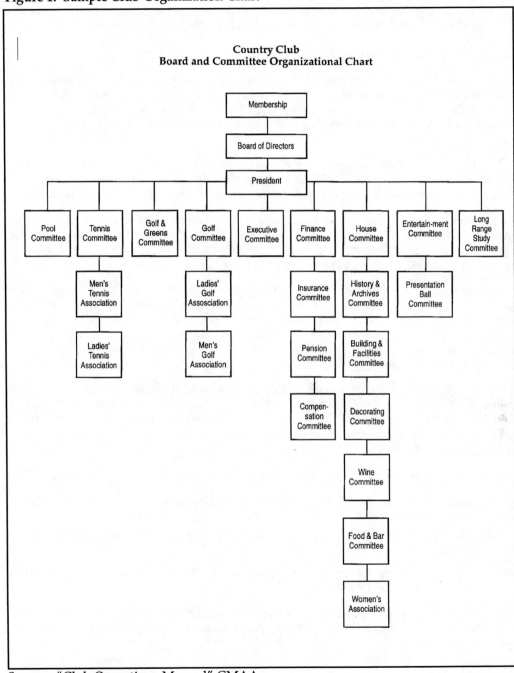

Source: "Club Operations Manual" CMAA.

These are the primary benefits of position descriptions that most GMs/COOs cite. Other benefits could include the resolution of conflicts over position perceptions, the clarification of committee roles and an increase in enthusiasm for club service.

Committee Member Descriptions

A board member or officer can find a fair number of resources in any library or association book catalog that delineate what is expected of him or her. Organizations such as the National Center for Nonprofit Boards have a wealth of materials for volunteer leaders. (See the list of resources at the back of this issue.) Information for committee members is much more scarce.

One of the reasons there is so little information available for committee members is the distinctiveness of committee structures in each club. Most clubs have a president, vice president and treasurer. But not every club has a squash committee or a library committee.

Even among more common committees such as the house committee, members do not necessarily have identical duties. A complete position description can enumerate the responsibility of committee members and highlight what is unique to that club. This can be especially useful for members who served on committees at other clubs.

Providing written position descriptions to committee members can help provide stability and continuity to an organization. A club that clearly defines each committee member's role will increase the comfort level members have with their responsibilities. Committee members can keep their position description on hand to help determine whether any given issue falls under their area of responsibility. Accurate position descriptions can help prevent the duplication of effort among committees.

It is especially important that the position descriptions of committee members stress that members always work in conjunction with the board and GM/COO. The GM/COO has valuable information to provide to committee members and he or she also needs to be kept apprised of committee work so that he or she can be effective in the club and carry out the club's objectives.

Position descriptions serve the following general purposes for all committees:

- Shorten the amount of time needed to learn the committee's function and role of committee members
- Provide continuity in committee's work despite changing membership in the committee
- Help committee members avoid duplication of efforts or conflicts with other governing bodies of the club

Figure 2: "Committee Types" shows a listing of several types of committees that can be found in private clubs. However, the list is by no means complete. There are three main types of committees:

- Standing
- Ad hoc
- Project

Figure 2: Committee Types

Types of Committees		
Standing	**Ad hoc**	**Project**
Athletic	Audit	Construction
Budget	Awards	Personnel
Building	Centennial	Public affairs
Bylaws	Executive search	Redecorating
Caddy	Nominating	Risk management
Employee benefit		Tournament
Entertainment		
Executive		
Finance		
Golf		
Greens		
Grounds		
Handicap		
Historical		
House		
Insurance		
Library		
Membership		
Planning		
Promotion		
Real estate		

Standing Committees

Standing committees meet on an ongoing basis and might include the greens committee, the house committee, membership committee and executive committee. The standing committees are typically established in the bylaws. Some bylaws even establish how many people must sit on each committee, how frequently the committees will meet and what their mission statements are.

The duties of standing committee members are usually well-established and easy to document. However, their very longevity can engender misconceptions among the membership. For example, an incoming member may believe that it is the house committee's duty to set the date for the member-guest banquet because it is always the house committee chair who acts as a master of ceremonies. However, in fact, it may be the duty of the membership committee. Position descriptions can help dispel these misconceptions.

Ad Hoc Committees

An ad hoc committee is formed to meet the needs of a particular purpose and its members serve for a specified period of time. Ad hoc committees might include nominating committees or renovation committees.

A position description might, at first glance, seem superfluous for what is often a short-term effort. However, the very nature of ad hoc committees makes brief position descriptions almost essential because such committees must be more focused. Position descriptions can help all members stay within the defined parameters of these committee positions. A position description for an ad hoc committee might include when to open the committee and when to close it. One GM/COO said it's important to immediately establish how long an ad hoc committee is expected to last. "Don't let (an ad hoc committee) become a standing committee. Make sure it serves its purposes and then ceases to exist."

Frequently, position descriptions are not developed for ad hoc committee members because of their temporary status. However, their temporary status makes several concerns inherent:

- Committee members must be more focused on their task
- Committee members must fully understand their mission
- Committee members must fully understand their limits
- Committee members need to have a clear understanding of when their job has ended

A position description, albeit a shorter version than that created for the board or a permanent committee, can help ad hoc committee members with each of the above concerns. The position description provides each member with a written version of the committee's task, mission, limits and tenure. Everyone is able to start out his or her service with a clear concept of what he or she needs to accomplish and what tools and resources are available.

Project Committees

Project or special committees are formed to respond to particular issues. While standing and ad hoc committees are usually provided for in the bylaws, project committees are less formal and their members tend to be directed toward a single task. Members are usually appointed by the board or the board president to oversee a particular project. For example, a club that is hosting a PGA tournament for the first time might appoint a PGA committee.

Position descriptions for project committee members can act as the forming document that is given everyone at the first meeting. They can serve as a blueprint for what committee members are expected to accomplish.

Position Description Information

Club industry experts and GMs/COOs have recommended that position descriptions include the following information:

Figure 3: Position Description Topics Checklist

<h2 style="text-align:center">Checklist</h2>

The following items can be included in a position description:

- ☐ List of duties
    - ☐ Financial duties
    - ☐ Structural and organizational duties
    - ☐ Human resources duties
- ☐ Structure of office
- ☐ Prerequisites
- ☐ Bylaws and rules
- ☐ Club policies

- ☐ Club budgets
    - ☐ Financial budgets
    - ☐ Personnel budgets
    - ☐ Time budgets
- ☐ Strategic plan goals
- ☐ Contracts and legal agreements
- ☐ Traditions
- ☐ Relationships
- ☐ Meeting agendas
- ☐ Biographical data

- List of duties
- Structure of office
- Prerequisites
- Bylaws and rules
- Club policies
- Club budgets
- Strategic plan goals
- Contracts and legal agreements
- Traditions/history of club
- Relationships
- Meeting agendas
- Biographical data

Figure 3: "Position Description Topics Checklist" is a checklist of all these categories that GMs/COOs can use when putting together position descriptions. The next several sections will address each of these categories in detail.

For many clubs, it is impractical to include all of the above information in the position description for every volunteer leader. Moreover, the amount of information in each category will vary from position to position and from club to club. Some clubs may distribute two booklets — one that can be given to all volunteer leaders and a second that contains information specific to a position.

List of Duties

The basic element and first section of a position description should be the list of duties each volunteer leader is expected to perform. This section can include both a list of skills and knowledge needed for the position and a list of tasks that must be performed.

Management consultant Philip C. Grant wrote in "Why Job Descriptions Don't Work" (*Personnel Journal*, January 1988, p. 53), "[A position description] must provide an accurate and comprehensive picture of the work design; typically it does not do this. Most [position descriptions] are too simplistic: They lack detail, they are out of date, they neglect many key structural elements of the job and they are unclearly written."

In order for a position description to be effective, the person developing it must make sure that it is sufficiently detailed, current and addresses all of the important structural elements of the position.

Grant suggests including the following things in the list of duties:

- How long it takes to perform each task
- Priorities of each task
- Environment or context of each task
- Degree of randomness of various tasks
- Key shared responsibilities that every one is held accountable for (supporting the mission, attending club functions, giving notice if unable to attend meetings, etc.)
- List of communications that must be given (reports, budgets, memos, etc.)
- Prohibitions on tasks that should not be done by this position
- Temporary assignments
- Group responsibilities section

Not all of the items in this list will apply to the list of duties for all board or committee positions. In addition, the degree of detail for each item will vary from club to club. For example, it is not usually necessary to specify down to the minute how long each task will take. However, most volunteers appreciate knowing approximately how much time commitment any task might require.

Figure 4 shows a sample list of duties that might be included in a position description for a board member.

When writing the list of duties, clubs may wish to keep the following in mind:

- Start each sentence with a verb.

  Example: *Notify the membership of the Annual Meeting date.*

  Not: *He or she should notify the membership of the Annual Meeting date.*

- Use the active voice.

  Example: *Sign all membership certificates.*

  Not: *All membership certificates must be signed by the president.*

- Use only one sentence per task.

  Example: *Promote adequate recordkeeping, course history information and a photographic record of the course.*

Figure 4: Sample Duty List

List of Duties		
Board Member		
Priority	**Duty/Environment**	**Time**
A	Chairs a specific committee and endeavors to satisfactorily obtain the committee's goals and objectives	3 hours/month
	Meetings are held in Green Room. Additional preparation and follow through can be done at club office or at home	
A	Attends monthly board meetings, specially called meetings, and the annual meeting	3 to 6 hours/ month
	Board meetings held in Trophy Room, annual meeting in ballroom	
A	Prepares a brief, concise report of committees' activities, programs, needs, etc.	1 hour/month
	Duty can be done in club office or at home	
B	Meets prospective new members	1 hour/month
	Duty performed in and around club. Member must also attend cocktail receptions	
B	Attends club functions	5 hours/ month
	Duty performed on club premises	
B	Supports club activities	ongoing
	Duty performed on club premises and in the community	
B	Sets an example by abiding by all club rules	ongoing
	Duty performed on club premises while in clubhouse, on golf course, at tennis facilities, etc.	
A	Is NOT involved in supervision of employees	ongoing
	Member defers supervision issues to the GM/COO	
A	Develops and implements policies	ongoing
	Member works with GM/COO and other board members throughout the club	

Not: *Promote adequate record keeping and keep the course history information and a photographic record of the course. Produce history booklets for important club anniversaries.*

Hint: If there is an *and* in the sentence that connects two verbs, it may be an indication that there are really two separate tasks.

Grant also suggests categorizing tasks chronologically, by priority, or by permanency of task. A club may also choose to categorize the tasks by area of responsibility. For example, a task list may begin with all of the duties that the board treasurer must perform as treasurer, then as chair of the finance committee, then as a board member.

Clubs may also wish to categorize duties based on three common areas of responsibility for club volunteer leaders:

- Financial duties
- Structural and organizational duties
- Human resources duties

Financial Duties

Directors frequently recognize budgeting and financial duties as their most important responsibility. In general, accounting is divided into two areas: financial and management. The majority of the financial accounting is done by club staff, with volunteer leaders reviewing those documents as needed. The financial duties of volunteer leaders are much more involved with managerial accounting.

In many clubs, the GM/COO will start the budgeting process by providing financial information to the committee or board. He or she may also provide the board or committees with a list of needs and projected costs.

A volunteer leader may typically:

- Review the balance sheet
- Review the income statement
- Review the cash flow statements
- Review solvency, activity and operating ratios
- Help determine pricing
- Perform cost-volume-profit analysis
- Forecast club usage and financial data
- Create an operations budget
- Oversee cash management
- Oversee internal control
- Create a capital budget
- Oversee payment of taxes and determine tax minimization methods

Structural and Organizational Duties

While many volunteer leaders see these duties as secondary to the financial ones, structural and organizational tasks often take up the majority of a volunteer leader's time. These duties are also most noticeable to non-board members who expect a responsive volunteer leader to help resolve problems.

Some typical structural and organizational duties may include:

- Admitting new members
- Determining club rules
- Responding to member needs
- Forming a strategic plan for the club
- Recommending menu changes
- Planning club events
- Determining land use
- Creating a remodeling plan
- Revising guest policies

Human Resources Duties

Many books have been devoted to the role boards play in human resources. The board is frequently in charge of hiring the GM/COO and approving other top management hirings and firings. Boards and committees may be charged with reviewing salary and benefit structures for all employees.

Human resources duties may include:

- Developing an organization chart
- Auditing the effectiveness of management
- Planning for future management resources
- Reviewing the organizational structure to see where teams could be effectively used
- Conducting management attitude surveys
- Providing continuous development opportunities for all employees

In this list of duties, it is also important to convey the limits on a volunteer leader's human resources function. For example, few clubs allow volunteer leaders to directly supervise any employee other than the GM/COO. Nor should volunteer leaders put an employee inthe uncomfortable position of having to follow conflicting orders from different volunteer leaders or from a volunteer leader and the employee's manager.

Clubs may also wish to list some of the duties that volunteer leaders do *not* have. Boards are policy-making bodies and committees are advisory bodies. Neither should interfere withthe day-to-day operations of the club. Some duties that volunteer leaders should refrain from include:

- Coaching or correcting employees
- Giving performance evaluations to employees other than the GM/COO
- Making hiring decisions

- Firing or disciplining employees
- Scheduling employees
- Rewarding or giving raises to individual employees

Structure of Office

Every volunteer leader needs to understand the structure of the office that he or she holds. There are many details that vary not only between clubs, but between positions at the same club. The position description should contain at least one section that answers the following questions:

- How long is a term for this position?
- How are the elections or selections staggered?
- How is continuity provided for?
- How is the person chosen for this position?
- Is the position advisory or does it set policy?
- What are the parameters of this position?

These are essential questions that help define the position. Putting the answers to these questions in the position description puts these facts at the fingertips of volunteer leaders and spares them from having to ask others. It can also safeguard them from overstepping their authority.

Prerequisites

If a position description is to be an effective recruitment and selection tool, it should also contain any prerequisites for a position. For example, at some clubs, service on each committee is required before becoming a board member. Other clubs may require that volunteer leaders be members of the club for a minimum number of years before being elected to a volunteer leader position.

One trend that club experts identified is that many members are no longer willing to put in long-term consecutive service to their club. Some clubs find it increasingly difficult to draw creative, committed leadership when they have lengthy service requirements. It is becoming more common to see members come in, serve for a few years and then take a break for a few years before resuming service. If a club's board or committe is able to accommodate this type of service, it should be spelled out in the position description.

Bylaws and Rules

After state and federal laws, a club's bylaws and rules are the source of authority for club volunteer leaders. Because of this, a position description should contain a reproduction of any bylaw or rule that directly affects the position the description was written for.

Many GMs/COOs place the bylaws and rules section of the position description immediately after a brief description or mission of the position. These are the inviolable parameters of the position unless the bylaws change. Typically, this happens only if the bylaws were written poorly to begin with, or the position has changed dramatically from when the bylaws were first written. (For more information on changing bylaws, see issue two of the *Topical Reference Series*, "Club Bylaws.")

The position description of a member of the nominating committee may contain bylaws similar to this one found in a city club:

> *It shall be the duty of the board of governors to appoint before the fourth Saturday of September in each year a committee on nominations of seven members whose names shall be posted immediately. No member of the board of governors shall be appointed a member of such committee. Such committee shall prepare and post for at least four weeks before the annual meeting a list of nominations for the places to be filled on the board of governors and the committee on admissions. Other nominations of such offices may be made by the membership in writing, signed by at least twenty members and delivered to the secretary at least three weeks before the annual meeting. The secretary shall post all such nominations together with the names of the first twenty members making such nominations at least ten days before the annual meeting.*

Club Policies

The role of volunteer leaders extends beyond merely the duties defined in the bylaws. Volunteer leaders are also expected to understand and enforce club policies. A policy is any decision that has been made collectively by the board. For example, the board may have voted in the previous year to send roses to each member on his or her first anniversary with the club. That action becomes a club policy. By including the policies in position descriptions, the club helps ensure that each new volunteer leader is aware of club policies and will carry them out or have the appropriate club staff members carry them out.

Including policies in position descriptions also ensures that volunteer leaders will not waste time trying to re-create existing policies. Likewise, writing out the policies and including them in the description facilitates a volunteer leader's making needed changes. After all, a volunteer leader cannot know if there is bad policy in place if the volunteer leader does not know what the policy is.

Including pertinent policies for a position description can be time-consuming if the club has not kept policy records. In such cases, the minutes of previous board meetings may need to be examined to identify policies to include. The policy section may be a brief description of each policy, or it may be an index listing each policy with the full text supplied in an appendix.

Policies should be included only in the position descriptions of the board positions most responsible for carrying them out. A person in such a position can also monitor new policies to make sure they are not in conflict with old ones. If they are, the board can address the problem. One club expert suggests putting a "sunset" date on each policy. After that date passes, the board will reconsider the policy and reconfirm it or let it die.

Some clubs break the policy section of the position description into several areas such as purchase order policies, committee meeting policies, capital expenditure policies and special event policies.

Club Budgets

Since not all board or committee members are CPAs, they may need extra time to analyze budgets. Even those volunteer leaders who deal with budgets in their businesses every day may need some additional information regarding the non-profit environment that most clubs work in. Some clubs may find it useful to list information about tax-exempt organizations in position descriptions.

Position descriptions should include samples of every type of budget that members might encounter. Actual budgets can be reviewed in the orientation session and included in the orientation packet or initial mailing.

Some of the budgets a volunteer leader might work with include:

- Financial budgets
- Personnel budgets
- Time budgets

Financial Budgets

Most people think of spreadsheets when they hear the word "budget." Certainly, financial statements are among the most common form of budgets, but club volunteer leaders will work with many budgets throughout their term and need to be familiar with which budgets the club uses and what their formats are.

The following financial budgets are among the most common that volunteer leaders use:

- *Operating.* This budget is sometimes called the revenue and expense budget. It outlines the club's plans for generating revenues and meeting expected expenses. It includes budgets for each department within the club (banquet, food and beverage, greens, pro shop, etc.) and planned overall expenses such as depreciation, interest expense and fixed charges.

- *Cash.* Cash budgeting and cash management involve the handling of all of the club's cash in whatever form. Cash could include cash in bank accounts, credit vouchers or petty cash.

- *Capital.* Capital budgets are typically prepared several years in advance. All construction projects, major equipment purchases and land purchases/sales are recorded on the capital budget. Clubs need to review their capital budgets annually to ensure that they still reflect the environment in which the club is working.

Typically, the financial budget has been formed before new volunteer leaders begin their term. One club expert advises giving actual budgets to incoming officers "so that they know how big they can dream." He adds that volunteer leaders need to know not only how much cash they have, but how they can change the previously formed budget if they need to.

Including financial budget information in position descriptions is important because it helps volunteer leaders make financially viable decisions. Budgets can also be key tools in strategic planning by forcing volunteer leaders to anticipate the future and examine how the economy, inflation, competition, membership changes, new facilities, etc., affect the club.

Personnel Budgets

A personnel budget is a schedule that tells volunteer leaders exactly what sort of staff assistance they can rely on. Knowing the personnel and the personnel hours available for each board or committee member can help that volunteer leader plan. Clubs should tell their volunteer leaders exactly which, if any, staff members are available to help the volunteer leaders carry out their duties.

A staff liaison usually helps committees perform their duties. For example, the club's:

- Controller works with finance committee
- Golf professional works with golf committee
- Tennis professional works with tennis committee
- Swimming pool manager works with pool committee
- Banquet manager works with catering committee

A good personnel budget establishes which staff position is assigned to work with each volunteer leader position and approximately how many hours that staff person can devote to the volunteer leader. The personnel budget may also specify which duties a staff member may perform. For example, a personnel budget might establish that the GM's/COO's secretary can be asked to type anddistribute board meeting minutes and agendas.

Personnel budgets are useful for two reasons: one, volunteer leaders are aware of what help they can count on from staff members; and two, they limit the abuse of staff members by volunteer leaders who require too much. These budgets can quickly establish the parameters of what volunteer leaders can and cannot ask staff members to do for them. Also, if the volunteer leader feels the personnel budget is insufficient or overly generous, alternate plans can be made well in advance.

Figure 5: "Sample Personnel Budget — Table" illustrates one possible personnel budget that could be included in a position description. Another example is shown in Figure 6: "Sample Personnel Budget — Chart." Yet another type of personnel budget might spell out which people are available for which tasks and for how long.

Time Budgets

A time budget can be either a list of dates and duties or an actual calendar for the year with events marked on it. See Figure 7 for a sample time budget that could be used in a position description.

A time budget differs from the club members' event calendar in that it is specific to the position. For example, in a president's position description, the time budget may show that the nominating committee must be chosen by Aug. 1 and that the president needs to send out letters by July 8. The event calendar, available to all members, would only show that the elections are on Nov. 1.

Many GMs/COOs say it is important to note meeting times in the time budgets. The times should include the length of the meeting, time it begins and time it ends. They also suggest scheduling when memos, notes and letters need to be sent; when to notify people of meeting times; and when to make reservations for meeting rooms. Some clubs may wish to record dates for every task.

Strategic Plan Goals

Clubs are increasingly forming strategic plans to help ensure that everyone in the club is working toward the same goals. The strategic plans are flexible and incorporate changing

Figure 5: Sample Personnel Budget — Table

Treasurer Personnel Budget	
Staff member	**Duties**
Controller	Supply financial information
	Fill out income tax forms
	File income tax forms after approved
	Review budget
	Create requested financial reports
Secretary	Type budgets
	Type and mail finance committee minutes
	Inform members of finance committee meetings
	Type agendas
GM/COO	Gather sales and operating expense information
	Provide projected revenue and expense information
	Provide salary and benefit information
	Attend meetings of finance committee

environments to fulfill the mission and vision of the club. Volunteer leaders are usually charged with determining what the club's basic values are, its mission and its vision. They are then able to work with the GM/COO to set goals for each department.

A strategic plan is most effective when everyone involved with the club knows what the club's mission is and what internal resources they have to accomplish the objectives. One club expert advises clubs to appoint a plan mentor who can help each person understand how to accomplish the long-term objectives assigned to his or her position.

One of the challenges clubs face in strategic planning is the turnover of club officers. One response to this challenge is to incorporate the goals of the strategic plan into the position descriptions of the volunteer leaders expected to carry them out. Some clubs also encourage new volunteer leaders to add their own annual objectives or goals to the strategic plan portion of the position description.

Figure 6: Sample Personnel Budget — Chart

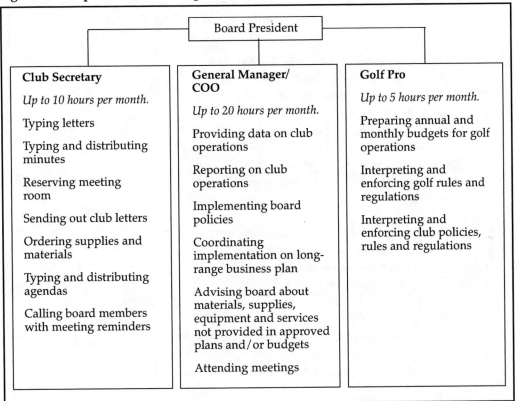

Contracts and Legal Agreements

Every club enters into numerous contracts on a regular basis. These contracts can restrict the decisions that volunteer leaders make. One club expert advises clubs to attach copies of any contracts or legal agreements to the position description of the position affected by the contract or agreement. This information tells the officer that he or she cannot do anything to violate these contracts or agreements.

Types of contracts might include:

- Lease of golf carts
- Pool liability insurance
- Directors and Officers insurance
- Purchase contract for sparkling wine
- Labor contract for dining room servers
- Contract for quality training

Figure 7: Sample Time Budget

Golf Committee Chair Calendar for May through August

May

6	Send out invitations to golf committee reception
7	Golf committee meeting — 6:30 p.m. to 8:30 p.m.
14	Check with Bar Manager about reception menu
15	Golf Committee Reception — 7 p.m. to 9 p.m.
16	Board meeting — 6 p.m. to 9 p.m.
24	President's Cup tournament (give opening speech)
25	Be present at President's Cup tournament
27	Mail out June agenda to golf committee members
31	Attend second weekend of President's Cup tournament

June

1	Give out awards at President's Cup tournament
3	Order trophies for Father-Son tournament
4	Golf committee meeting — 6:30 p.m. to 8:30 p.m.
11	Attend Ladies Tournament and Barbecue
12	Confirm Father-Son buffet arrangements with catering manager
13	Board meeting — 6 p.m. to 9 p.m.
14	Attend Father-Son Championship and awards presentation
22	Attend first Member-Guest tournament
24	Mail out July agenda to golf committee members

July

2	Golf committee meeting — 6:30 p.m. to 8:30 p.m.
3	Confirm accommodations for LPGA tournament organizers
5	Men's Guest Day
7	Ladies Guest Day
8	Tour greens with LPGA officials
	Hold news conference on LPGA tournament
9	Attend welcoming lunch for LPGA tournament participants
10	LPGA tournament begins
11	Board meeting — 6 p.m. to 9 p.m.
14	LPGA tournament ends — attend awards banquet
25	Men's Guest Day
29	Mail out August agenda to golf committee members

August

6	Golf committee meeting — 6:30 p.m. to 8:30 p.m.
7	Seniors Championship with dinner and awards ceremony
8	Board meeting — 6 p.m. to 9 p.m.
16	Sun Classic begins
17	Sun Classic ends

Including the contracts and agreements in the position descriptions can also help clubs avoid legal tangles. One GM/COO points out that new committee chairs often want to make their mark on the club. This can create expensive tangles such as the one made by a new entertainment chair who decided to book a band he liked for one of the club events. While booking bands was one of the chair's duties, the previous chair had already booked one for that particular event, leaving the club stuck paying for two bands.

For many clubs, the sheer bulk of contracts may make including copies of all of them in position descriptions impractical. These clubs may prefer to include an annotated table of contents or bibliography of all contracts and legal agreements. The annotation could include where the full text can be found, the promises or agreements of the contracts, who the contract or agreement is with, who signed it and when it expires.

Traditions/History of Club

When identifying the roles and responsibilities of board and committee members, clubs should include their traditions. If the golf committee chair, for example, has traditionally teed off the first ball of the season, this privilege should be included in his or her position description.

If a tradition has a negative effect, says a club expert, the volunteer leader who is supposed to carry it out needs to propose a new tradition to replace it.

Because traditions are rarely written down, they can be difficult for a new volunteer leader to uphold. Documenting the tradition in a position description doesn't turn the tradition into a policy or rule, but it does keep everyone aware of it that needs to be.

Relationships

The position description should contain a list of the other board or committee positions that the officer needs to interact with. This list differs from the main organization chart as seen in Figure 1 in that it is personalized to each volunteer leader. Figure 8: "Sample Relationship Chart" shows a sample position relationship chart.

Frequently, the quality of a volunteer leader's relationships and team efforts determine whether he or she is successful. An explanation of the relationships a given position has can help that volunteer leader know with whom to work. This list can tell a volunteer leader whom to turn to for help and who will be expecting assistance from him or her.

Meeting Agendas

Every incoming volunteer leader knows that attending meetings is a primary responsibility. However, the volunteer leader may not necessarily know what type of topics are covered at meetings, the style of meetings or the order in which business is conducted. Therefore, many GMs/COOs recommend including sample agendas in the position description.

Clubs may wish to include sample agendas in the position descriptions of volunteer leaders who are not responsible for creating an agenda as well. Sample agendas, or copies of agendas from previous meetings, can help give volunteer leaders an idea of what topics are typically discussed and how many subjects are dealt with on average in a given meeting.

Clubs can also provide agenda forms to save volunteer leaders time and to ensure that essential topics are covered at each meeting. These forms could be created with the main

Figure 8: Sample Relationship Chart

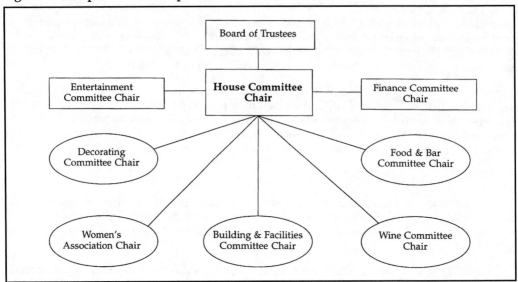

topic headings (such as Minutes, Reports, Old Business, New Business, etc.) and times typed in. Under each heading could be blank lines that the committee or board chair could use to fill in the details of each agenda. The completed agenda form could be given to the person responsible for printing and distributing it. See Figure 9: "Sample Agenda for Meetings."

Several GMs/COOs say they find that agenda forms have the added benefit of making the meetings move more quickly and smoothly. The position description should also contain the club's policies on meeting agendas. (Effective meetings will be discussed in a future issue of the *Topical Reference Series*.)

Biographical Data

The people and personalities of a board or committee can make or break it. Even when the structure, duties and issues under consideration remain constant, a change in members can take a board or committee from one that is impotent to one that is radically successful in a single year.

Not all GMs/COOs believe this information is necessary. Certainly, including it in the position description mandates extensive updating on an annual basis. It is recommended that the position description include only brief biographical data that can provide some basic information. This information can help new members gain some knowledge of the people with whom they will be working. The biographies can include a picture of each volunteer leader along with the volunteer leader's:

- Name, title and affiliation
- Personal background, such as education, careers, hobbies
- Length of membership in the club
- Names of family members, especially other club members

Figure 9: Sample Agenda for Meetings

MEETING AGENDA					**The Country Club** 123 Country Club Drive Anytown, USA 48826	

Meeting Description Golf Committee
Results Desired Plan for upcoming member-guest tournament
Date May 15, 199X   **Time** 6:30 p.m.   **Location** The Oliver Room

Scheduled Time			Actual Time			
Start	Stop	Total Hours	Start	Stop	Total Hours	
6:30	8 p.m.	1 ½				

Persons Attending

1	Jerry Town, chairman
2	Phillip Grawson, secretary
3	Sanchez Hernandez
4	Ray Forth
5	Terry Korval
6	Tina Forsyth, GM/COO
7	
8	
9	

Items To Be Discussed ✓

1	Present minutes of previous meeting
2	Chairman's report
3	Replacement of worn seats on golf carts
4	Hiring caddies for member-guest tournament
5	Selection of menu for post-tournament dinner
6	Prizes for tournament winners
7	
8	
9	

Materials Needed	Person Responsible
Pens	Grawson
Notepads	Grawson
Minutes of previous meeting	Grawson
Copies of chairman's report	Town
Bids for golf cart seats	Hernandez

- Interests related to the club
- Past service to the club
- Personal mission statement/quote from the volunteer leader

Including this biographical data can let potential volunteer leaders know whom they will be serving with and what type of backgrounds each person has. Likewise, the biographies help new volunteer leaders get to know the others with whom they are working.

Position Description Formats

Position descriptions may take several different formats, ranging from a one-paragraph sheet to a short booklet. The appendix of this issue contains several sample descriptions, including short ones.

Most modern computer software can produce handsome documents. The binding and presentation of the position description will depend largely on the resources available at the club. Some factors that GMs/COOs recommend that clubs take into consideration include the following:

- *Make sure there is room to update the position description on an annual basis.* Most experts advise updating the position description on an annual basis. Even if a club doesn't expect to make any changes, it can still be useful to review each position description at a regular time each year. This can help ensure that the description does not become outdated or lose credibility.

- *Provide an index or tabs for lengthy documents.* The longer a document gets, the more daunting it can be for busy executives. Keep the description brief, easy to read and attractive.

- *Make all position descriptions consistent so that they will be easier to update.* If each description has the same format, same headings and same organization, it will be easier to make changes to all descriptions to accommodate policy revisions, new goals or anything else that needs updating.

Sources of Information

The task of compiling detailed position descriptions can be daunting to a club that has never produced such documents. However, few descriptions need to be written from scratch. Clubs without position descriptions for their volunteer leaders usually have some documentation of what duties need to be performed. This documentation can be a useful source for anyone creating or updating a position description.

There are two major sources of information that can be used in position descriptions:

- Written sources
- Unwritten sources

Written Sources

Frequently, the constitution, bylaws or rules of the club will define the roles and responsibilities of board and committee members. The person compiling a position description will first want to read what these documents have to say about the position.

For example, when compiling the position description for the chair of the house committee, it would be essential to have this information from the club's bylaws:

> *The house committee shall advise the GM/COO on the operation and upkeep of the clubhouse and locker room including prices charged for food, bar and use of clubhouse facilities; shall recommend for board concurrence all house rules and shall enforce such rules. The house committee shall periodically review wages, salaries and benefits paid all clubhouse employees except the GM/COO and shall, with the concurrence of the GM/COO, recommend changes as appropriate to the board.*

From this, the person compiling the position description can make the following list of duties for a house committee member:

- Advise the GM/COO on the operation and upkeep of the clubhouse and locker room
- Advise the GM/COO on prices charged for food, bar and use of clubhouse facilities
- Recommend house rules
- Enforce house rules
- Review wages, salaries and benefits paid all clubhouse employees except the GM/COO
- Recommend, with the agreement of the GM/COO, changes to policy and operations as appropriate

Figure 10: "Bylaw Diagram" diagrams the ways that clubs can pull duty lists from their bylaws and rules, using the board secretary position as an example.

Other documents that can help someone compile position descriptions may include:

- Policy statements
- Contracts
- Meeting minutes
- Budgets
- Organization charts

Unwritten Sources

Not all GMs/COOs rely solely on written documentation to compile position descriptions for their club's volunteer leaders. Outdated documentation can misrepresent the true status or duties of a position. Some clubs neglect to write much of the volunteer leader information down — relying on members to share their knowledge on an informal mentorship basis.

One GM/COO said he gets nearly all of the information he needs from other club managers, books, staff knowledge, personal experience and talking to members. (See the list of resources at the end of this issue for some book resources.)

There are several ways to find the specific information needed for a particular position description from a club's oral tradition, including surveys, focus groups, interviews and discussions. See Figure 11: "Unwritten Sources for Position Descriptions" for more detail on these methods.

Position Description Uses

Position descriptions can be used for several purposes. The most obvious is as a board or committee handbook that volunteer leaders can use throughout their term. However, it has other uses as well, including:

- Recruitment and selection of new volunteer leaders
- Orientation of volunteer leaders
- Board and committee meetings

Figure 10: Written Sources for Position Descriptions — Bylaw Diagrams

Breaking Down a Bylaw

1. Underline all verbs that pertain to the position.

   Secretary — The secretary shall <u>keep</u> minutes of the board meetings, <u>conduct</u> correspondence as directed by the board and <u>keep</u> club records. Pursuant to board approval and a reasonable time prior to the annual meeting, the secretary shall <u>mail</u> ballots and appropriate accompanying information to members who are eligible to vote in the election of board members. He or she shall <u>attest</u> to the president's execution of all obligations and contracts of the club as necessary and shall <u>perform</u> such other duties as may be required by the bylaws or the board.

2. Use the verb to begin each task on the list of duties.

   - *<u>Keep</u>* minutes of the board meetings
   - *<u>Conduct</u>* correspondence as directed by the board
   - *<u>Keep</u>* club records
   - *<u>Mail</u>* ballots and appropriate accompanying information to members who are eligible to vote in the election of board members
   - *<u>Attest</u>* to the president's execution of all obligations and contracts of the club
   - *<u>Perform</u>* other duties as may be required by the bylaws or the board

Recruitment and Selection

Once the position description for a particular office is compiled, it can be distributed to all potential candidates for that office. Clubs can ask nominees for each office to read the office's position description to determine whether the job is one that they have the time and ability to do. This allows candidates a chance to evaluate whether they are fit for the position.

One club management expert advises clubs to ask all candidates to sign a statement that they have read the description and agree to perform all of the outlined duties. The expert also suggests asking candidates to attach to the description a list of goals that they want to accomplish if they are chosen for the office. He said this lets everyone in the club know what a candidate's personal agenda is and helps determine whether the person is a good match for the position.

Orientation

Position descriptions can be used as checklists during orientation sessions or as the orientation manual. The person conducting the orientation can make sure that each duty listed in the position description is covered during orientation.

GMs/COOs can also advocate particular concepts or philosophies in their club's position descriptions. For example, if the club's board has agreed to adopt the COO concept for the

Figure 11: Unwritten Sources for Position Descriptions

Methods of Gathering Position Description Information	
Method	**Definition**
Surveys	For specific questions with very measurable answers, a survey of the membership or of current and former volunteer leaders can help record club policies, lists of duties and relationships.
Focus Groups	This method can help a club gather information on traditions, club goals, club policies and structures of office.
Interviews	This method is most effective when the people participating have had extensive direct experience with club governance. It can be important to interview a cross-section of people in the club so that the function profile does not represent a single political faction.
Informal Discussions	A GM/COO may find out valuable information simply by playing a round of golf with members or sharing a meal with them after the game.

club, that concept could be explained in the board's position descriptions and highlighted during the orientation session for new board members. One GM/COO says it is the club executive's role to educate the board members and to give them the information they need to assist the executive.

For more about orientations, see the first issue in this series, "Club Board and Committee Orientation."

Meetings

Volunteer leaders are always concerned with the effectiveness of their meetings. Much planning needs to go into meetings in order to make them run smoothly, stay on track and be productive. One GM/COO says he puts each person's position description in front of him or her at every meeting. He says it helps them stay focused on what their job is and what they're supposed to accomplish. The next issue in the *Topical Reference Series* will discuss ways to make meetings more effective and what prevents meetings from being productive.

Updating Position Descriptions

The GM/COO needs to update position descriptions on a regular basis. If a position description is never reviewed, it quickly becomes outdated as policies, rules, duties and traditions change. A document that is outdated lacks credibility and nullifies its benefits.

Some GMs/COOs recommend an annual review of position descriptions. A club can pick an arbitrary week and always set aside a day in that week to review and update its descriptions. Other GMs/COOs say that it is only necessary to update descriptions before an election — and that only the positions that are up for election need be reviewed.

The design of the position description will typically dictate how it should be updated. Many GMs/COOs find it useful to keep each description on a computer disk so that changes can be easily made and printed out. This method can be especially cost-effective if each description is kept in a three-ring binder so that pages can be removed and replaced without reprinting and rebinding the entire manual.

Pulling It All Together

Compiling a position description can be a time-consuming task, but one that pays dividends in increased volunteer leader productivity, happier members and improved relations between volunteer leaders and staff. This issue has outlined some of the material that can be included in a description and can be used as a guide for clubs. The appendix contains sample position descriptions that can be adapted to an individual club's needs and positions.

However, whether the club uses the format described in this issue, or creates a format customized to its individual needs, the position descriptions will be tools that are much used and much appreciated.

ACKNOWLEDGEMENTS

The following individuals generously donated their expertise and time to make this issue possible:

Dennis Ahearn, CCM
Jay DiPietro, CCM
Charles Dorn, CCM
Terry Gilmer, CCM
Charles Hoare, CCM
John Hudson, CCM
Brian Kroh, CCM
Pasquale La Rocca, CCM
William Schulz, CCM
Richard Smetana, CCM
Daniel Urbin, CCM
Peter Young, CCM

SPECIAL THANKS

Special thanks are due to the faculty of the 1995 Premier Club Services Club Issues Forum:

Gerald F. Hurley, CAE
Tarun Kapoor, CHA, CHE
Charles D. Rumbarger, CAE

Additional Resources

Dorsey, Eugene, *The Role of the Board Chairperson*, Washington D.C.: National Center for Nonprofit Boards, Governance Series Booklet, 1992.

Grant, Philip C., PhD, *What Use is a Job Description?* Personnel Journal, February 1988, pp. 45-53.

Grant, Philip C., PhD, *Why Job Descriptions Don't Work*, Personnel Journal, January 1988, pp. 52-59.

Houle, Cyril O., *Governing Boards: Their Nature and Nurture*, San Francisco, CA: Jossey-Bass Publishers, 1990.

Ingram, Richard T., *Booklet #1 Ten Basic Responsibilities of Nonprofit Boards*, National Center for Nonprofit Boards, Washington D.C., 1988.

Leadership Guide for Board Presidents and Committee Chairpersons, Aspen Publishers, Inc., Maryland, 1993.

1995 Board Member Manual, Aspen Publishers, Inc., Maryland, 1994.

The Corporate Director, Corporate Directors Conference, Boston, MA: Cahners Books, 1975.

Discussion Questions

1. How can position descriptions make volunteers more effective?
2. What type of information should be included in a position description?
3. What are some ways a club can use position descriptions?

Additional Activities

1. Develop a position description for a Finance Committee Chairperson.
2. In a small group, critique one of the position descriptions in the appendix. Discuss how it could be made more specific or whether certain information should be excluded. If all members of the group are associated with a club, customize it to reflect the particulars of that club.

Appendix

This appendix contains *sample* position descriptions compiled from several different city and country clubs. All but the final two follow the format described in this issue. The final two, position descriptions for a recreation committee member and a centennial committee member, are samples taken directly from a club and follow a slightly different format. At the very end of the section is a template for a position description that may be copied and customized for any club.

Included in this appendix are sample position descriptions for:

Sample Position Description for Board President

The president is the chief executive officer of the club and, as such, in addition to his or her powers and duties under the bylaws, is the principal officer in correlating the activities of the committees and departments of the club. In emergencies, when action is required and board authority is not available, he or she shall act at his or her discretion and report to the board as soon as practicable. The president shall maintain close liaison with all committee chairpersons and the General Manager/Chief Operating Officer, GM/COO.

List of Duties

President only:

Critical duties

1. Hold a Board Orientation Day at the club.

    a. Tour the facilities with the GM/COO.

    b. Review the accounting methods and monthly statements provided by the business manager.

    c. Review the next year's capital and operating budgets.

    d. Review the contracts in force, liabilities, insurance, etc.

    e. Describe volunteer leaders' responsibilities as they relate to club functions, members, and employees.

    f. Discuss duties volunteer leaders do NOT have, such as: discussing board agendas with third parties; public discipline of members or employees; revealing matters under discussion by the board before they have been decided.

2. Chair the meetings of the board.

3. Execute papers and documents requiring execution in the name of the club.

4. Establish committees.

5. Serve as senior officer of the corporation and of the club.

6. Exercise control over methods of capital financing and disposal of major assets.

7. Help review and recommend salary levels for the club's senior operating personnel and participate in the development and implementation of insurance and pension plans.

Important duties

1. Receive reports from committee chairpersons.

2. Remove any volunteer leader who shall fail to attend fifty percent of the regular board meetings in one year.

3. Attend committee meetings.

4. Handle special requests for information from the volunteer leaders or the members working through the GM/COO.

Incidental duties

1. Counsel with officers, volunteer leaders, and management on specific problems wherein his or her experience may be helpful.

Additional duties as a board member include:

Critical duties

1. Establish policy.
2. Oversee the fiscal management of the club.
3. Enact regulations (bylaws, rules, resolutions).
4. Adopt budget plans.
5. Approve membership applications.
6. Appoint the GM/COO.
7. Meet prospective new members.

Important duties

1. Oversee the administration of policies.
2. Fill vacancies on the board.
3. Supervise the administration and enforcement of club regulations.
4. Discipline, suspend or expel a member, family member or guest.
5. Approve programs submitted by committees.
6. Oversee transfers of memberships.
7. Attend special meetings.
8. Supervise club elections.
9. Set an example by abiding by all club rules.

The president, acting alone, canNOT:

1. Approve or recommend proposals which require approval by the members.
2. Amend, repeal or adopt bylaws.
3. Pass capital assessments.
4. Borrow for capital purposes.
5. Authorize capital expenditures.
6. Conflict with the recommendation of standing committees given specific authority.

Prerequisites and Office Structure

A member must have served three consecutive years on the board before being chosen as president. No volunteer leader may serve in the same officer capacity for more than three consecutive full one-year terms of office. An individual volunteer leader who has served as an officer the preceding three successive years shall nevertheless be eligible to serve additional successive years in another office, provided that the individual shall have been elected a volunteer leader by the membership, and the individual serves in an office which has higher seniority than the office served in during the last full one-year term within the preceding three years.

Bylaws and Rules

The following bylaws and rules directly affect this position:

I.2   As a matter of law, the directors have the power and duty of management which cannot be generally delegated, and they are in a fiduciary relationship to the club's members or shareholders.

The general management of the affairs of a corporation having been entrusted by the legislature to the board of directors, it accords with general principle to hold that their functions may not be delegated to others.

Undoubtedly the board can appoint agents, to transact the ordinary business of the corporation, but generally directors cannot confer upon others the power to discharge duties which involve the exercise of judgment and discretion, except in the transaction of the ordinary business of the corporation.

In addition to the statutes, the bylaws fix the responsibility of the volunteer leaders. The bylaws of this club provide that "The management of this club shall be vested in a board of thirteen (13) members" and "The board of directors shall have the general management of the property, affairs and membership of the club, and shall have the power to adopt such rules and regulations as they may deem necessary for the government of the club."

I.3   The officers are a president, vice president, secretary and treasurer, elected by the board from their number with certain specific duties provided in the bylaws.

Except as authorized by law, in the bylaws or by the board, an officer is otherwise empowered to act only as any other volunteer leader. The board of this club can and has, from time to time, properly constituted the officers and executive committee to act in emergency or routine matters.

II.2   The officers of the club must be members of the board of directors, which elects them annually, but an assistant secretary (the club's general manager) may be selected by the board who is not a board member.

III.2   The president shall be the senior officer of the club. He or she shall preside at all meetings of the members of the club and of the board of directors. He or she shall see that the bylaws and rules of the club are enforced and shall perform such other duties as the board of directors may assign to him or her. He or she shall be an ex-officio member of all committees except the admissions committee.

Club Policies

This position is expected to understand and enforce the following policies:

1. It has been accepted as board policy for a number of years that a volunteer leader, due to his or her sensitive position in the acceptance process, does not sponsor persons for membership. It has not been required in the past that new volunteer leaders drop their sponsorship of persons already on the list at the time of their ascendancy to a board position. However, some have disqualified themselves from voting on the membership of a person they have sponsored.

2. The board has designated Thursday as the only day in which Prospective Member Cocktail Parties will be scheduled. Up to five prospectives are invited with their sponsors. It has been the practice to encourage all volunteer leaders to meet as many prospectives as possible and return evaluation sheets on all of them shortly after the cocktail party. Generally, no cocktail party is scheduled within two weeks of any board meeting.

3. All communications with the media or the wider community shall be referred first to the GM/COO and then handled by the president. The club's policy is to be open and forthright with the media, while respecting the privacy and exclusivity of the club and its members.

4. The policy of non-member use of facilities has generally been that the board must approve all outside or non-member uses of the club's facilities by the board at a regular meeting. All non-members except those who receive prior approval from the board or the athletic chairman, must be accompanied by a member.

Club Budgets

Operating Budget

The fiscal year generally runs from March 1 to February 28. This will vary, however, since the club follows a four week, four week, five week quarter. Operating budgets are prepared in early January for the review and recommendations of the finance committee. The board generally approves the operating budget in February. The finance committee will carefully review and consider each proposed figure of each budget. A properly prepared, well-thought-out budget is more apt to receive quick approval than one loosely constructed with built-in "fat."

The operating budget must be strictly adhered to once it is approved by the finance committee and the board. Any deviations must have both the finance committee's and board's approval.

See the attached operating budget.

Capital Budget

Capital budgets are prepared on the Capital Appropriation Request form and presented to the capital improvements and appropriations committee for its consideration and subsequent recommendation to the board. Generally, three bids must be obtained on items of capital expenditures. These bids are attached to the Capital Appropriation Request form.

For a sample personnel budget for a club president, see Figure 6 on page 13 of Roles and Responsibilities of Club Volunteer Leaders.

Operating Budget Summary

6 years ($ 000's)

	PRIOR YEAR Actual 19XX/0		CURRENT: Projected Actual		Budget 19X0/1		NEW BUDGET 19X1/X2		FORECAST: YR-1 Budget		YR-2 Budget		YR-3 Budget	
INCOME														
Member Dues	$ 3,193	0.93	$ 3,510	0.93	$ 3,450	0.93	$ 3,961	0.94	$ 4,077	0.93	$ 4,268	0.93	$ 4,467	0.93
Pro Shop	$ 33	0.01	$ 28	0.01	$ 37	0.01	$ 40	0.01	$ 43	0.01	$ 44	0.01	$ 45	0.01
Food & Beverage	$ 15	0.00	$ (63)	0.00	$ 31	0.01	$ 33	0.01	$ 34	0.01	$ 34	0.01	$ 35	0.01
Sports Dept.	$ 10	0.00	$ 7	0.00	$ 7	0.00	$ 11	0.00	$ 12	0.00	$ 12	0.00	$ 13	0.00
Other Income	$ 180	0.05	$ 207	0.05	$ 202	0.05	$ 177	0.04	$ 234	0.05	$ 236	0.05	$ 238	0.05
Total Income	$ 3,431	1.00	$ 3,689	1.00	$ 3,727	1.00	$ 4,222	1.00	$ 4,400	1.00	$ 4,594	1.00	$ 4,798	1.00
EXPENSE:														
Payroll and benefits	$ 1,943	0.56	$ 2,128	0.56	$ 2,106	0.57	$ 2,409	0.57	$ 2,529	0.57	$ 2,656	0.58	$ 2,789	0.58
Utilities and Taxes	$ 498	0.14	$ 567	0.14	$ 566	0.15	$ 600	0.14	$ 654	0.15	$ 713	0.16	$ 777	0.16
Operating Costs	$ 387	0.11	$ 430	0.11	$ 414	0.11	$ 450	0.11	$ 464	0.11	$ 477	0.11	$ 492	0.10
Administration Costs	$ 260	0.08	$ 257	0.08	$ 230	0.06	$ 270	0.06	$ 275	0.06	$ 281	0.06	$ 287	0.06
Contingency	$ -	0.00	$ -	0.00	$ 100	0.03	$ 42	0.01	$ 44	0.01	$ 46	0.01	$ 49	0.01
Total Expense	$ 3,088	0.89	$ 3,382	0.89	$ 3,416	0.92	$ 3,771	0.89	$ 3,966	0.90	$ 4,173	0.91	$ 4,393	0.92
OPERATING INCOM	$ 343	0.10	$ 307	0.10	$ 311	0.08	$ 451	0.11	$ 434		$ 421		$ 405	
INTEREST EXPENS	$ 370	0.11	$ 309	0.11	$ 311	0.08	$ 450	0.11	$ 433	0.10	$ 420	0.09	$ 404	0.08
GROSS EXPENSE =	$ 3,458	1.00	$ 3,691	1.00	$ 3,727	1.00	$ 4,221	1.00	$ 4,399	1.00	$ 4,593	1.00	$ 4,797	1.00
NET OPERATING														
INCOME(LOSS)=	$ (27)		$ (2)		$ -		$ 1		$ 1		$ 1		$ 1	

Expense forecasting assumptions for years following new budget:

Payroll & Benef =	5%	Operating Costs = 3%
Utilities & Taxe =	9%	Administration C = 2%

Time Budget (partial)

Jan. 1	New Year's Day Open House
Jan. 9	Prepare and mail out January meeting agenda
Jan. 21	January Board Meeting
Jan. 28	Finance Committee Meeting
Feb. 14	Valentine's Day Candlelight Dinner and Dance
Feb. 9	Prepare and mail out February meeting agenda
Feb. 21	February Board Meeting
Feb. 28	Preliminary Operating Budget due
March 9	Prepare and mail out March meeting agenda
March 14	Shore dinner
March 19	March Board Meeting (present budget)
April 9	Prepare and mail out April meeting agenda
April 12	Palm Sunday Brunch
April 16	Easter Dinner
April 19	April Board Meeting
April 26	Golf Season opener
May 9	Prepare and mail out May meeting agenda
May 10	Mother's Day Brunch
April 26	Golf Season opener
May 9	Prepare and mail out May meeting agenda
May 10	Mother's Day Brunch
May 19	May Board Meeting
May 20	Mixed Golf Guest Day
May 27	Swimming pool and tennis shop opens
June 2	Nine Holer Opening Day golf and luncheon
June 9	Prepare and mail out June meeting agenda
June 11	Opening Family Tennis Event
June 15	Swim meet
June 19	June Board Meeting
June 21	Father's Day Outing

Strategic Plan Goals

The president is expected to take ownership of the following strategic plan goals:

1. Constituent satisfaction
2. Membership attraction and retention
3. Ongoing facility maintenance and development
4. Establishing spending priorities that keep the club financially viable

Contracts and Legal Agreements

The following contracts and legal agreements affect the president's position at this club:

1. Leases for major equipment such as golf carts or housekeeping equipment

2. Employment contracts for:

    GM/COO (exp. 5/9X)
    Golf Pro (exp. 10/9X)
    Tennis Pro (exp. 2/9X)
    Clubhouse Manager (exp. 7/9X)
    Swimming Pro (exp. 10/9X)

3. Floral arrangements with Smith Florals for the following events:

    Valentine's Day Ball
    Mother-Daughter Banquet
    Father-Daughter Dance
    Grandparent's Day Tea
    Memorial Day Golf Banquet

4. Banquet contracts for club function rooms:

    Weddings on Jan. 12, 19, 26 Feb. 14, 17, 24, March 23, April 27 June 15, 22, 29
        Sept. 14, 21
    Graduation Parties: June 1, 8
    Retirement Parties: April 6, 20 Oct. 19 Dec. 14
    Anniversaries: Nov. 2

5. Entertainment contracts with:

    BMI
    ASCAP
    SESAC

Submit any requests for copies of these documents to the GM/COO or his or her secretary.

Traditions

The following traditions are associated with this position:

1. The president and golf committee chairperson play the first round of golf on opening day and the last round of golf on the closing day.

2. The president typically dresses up as Santa for the two brunches with Santa in December.

3. The president presides at New Year's Day Open House and typically makes welcoming remarks.

4. The president typically meets with all nominees for the board and discusses board duties with them before nominations are accepted.

Relationships

To The Board

The president is the chief executive officer. He or she is the top level in the chain of administrative command; presides at all meetings of the members of the board; and has the power to call special meetings of the board. He or she is the chairperson of the executive committee and may call meetings of that committee as well. He or she has the power to create committees, subject to the approval of the board, and designate the chairperson and vice-chairperson, if any, of all committees other than the nominating committee.

To Committees

Each of the committees, subject to approval of the board, shall formulate programs and submit them with recommendations to the board for approval. The officers of the club shall have control of the execution of such programs and recommendations as are approved by the board. The committees shall act only as consultants and advisors to the board and officers. The president should be available to provide advice and counsel to all committees. The president is considered an ex-officio member of each committee.

To Employees

The president may call upon the following employees to assist in the execution of his or her duties:

- GM/COO
- Club accountants/chief financial officer
- Clubhouse manager
- Club secretary

The following is expected of the president when working with the GM/COO:

1. Provide counsel and advice, giving the benefit of your judgment, expertise and familiarity with club operations.
2. Consult with the GM/COO on all matters which the board is considering.
3. Delegate responsibility for all executive and operational functions.
4. Refrain from handling administrative details.
5. Make all staff responsible to the GM/COO.
6. Share all communications with the GM/COO.
7. Provide support to the GM/COO and staff in carrying out their professional duties.
8. Support the GM/COO in all decisions and actions consistent with the policies of the board and the standards of the club.
9. Hold the GM/COO accountable for the supervision of the organization.
10. Evaluate the work of the GM/COO.

Meeting Agendas

For the 199X–9X year, the board meeting dates have been set as the first Thursday of every month. Meetings begin at 6 p.m. and run between an hour and an hour and a half. Each meeting is followed by a dinner, which is optional.

The following tips will help you run effective meetings:

1. Know the main purpose of each of your meetings.

2. Keep your meeting time reasonable — the shorter the better.

3. Start your meetings on time and end on time.

4. Take charge of your meetings.

5. Stick to the agenda.

Here is a sample meeting agenda which you may wish to follow:

5 min	Greetings from the president, along with a statement of objective(s) of the meeting or a brief review of the agenda.
1 min	Roll call, oral or observed
5–10 min	Review dates of future meetings and minutes of previous meeting
35 min	Discussion on agenda topics
30 min	Unfinished business and new business
2 min	Adjournment, with thanks from the president for the time and effort that the board members devoted to accomplishing the meeting's objectives

NOTE: Be sure that someone is taking minutes. This probably should not be the president, who must guide the discussion, summarize key points and keep the meeting on track.

Sample Position Description for Board Vice President

The vice president acts as the chief executive officer in the president's absence, and assists the president as he or she may request. The vice president frequently has committee responsibilities.

List of Duties

Vice president only:

Critical duties

1. Act for the president in his or her absence or incapacity.
2. Attend executive committee meetings.

Important duties

1. Assume, at the president's request, responsibility for an especially important area of activity or study.
2. Chair long-range planning committee.

Additional duties as a board member include:

Critical duties

1. Establish policy.
2. Oversee the fiscal management of the club.
3. Enact regulations (bylaws, rules, resolutions).
4. Adopt budget plans.
5. Approve membership applications.
6. Appoint the GM/COO.
7. Meet prospective new members.

Important duties

1. Oversee the administration of policies.
2. Fill vacancies on the board.
3. Supervise the administration and enforcement of club regulations.
4. Discipline, suspend or expel a member, family member or guest.
5. Approve programs submitted by committees.
6. Oversee transfers of memberships.
7. Attend special meetings.
8. Supervise club elections.
9. Set an example by abiding by all club rules.

The vice president, acting alone, canNOT:

1. Approve or recommend proposals which require approval by the members.
2. Amend, repeal or adopt bylaws.
3. Pass capital assessments.
4. Borrow for capital purposes.
5. Authorize capital expenditures.
6. Conflict with the recommendation of standing committees given specific authority.

Prerequisites and Office Structure

A member must have served three consecutive years on the board before being chosen as vice president. No volunteer leader may serve in the same officer capacity for more than three consecutive full one-year terms of office. An individual volunteer leader who has served as an officer the preceding three successive years shall nevertheless be eligible to serve additional successive years in another office, provided that the individual shall have been elected a volunteer leader by the membership, and the individual serves in an office which has higher seniority than the office served in during the last full one-year term within the preceding three years.

Bylaws and Rules

The following bylaws and rules directly affect this position:

I.2 As a matter of law, the volunteer leaders have the power and duty of management which cannot be generally delegated, and they are in a fiduciary relationship to the club's members or shareholders.

The general management of the affairs of a corporation having been entrusted by the legislature to the board of directors, it accords with general principle to hold that their functions may not be delegated to others.

Undoubtedly the board can appoint agents, to transact the ordinary business of the corporation, but generally volunteer leaders cannot confer upon others the power to discharge duties which involve the exercise of judgment and discretion, except in the transaction of the ordinary business of the corporation.

In addition to the statutes, the bylaws fix the responsibility of the volunteer leaders. The bylaws of this club provide that "The management of this club shall be vested in a board of thirteen (13) members" and "The board of directors shall have the general management of the property, affairs and membership of the club, and shall have the power to adopt such rules and regulations as they may deem necessary for the government of the club."

I.3 The officers are a president, vice president, secretary and treasurer, elected by the board from their number with certain specific duties provided in the bylaws.

Except as authorized by law, in the bylaws or by the board, an officer is otherwise empowered to act only as any other volunteer leader. The board of this club can and has, from time to time, properly constituted the officers and executive committee to act in emergency or routine matters.

IX.8   If the president is absent, disabled or otherwise unable to perform the duties of office, the vice president shall perform all of the duties of the president, and when so acting, shall have all the powers of and be subject to all the restrictions upon the president. The vice president shall have such powers and perform such other duties as from time to time may be prescribed for him or her by the board, the bylaws, or the president.

Club Policies

This position is expected to understand and enforce the following policies:

1. It has been accepted as board policy for a number of years that a volunteer leader, due to his or her sensitive position in the acceptance process, does not sponsor persons for membership. It has not been required in the past that new volunteer leaders drop their sponsorship of persons already on the list at the time of their ascendancy to a board position. However, some have disqualified themselves from voting on the membership of a person they have sponsored.

2. The board has designated Thursday as the only day in which Prospective Member Cocktail Parties will be scheduled. Up to five prospectives are invited with their sponsors. It has been the practice to encourage all volunteer leaders to meet as many prospectives as possible and return evaluation sheets on all of them shortly after the cocktail party. Generally, no cocktail party is scheduled within two weeks of any board meeting.

3. All communications with the media or the wider community shall be referred first to the GM/COO and then handled by the president. The club's policy is to be open and forthright with the media, while respecting the privacy and exclusivity of the club and its members.

4. The policy of non-member use of facilities has generally been that the board must approve all outside or non-member uses of the club's facilities by the board at a regular meeting. All non-members except those who receive prior approval from the board or the athletic chairman, must be accompanied by a member.

Club Budgets

Operating Budget

The fiscal year generally runs from March 1 to February 28. This will vary, however, since theclub follows a four week, four week, five week quarter. Operating budgets are prepared in early January for the review and recommendations of the finance committee. The board generally approves the operating budget in February. The finance committee will carefully review and consider each proposed figure of each budget. A properly prepared, well-thought-out budget is more apt to receive quick approval than one loosely constructed with built-in "fat."

The operating budget must be strictly adhered to once it is approved by the finance committee and the board. Any deviations must have both the finance committee's and board's approval.

See the sample operating budget in the sample position description of the board president.

Capital Budget

Capital budgets are prepared on the Capital Appropriation Request form and presented to the capital improvements and appropriations committee for its consideration and subsequent recommendation to the board. Generally, three bids must be obtained on items of capital expenditures. These bids are attached to the Capital Appropriation Request form.

Strategic Plan Goals

The vice president is expected to take ownership of the following strategic plan goals:

1. Ensure that the club's leadership consistently carries out the club's long-term plan.
2. Ensure that the club's risk management program is cost effective and provides adequate protection for the club.

Relationships

The vice president typically works with the following volunteer leaders and employees:

President: The vice president assists the president as needed, and steps in when the president can not be present. The president provides training and succession planning information to the vice president. The vice president should help the president be the best president he or she can be.

Long-Range Planning Committee: The vice president chairs this committee. Its purpose is to study and recommend long-range plans to the board of directors and complete special studies as requested by the board. It concerns itself with projects over the coming three- to five-year period.

GM/COO: The following is expected of the vice president when working with the GM/COO:

1. Provide counsel and advice, giving the benefit of your judgment, expertise and familiarity with club operations.
2. Consult with the GM/COO on all matters which the board is considering.
3. Delegate responsibility for all executive and operational functions.
4. Refrain from handling administrative details.
5. Make all staff responsible to the GM/COO.
6. Share all communications with the GM/COO.
7. Provide support to the GM/COO and staff in carrying out their professional duties.
8. Support the GM/COO in all decisions and actions consistent with the policies of the board and the standards of the club.
9. Hold the GM/COO accountable for the supervision of the organization.
10. Evaluate the work of the GM/COO.

Meeting Agendas

For the 199X–9X year, the board meeting dates have been set as the first Thursday of every month. Meetings begin at 6 p.m. and run between an hour and an hour and a half. The meeting is followed by dinner, which is optional.

The following tips will help you run effective committee meetings:

1. Know the main purpose of each of your meetings.

2. Keep your meeting time reasonable — the shorter the better.

3. Start your meetings on time and end on time.

4. Take charge of your meetings.

5. Stick to the agenda.

Here is a programmed sample agenda which you may wish to follow:

5 min.	Greetings from the chairperson, along with a statement of objective(s) of the meeting or a brief review of the agenda
1 min	Roll call, oral or observed
5–10 min	Review dates of future meetings and minutes of previous meeting
35 min	Discussion on agenda topics
30 min	Unfinished business and new business
2 min	Adjournment, with thanks from the chairperson for the time and effort that the committee members devoted to accomplishing the meeting's objectives

Sample Position Description for Board Secretary

The secretary is responsible for the duties delegated to him or her in the bylaws and will not normally be given any committee assignment. The secretary will take the minutes during each board and executive committee meeting and be responsible for agendas. The secretary is a member of the board and executive committee and has custody of the seal of the club.

List of Duties

Secretary only:

Critical duties

1. Attend board meetings.
2. Keep minutes of all board and executive committee meetings.
3. Prepare agendas for each board and executive committee meeting.
4. Send out announcements of special meetings and annual meetings.
5. Mail and post all required notices.
6. Bill all members and guests for their fees, dues and fines.

Important duties

1. Prepare ballots for annual elections.
2. Conduct the correspondence of the corporation at the direction of the board.
3. Sign all written contracts and obligations.
4. Sign, with the president, all membership certificates, obligations, contracts, deeds, mortgages, promissory notes and other instruments.
5. Maintain a list of all club members.
6. Notify the treasurer of all changes to the membership list.

Additional duties as a board member include:

Critical duties

1. Establish policy.
2. Oversee the fiscal management of the club.
3. Enact regulations (bylaws, rules, resolutions).
4. Adopt budget plans.
5. Approve membership applications.
6. Appoint the GM/COO.
7. Meet prospective new members.

Important duties

1. Oversee the administration of policies.
2. Fill vacancies on the board.
3. Supervise the administration and enforcement of club regulations.
4. Discipline, suspend or expel a member, family member or guest.
5. Approve programs submitted by committees.
6. Oversee transfers of memberships.
7. Attend special meetings.
8. Supervise club elections.
9. Set an example by abiding by all club rules.

The secretary, acting alone, canNOT:

1. Approve or recommend proposals which require approval by the members.
2. Amend, repeal or adopt bylaws.
3. Pass capital assessments.
4. Borrow for capital purposes.
5. Authorize capital expenditures.
6. Conflict with the recommendation of standing committees given specific authority.

Prerequisites and Office Structure

A member must have served two consecutive years on the board before being chosen as secretary. No volunteer leader may serve in the same officer capacity for more than three consecutive full one-year terms of office. An individual volunteer leader who has served as an officer the preceding three successive years shall nevertheless be eligible to serve additional successive years in another office, provided that the individual shall have been elected a volunteer leader by the membership, and the individual serves in an office which has higher seniority than the office served in during the last full one-year term within the preceding three years.

Bylaws

The following bylaw directly affects this position:

III.e The secretary shall have, in addition to all other powers and duties granted by law and by the articles of incorporation and the bylaws of the corporation, the following powers and duties:

A. To affix the corporate seal to instruments and attest the same.

B. To keep minutes of all meetings of the active members of the club and of the board of governors.

C. To conduct the correspondence of the corporation at the direction of the board of governors.

D. To mail and post all notices required to be mailed or posted by the provisions of these bylaws. Such notices are presumed to have been given when mailed to the member or other person at the address shown on the records of the corporation.

E. To bill all members and persons granted club privileges for fees, dues and fines, and to perform such other duties as the president or board of governors may from time to time prescribe.

Club Policies

This position is expected to understand and enforce the following policies:

1. It has been accepted as board policy for a number of years that a volunteer leader, due to his or her sensitive position in the acceptance process, does not sponsor persons for membership. It has not been required in the past that new volunteer leaders drop their sponsorship of persons already on the list at the time of their ascendancy to a board position. However, some have disqualified themselves from voting on the membership of a person they have sponsored.

2. The board has designated Thursday as the only day in which Prospective Member Cocktail Parties will be scheduled. Up to five prospectives are invited with their sponsors. It has been the practice to encourage all volunteer leaders to meet as many prospectives as possible and return evaluation sheets on all of them shortly after the cocktail party. Generally, no cocktail party is scheduled within two weeks of any board meeting.

3. All communications with the media or the wider community shall be referred first to the GM/COO and then handled by the president. The club's policy is to be open and forthright with the media, while respecting the privacy and exclusivity of the club and its members.

Club Budgets

Operating Budget

The fiscal year generally runs from March 1 to February 28. This will vary, however, since the club follows a four week, four week, five week quarter. Operating budgets are prepared in early January for the review and recommendations of the finance committee. The board generally approves the operating budget in February. The finance committee will carefully review and consider each proposed figure of each budget. A properly prepared, well-thought-out budget is more apt to receive quick approval than one loosely constructed with built-in "fat."

The operating budget must be strictly adhered to once it is approved by the finance committee and the board. Any deviations must have both the finance committee's and board's approval.

See the sample operating budget in the sample position description of the board president.

Capital Budget

Capital budgets are prepared on the Capital Appropriation Request form and presented to the capital improvements and appropriations committee for its consideration and subsequent recommendation to the board. Generally, three bids must be obtained on items of capital expenditures. These bids are attached to the Capital Appropriation Request form.

Personnel Budget

The board secretary may ask the club secretary for assistance in preparing agendas, mailing out notices and mailing out club correspondence. This assistance should not exceed five hours per week.

The board secretary may also seek assistance on an as-needed basis from the GM/COO to explain club documents and correspondence or to clarify membership matters.

Time Budget (partial)

Time	When	Task
2 hours/month	1 week before each board meeting	Prepare agenda and mail out to board members
3 hours/month	Date of board meeting	Take minutes of meeting and type up for files
5 hours/month	As needed	Write correspondence for board or membership matters
2 hours/year	Nov. 1	Prepare ballots for elections
½ hour/year	Jan. 2	Post election results in clubhouse

Contracts and Legal Agreements

The following contracts and legal agreements affect the secretary's position at this club:

1. Leases for major equipment such as golf carts or housekeeping equipment

2. Employment contracts for:

   GM/COO (exp. 5/9X)
   Golf Pro (exp. 10/9X)
   Tennis Pro (exp. 2/9X)
   Clubhouse Manager (exp. 7/9X)
   Swimming Pro (exp. 10/9X)

3. Floral arrangements with Smith Florals for the following events:

   Valentine's Day Ball
   Mother-Daughter Banquet
   Father-Daughter Dance
   Grandparent's Day Tea
   Memorial Day Golf Banquet

4. Banquet contracts for club function rooms:

> Weddings on Jan. 12, 19, 26; Feb. 14, 17, 24; March 23; April 27; June 15, 22, 29; Sept. 14, 21
> Graduation Parties: June 1, 8
> Retirement Parties: April 6, 20; Oct. 19; Dec. 14
> Anniversaries: Nov. 2

5. Entertainment contracts with:

> BMI
> ASCAP
> SESAC

Submit any requests for copies of these documents to the GM/COO or his or her secretary.

Relationships

The secretary typically works with the following volunteer leaders and employees:

President: The secretary provides the president with informational support and works with him or her to develop agendas and membership letters.

Treasurer: The secretary informs the treasurer of any changes in membership lists.

Nominating Committee: The secretary helps the nominating committee prepare and mail ballots once nominations are made.

Board of Directors: The secretary keeps minutes of board meetings and provides copies at each meeting and upon request. The secretary is also responsible for mailing out meeting notices and agendas prior to each meeting.

GM/COO: The secretary provides copies of all relevant documents to the GM/COO. The secretary signs documents provided by the GM/COO as needed and shares all communications with the GM/COO.

Meeting Agendas

For the 199X–9X year, the meeting dates have been set as the first Thursday of every month. Meetings begin at 6 p.m. and run between an hour and an hour and a half. The meeting is followed by dinner, which is optional.

Here is a sample meeting agenda which you may wish to follow:

5 min	Greetings from the president along with a statement of objective(s) of the meeting or a brief review of the agenda
1 min	Roll call, oral or observed
5–10 min	Review dates of future meetings and minutes of previous meeting
35 min	Discussion on agenda topics (list specific topics here)
30 min	Unfinished business and new business (list specific business here)
2 min	Adjournment

Possible format for taking the minutes of a meeting:

Name of governing body:
Date of meeting:
Time called to order:

Members of board or committee	Present	Absent

Statement of objective(s) of meeting or brief review of agenda:

Review date(s) of future meetings:

Discussion of agenda items	Who to handle	By when
Unfinished business	**Who to handle**	**By when**
New business:	**Who to handle**	**By when**

Adjournment time: **Signed:**

Sample Position Description for Board Treasurer

The treasurer is responsible for the duties delegated to him or her in the bylaws, and usually will serve as chairperson of the finance committee, but on no other committee. He or she will direct, in liaison with the GM/COO and the business manager, duties of a financial nature.

List of Duties

Treasurer only:

Critical duties

1. Responsible for the monies of the club.
2. Responsible for the keeping of regular accounts.
3. Responsible for seeing that due dates are met for income tax, insurance and other fiscal matters.
4. Chair the finance committee.
5. Collect all the amounts due the club.
6. Disburse funds as directed by the board.
7. Keep all the accounts of the club in books belonging to it.
8. Prepare and present a report on the finances of the club at the annual meeting and at board meetings.

Important duties

1. Keep custody of the funds and securities of the club.
2. Keep the funds and securities of the club in the designated depository.
3. Evaluate budget variances and review procedures when necessary.
4. Recommend investment accounts and custodians.
5. Enforce the tax, government and accounting rules and regulations.
6. Make sure that the club finances are audited annually by an outside auditor.

Incidental duties

1. Furnish bond when required.

Additional duties as a board member include:

Critical duties

1. Establish policy.
2. Oversee the fiscal management of the club.
3. Enact regulations (bylaws, rules, resolutions).
4. Adopt budget plans.

5. Approve membership applications.

6. Appoint the GM/COO.

7. Meet prospective new members.

Important duties

1. Oversee the administration of policies.

2. Fill vacancies on the board.

3. Supervise the administration and enforcement of club regulations.

4. Discipline, suspend or expel a member, family member or guest.

5. Approve programs submitted by committees.

6. Oversee transfers of memberships.

7. Attend special meetings.

8. Supervise club elections.

9. Set an example by abiding by all club rules.

The treasurer, acting alone, canNOT:

1. Approve or recommend proposals which require approval by the members.

2. Amend, repeal or adopt bylaws.

3. Pass capital assessments.

4. Borrow for capital purposes.

5. Authorize capital expenditures.

6. Conflict with the recommendation of standing committees given specific authority.

Prerequisites and Office Structure

A member must have served two consecutive years on the board before being chosen as treasurer. No volunteer leader may serve in the same officer capacity for more than three consecutive full one-year terms of office. An individual volunteer leader who has served as an officer the preceding three successive years shall nevertheless be eligible to serve additional successive years in another office, provided that the individual shall have been elected a volunteer leader by the membership, and the individual serves in an office which has higher seniority than the office served in during the last full one-year term within the preceding three years.

Bylaws

The following bylaw directly affects this position:

V.4   The treasurer shall be a member of the board. He or she shall have custody of the funds and securities of the club and shall keep them in such depository or depositories as the board may, from time to time, designate. He or she shall attend to the collection of all amounts due the club and shall disburse the funds of the club as may be directed by the board. He or she shall keep all accounts of the club in books belonging to it and report on the finances of the club at the annual meeting and to the board as it may direct. If required by the board, he or she shall furnish bond in such amount and with such surety as the board may direct, the cost of which shall be paid by the club. He or she shall perform the duties that generally pertain to the office of treasurer and such other duties as the board may assign.

Club Policies

This position is expected to understand and enforce the following policies:

1. It has been accepted as board policy for a number of years that a volunteer leader, due to his or her sensitive position in the acceptance process, does not sponsor persons for membership. It has not been required in the past that new volunteer leaders drop their sponsorship of persons already on the list at the time of their ascendancy to a board position. However, some have disqualified themselves from voting on the membership of a person they have sponsored.

2. Funds derived from transfer fees and all other "non-operating income" should be primarily dedicated to permanent improvements, additions, renewals, re-habilitation of fixtures and equipment and replacements of substantial nature. Realizing that the distinction between these expenditures and certain operating expenses may be vague, caution should be exercised to prevent operating expenses from being budgeted as one of the above, especially if it is solely to produce a balanced operating budget.

3. Operating expenses should be budgeted and managed so as to be equal to or slightly less than dues and operating revenues. In essence, a balanced operating budget is highly desirable, but not through a reduction in the quality of services.

4. Membership assessment is the most attractive route for funding capital additions and replacements. Assessments provide the equivalent of interest-free loans. The assessment may be added to the member's equity and later recovered by the member when he or she resigns or transfers to another membership category. However, care should be taken to prevent the equity portion of the total cost of an active membership from becoming too large, because for each dollar increase in equity tends to restrict the amount by which the transfer fee can be increased.

5. A major capital asset replacement fund may be established, funded from time to time by board action from excess membership transfer fees, so long as the debt of the club is nil.

Club Budgets

Operating Budget

The fiscal year generally runs from March 1 to February 28. This will vary, however, since the club follows a four week, four week, five week quarter. Operating budgets are prepared in early January for the review and recommendations of the finance committee. The board generally approves the operating budget in February. The finance committee will carefully review and consider each proposed figure of each budget. A properly prepared, well-thought-out budget is more apt to receive quick approval than one loosely constructed with built-in "fat."

The operating budget must be strictly adhered to once it is approved by the finance committee and the board. Any deviations must have both the finance committee's and board's approval. If a particular committee's operation has been so efficient that it is operating below the approved budget, the committee is to be commended. However, "excess" operational monies may not be spent for the sake of spending them, nor may these "excess" funds be used in any way without prior finance committee and board approval.

See the sample operating budget in the sample position description of the board president.

Capital Budget

Capital budgets are prepared on the Capital Appropriation Request form and presented to the capital improvements and appropriations committee for its consideration and subsequent recommendation to the board. Generally, three bids must be obtained on items of capital expenditures. These bids are attached to the Capital Appropriation Request form.

For a sample personnel budget for treasurer, see Figure 5 on page 12 of the Roles and Responsibilities of Club Volunteer Leaders *issue.*

Time Budget (partial)

The following schedule has been established for the filing of financial statements:

Jan. 3	File fourth quarter tax bill
Jan. 5	Review December's income statement
Jan. 15	Submit preliminary operating budget to the finance committee
Feb. 3	Submit operating budget to board of governors
Feb. 5	Review January's income statement
Feb. 8	Prepare and present treasurer's report for board meeting
April 1	File first quarter tax bill
June 1	Review new capital budget
July 1	File second quarter tax bill
Sept. 1	Recommend to board goals for membership and club usage
Oct. 1	Complete first draft of financial plan for following year
	File third quarter tax bill
Nov. 15	Review, with finance committee, final draft of financial plan

Strategic Plan Goals

The treasurer is expected to take ownership of the following strategic plan goals:

1. Ensure the financial viability of the club through careful budgeting.

2. Keep membership dues increases to a maximum of 5 percent over the next three years.

3. Reduce debt by 35 percent over the next three years.

4. Increase pro salaries to a more competitive level over the next five years.

Relationships

The treasurer typically works with the following volunteer leaders and employees:

President: The treasurer provides the president with all needed financial information and presents all of the finance committee's proposals to the president and board. The treasurer is responsible for providing finance reports to the president on an as-needed basis.

Secretary: The treasurer works with the secretary to keep billing and membership status lists up to date.

Finance Committee: The treasurer orients new members to the finance committee, provides agendas, runs efficient meetings and provides necessary information.

Board of Directors: The treasurer prepares and presents the finance report and provides other information as needed. He or she also presents the finance committee's proposals and recommendations. He or she answers any questions the board may have.

GM/COO: The treasurer works closely with the GM/COO to make sure he or she has input on all policy decisions made by the board. The treasurer keeps the GM/COO informed of finance committee actions and invites the GM/COO to all meetings.

Club Controller: The treasurer works with the club controller to analyze and produce financial statements. The treasurer reviews board and committee policies with the club controller and oversees their implementation.

Meeting Agendas

For the 199X–9X year, the board meeting dates have been set as the first Thursday of every month. Meetings begin at 6 p.m. and run between an hour and an hour and a half. Each meeting is followed by a dinner, which is optional.

The following tips will help you run effective meetings:

1. Know the main purpose of each of your meetings.
2. Keep your meeting time reasonable — the shorter the better.
3. Start your meetings on time and end on time.
4. Take charge of your meetings.
5. Stick to the agenda.

Here is a sample meeting agenda which you may wish to follow:

5 min	Greetings from the committee chairperson, along with a statement of objective(s) of the meeting or a brief review of the agenda
1 min	Roll call, oral or observed
5–10 min	Review dates of future meetings and minutes of previous meeting
35 min	Discussion on agenda topics

30 min   Unfinished business and new business

2 min   Adjournment, with thanks from the committee chairperson for the time and effort that the committee members devoted to accomplishing the meeting's objectives

NOTE: Be sure that someone is taking minutes. This probably should not be the chairperson, who must guide the discussion, summarize key points, and keep the meeting on track.

Sample Position Description for House Committee Chairperson

The house committee is charged with the proper operation of the clubhouse. The chairperson of the committee directs all meetings and reports on committee actions to the board of governors. The GM/COO is responsible for the daily operations of the clubhouse. The house committee supervises these operations. In many respects, it is a liaison committee, coordinating member desires with the capabilities of management and facilities.

List of Duties

House committee chairperson only:

1. Schedule meetings of the house committee.
2. Prepare agendas for house committee meetings.
3. Chair all meetings of the house committee.
4. Report on committee proceedings to the board of governors.
5. Work with the GM/COO on all committee initiatives.
6. Appoint members of the house committee.
7. Establish subcommittees as needed.
8. Choose chairpersons for subcommittees.

Additional duties as a member of the house committee include:

1. Survey the kitchen, dining room and grill rooms, bar and locker rooms.
2. Book social events.
3. Establish prices for food, drinks and confections.
4. Enforce all rules governing the use of the clubhouse.
5. Prepare the annual budget for the maintenance, upkeep and improvement of the clubhouse, roadways, parking areas and landscaping in the clubhouse area not considered part of the golf course.
6. Coordinate the use of the clubhouse with the activities of all other committees.
7. Maintain the clubhouse facilities and services at the highest possible level consistent with overall club objectives.
8. Recommend improvements and renovations to the clubhouse and its equipment and furnishings.
9. Propose regulations concerning the use of the club.
10. Address reported violations of clubhouse rules.
11. Recommend hours of service, food and beverage price structures, locker room and other fees for use of clubhouse facilities.
12. Recommend to finance or insurance committee any insurance coverage or changes therein pertaining to the portion of the club under its jurisdiction and assist in the development of the annual budget insofar as it concerns this committee's functions.

13. Recommend personnel policies for the clubhouse staff.

14. Maintain a roster of members.

15. Distribute rosters annually to each member.

16. Post clubhouse rules.

Prerequisites

1. Prior service on at least one other committee.

2. Membership in the club for at least five years.

3. Active in club activities.

4. A minimum of three years service on the house committee.

Structure of Office

1. House committee chair is appointed by the board president.

2. Term of service is for one year, up to three consecutive years.

3. The committee will continue to function until March 31 of each year — or until such a time as a reconstituted committee is announced.

4. The house committee chairperson oversees the following subcommittees: decorating committee, women's association, building and facilities committee, wine committee, food and bar committee and others as appointed.

Bylaws and Rules

The following bylaws and rules directly affect this position:

IX. The members of all committees (other than the nominating and grievance committees) serve at the pleasure of the board of governors.

The committees shall act only as consultants and advisors to the board of governors and officers. Each of the several committees shall act only as a committee and the individual members thereof shall have no power or authority.

The chairman of each committee may appoint such subcommittees as he or she deems desirable.

XI. (a) The house committee shall have the general supervision over the operations of the clubhouse, including the swimming pool, the patio areas and the sanitation system. Additionally it shall have the general charge and supervision of all maintenance, repair and replacement of real and personal property of the club except the golf course and golf course maintenance equipment. It may appoint a subcommittee for the repairs and maintenance portion of its duties and may make expenditures for the maintenance, repair or replacement of the real or personal property over which it has responsibility, subject to the approval of the board of governors.

Further, it shall recommend rules governing the conduct of members, visitors and employees and such rules, on approval of the board of governors, shall be published for the members, posted and enforced by this committee.

All policy directives by this committee which affect personnel shall be made to the GM/COO and through him or her to the affected personnel, whose performance of their club duties is the ultimate responsibility of the GM/COO.

(b)   This committee shall be responsible for keeping and maintaining a roster of club members. The club roster shall be distributed annually to each member and listed therein shall be identification as to the classification of membership. The roster shall also contain the chairpersons and members of each committee (except the admissions committee), the current code of regulations, and bylaws, all existing committee rules or rules promulgated by the board of governors. The roster shall be distributed to all members on or before May 15 of each year or as soon thereafter as practicable.

Club Policies

This position is expected to understand and enforce the following policies:

1. The clubhouse building architecture and interior design standards should project a theme of quiet, tasteful elegance. Every effort should be made to blend the clubhouse and other structures into the natural setting at the club.

2. Golf bag storage should be available to all members. Bags and clubs should be stored with high regard for security, cleaning and damage control. Sufficient space should be provided for repairing and renovating golf clubs.

3. A lockers should be available to all members who desire one.

4. Youth rooms should be available to members' children, and, as now, they should be located close to the swimming pool and/or tennis courts.

5. Functional, productive administrative offices should be maintained.

6. Effective flood control measures should be taken to minimize potential losses of facilities, equipment and awards.

Strategic Plan Goals

The house committee chairperson is expected to take ownership of the following strategic plan goals:

1. Provide the highest quality food and beverage service to members.

2. Maintain the facilities at the highest quality consistent with financial viability.

3. Provide unique entertainment that appeals to as many of the club's constituents as possible.

Traditions

The house committee chairperson typically sits at the head table for the Opening Day Banquet, Be My Guest Day, and the Guys and Dolls Dinner Dance.

Relationships

The house committee chairperson typically works with the following volunteer leaders and employees:

President: The committee chairperson presents all of the house committee's proposals to the president and board. The house committee chairperson is responsible for providing house reports to the president on an as-needed basis.

Secretary: The committee chairperson keeps the secretary apprised of all membership changes and works with the secretary to publish the yearly roster and directory.

House Committee: The committee chairperson orients members to the committee, provides agendas, runs efficient meetings and provides necessary information.

Board of Governors: The committee chairperson presents committee's proposals and recommendations. He or she answers any questions the board may have.

GM/COO: The committee chairperson works closely with the GM/COO to make sure he or she has input on all policy decisions made by the board. The committee chairperson keeps the GM/COO informed of committee actions and invites the GM/COO to all meetings. The GM/COO is the primary information source for the committee chairperson and helps the chairperson perform duties as necessary.

Also, see Figure 8 on page 16 of the Roles and Responsibilities *issue for another sample relationship chart for the house committee chairperson.*

Meeting Agendas

For the 199X–9X year, the committee meeting dates have been set as the first Wednesday of every month. Meetings begin at 6 p.m. and run between an hour and an hour and a half.

The following tips will help you run effective meetings:

1. Know the main purpose of each of your meetings.
2. Keep your meeting time reasonable — the shorter the better.
3. Start your meetings on time and end on time.
4. Take charge of your meetings.
5. Stick to the agenda.

Here is a sample meeting agenda which you may wish to follow:

5 min	Greetings from the chairperson, along with a statement of objective(s) of the meeting or a brief review of the agenda
1 min	Roll call, oral or observed
5–10 min	Review dates of future meetings and minutes of previous meeting
35 min	Discussion on agenda topics
30 min	Unfinished business and new business
2 min	Adjournment, with thanks from the chairperson for the time and effort that the house committee members devoted to accomplishing the meeting's objectives

Sample Position Description for Golf Committee Chairperson

The golf committee chairperson directs the golf committee. This committee is responsible for all golf tournaments and the entertainment connected with them, except the details of those authorized to the Women's Golf Association and the annual Member-Guest Tournament. The committee is responsible for men's golf handicaps, golf score cards, local rules and tee-off times. It screens for the board applications for any group play or blocked-off tee time requests for the golf course. It also reviews reported violations and responds as needed.

List of Duties

Golf committee chairperson only:

1. Invite the board president to all committee meetings.
2. Work with the GM/COO and golf pro.
3. Keep records of the committee's meetings, policies, and authorities.
4. Prepare reports for the board.
5. Identify services desired by the membership.
6. Choose chairpersons of the subcommittees.
7. Delegate jobs to committee members.
8. Prepare agendas for committee meetings.
9. Conduct golf committee meetings.
10. Submit committee recommendations to the board in writing.
11. Supervise all subcommittee activity.
12. Assign duties to subcommittees.
13. Select, upon recommendation by the subcommittee chairpersons, subcommittee members.

Additional duties as a member of the golf committee include:

1. Schedule golf tournaments.
2. Schedule entertainment to accompany golf tournaments.
3. Work with golf pro to schedule golf tournaments.
4. Maintain the system of golf handicaps and score cards.
5. Establish local golf rules.
6. Establish tee-off times.
7. Screen applications for group play or blocked-off tee time requests.
8. Review golf rule violations and penalize where necessary.
9. Recommend to the board the employment of a golf professional and monitor that professional's performance.

10. Recommend to the GM/COO how the pro shop should be operated and how to maintain and operate the golf carts.

11. Publish the rules for all golf playing on the course, including the use of carts.

12. Decide all questions which may arise regarding the rules of golf.

13. Receive and consider all complaints made against members or guests for violating the rules and etiquette of golf.

14. Recommend the fees to be paid for various outdoor games, including all tournaments.

15. Prepare and publish schedules of all golf events.

16. Purchase all golf prizes and trophies given at the club.

17. Provide for the reception of visiting golfers and teams on days of special golfing competitions.

Prerequisites

1. Golf committee chairperson must be a member of the board.

2. The committee chairperson must have served on a golf subcommittee for a minimum of three years, with at least one year as chairperson.

Office Structure

The golf committee consists of:

- Chairperson of the tournament subcommittee
- Chairperson of the rules subcommittee
- Chairperson of the handicap subcommittee
- Chairperson of the women's golf subcommittee
- Chairperson of the junior golf subcommittee
- Team captain

The golf committee chairperson will stay in his or her position until a replacement is selected by the president of the board. The golf committee is organized with an uneven number of members. The chairperson is appointed by the president and is a member of the board of governors. The term of office for the chairperson shall be one year. The term of each member of the committee shall be one year.

Bylaws

The following bylaw directly affects this position:

VI.7 The golf committee shall consist of not less than five (5) members, at least (3) of whom shall be members of the board. Subject to the control of the board, the golf events of the club will be under the supervision of the golf committee and it shall be its duty to determine and schedule the time and type of competitions, to formulate and operate a handicap system and assign handicaps to members, to establish local rules and the conditions of play and to determine and adjust questions and disputes arising from play in competition.

By and with the approval of the board, the golf committee may appoint a subcommittee to attend to the details of the handicap system, and may appoint any other subcommittees which it deems necessary.

The golf committee shall have the authority to engage and discharge golf professionals and assistants, golf shop employees, caddy masters and starters and to regulate the employment and training of caddies, subject to the approval of the board.

Club Policies

This position is expected to understand and enforce the following policies:

1. Season golfing privileges are currently limited to 857 members annually. Members generally register for season golf during March of each year and are billed accordingly.

2. The annual golfing fee includes unlimited golf, use of the club's driving range, and the opportunity, at some additional cost, to rent a locker and store clubs.

3. Non-season golf members are entitled to golf privileges but must pay a greens fee each time they play. Golf members are entitled to play any time, but non-golf members are entitled to play only once a month and must play with a golfing member.

4. In the interest of all, players should play without delay. Under normal circumstances, no round should take more than four hours to complete.

5. Golfers should replace all divots and/or use the divot mix provided on each cart.

6. Observe signs controlling cart operations and never drive closer than 10 yards from tees, greens or bunkers.

7. A non-member or non-golfing member can only play golf once every thirty days as the guest of a golfing member. It is your responsibility to ask your guest whether he or she has played the course recently as a guest of another member. This rule does not apply to any guest tournaments sponsored by the golf committee. All members are expected to use good judgment in the selection of their golfing guests. As the hosting member is responsible for his or her guests at all times, please inform guests of our conservative dress code and monitor their pace of play. Many guests are not accustomed to playing such challenging courses, so if you are concerned that your guests are inexperienced players, please consider playing at a time when you know the course will not be busy.

8. Our tournament schedule has been designed to offer a variety of events for those members who enjoy structured play. The schedule is distributed to all golfing members in advance of the season each year. You may sign up to participate when the notice relating to thespecific event is mailed to you or is posted in the Golf Pro Shop.

Club Budgets

Operating Budget

The fiscal year generally runs from March 1 to February 28. This will vary, however, since the club follows a four week, four week, five week quarter. Operating budgets are prepared in early January for the review and recommendations of the finance committee. The board generally approves the operating budget in February. The finance committee will carefully review and consider each proposed figure of each budget. A properly prepared, well-thought-out budget is more apt to receive quick approval than one loosely constructed with built-in "fat."

The operating budget must be strictly adhered to once it is approved by the finance committee and the board. Any deviations must have both the finance committee's and board's approval. If a particular committee's operation has been so efficient that it is operating below the approved budget, the committee is to be commended. However, "excess" operational monies may not be spent for the sake of spending them, nor may these "excess" funds be used in any way without prior finance committee and board approval.

See the sample operating budget in the sample position description of the board president.

Capital Budget

Capital budgets are prepared on the Capital Appropriation Request form and presented to the capital improvements and appropriations committee for its consideration and subsequent recommendation to the board. Generally, three bids must be obtained on items of capital expenditures. These bids are attached to the Capital Appropriation Request form.

Time Budget (partial)

Items in bold are listed on the general golf season schedule.

March 17	Reserve banquet room for golf committee reception
	Send out invitations for golf committee reception
March 24	Order Frostbreaker trophies and reserve breakfast and luncheon rooms.
March 31	**Golf committee reception;** cocktails from 6 p.m. to 8 p.m.
April 1	**Frostbreaker tournament**
April 6	Board meeting 7 p.m. to 8:30 p.m.
April 11	Reserve room for Men's Guest Day dinner
April 15	**Spring 4-Ball**
April 21	Order trophies for President's Cup tournament; order trophies for Men's Guest Day.
May 6 & 7	**President's Cup Opening Weekend**
May 10	Pick up trophies for Men's Guest Day
May 11	Board meeting 7 p.m. to 8:30 p.m.
May 11	**First Men's Guest Day; dinners and awards following**
May 12	Pick up trophies for President's Cup tournament
May 13 & 14	**President's Cup closing weekend.**
May 18	Golf committee meeting 7 p.m. to 8:30 p.m.

May 19	Order trophies for Men's Member Guest
May 22	Reserve room for cocktail party, discuss hors d'oeuvres menu with banquet manager
June 7	Pick up trophies for Men's Member Guest
June 9	**Men's Member-Guest; cocktail party in the evening**
June 15	Board meeting 7 p.m. to 8:30 p.m.
June 18	Golf committee meeting
June 19	Order trophies for Rosson Cup and Father-Son Championship
July 1	Reserve room for buffet dinner for Father-Son Championship and discuss arrangements with banquet manager
July 13	Pick up trophies
July 14	**Father-Son Championship**
July 15 & 16	**Rosson Cup**

Strategic Plan Goals

The golf committee chairperson is expected to take ownership of the following strategic plan goals:

1. Promote an approach to course architecture, maintenance and play which promotes the best traditions of the game.

2. Refine and put final touches on new golf course.

3. Produce well-rounded golf programs stressing membership interaction.

4. Employ an adequate staff to work the golf shop, provide golf instructions to the members and their families, conduct golf programs and tournaments, run the driving range and marshal play on the course.

Contracts and Legal Agreements

The following contracts and agreements affect the golf committee chairperson's position:

1. Golf professional contract

2. Caddy master contract

3. Golf cart rental contract

4. Refreshment cart exclusive provider contract

Traditions

The golf committee chairperson always plays the first round of golf with the board president on opening day and the last round of golf on the closing day. He or she is also expected to present trophies at all of the major tournaments.

Relationships

The golf committee chairperson typically works with the following volunteer leaders and employees:

President: The committee chairperson provides the board president with event schedules and golf committee proposals. The chairperson submits monthly reports to the board and reports on committee action.

Golf Committee: The committee chairperson orients members to the committee, provides agendas, runs efficient meetings and provides necessary information. He or she also picks members and appoints subcommittees. The chairperson is an ad hoc member of each subcommittee.

GM/COO: The committee chairperson works closely with the GM/COO to make sure he or she has input on all policy recommendations made by the committee. The committee chairperson keeps the GM/COO informed of golf committee actions and invites the GM/COO to all meetings.

Golf Professional: The committee chairperson works with the golf professional to ensure the success of tournaments and the efficient running of golf programs. The committee chairperson reviews committee recommendations with the golf professional and oversees their implementation.

Meeting Agendas

For the 199X–9X year, the committee meeting dates have been set as the first Tuesday of every month. Meetings begin at 6 p.m. and run between an hour and an hour and a half. Each meeting is followed by a dinner, which is optional.

The following tips will help you run effective meetings:

1. Know the main purpose of each of your meetings.
2. Keep your meeting time reasonable — the shorter the better.
3. Start your meetings on time and end on time.
4. Take charge of your meetings.
5. Stick to the agenda.

Here is a sample meeting agenda which you may wish to follow:

5 min	Greetings from the chairperson, along with a statement of objective(s) of the meeting or a brief review of the agenda
1 min	Roll call, oral or observed
5–10 min	Review dates of future meetings and minutes of previous meeting
35 min	Discussion on agenda topics
30 min	Unfinished business and new business
2 min	Adjournment, with thanks from the chairperson for the time and effort that the committee members devoted to accomplishing the meeting's objectives.

NOTE: Be sure that someone is taking minutes. This probably should not be the chairperson who must guide the discussion, summarize key points and keep the meeting on track.

Sample Position Description for Membership Committee Member

The membership committee is expected to receive, screen and process confidentially all membership applications, insuring compliance with bylaws and rules of the club; to maintain a waiting list of prospective members; to recommend acceptance or rejection of applicants; to advise sponsors of rejected applicants; and to maintain a current roster of all members and their categories.

List of Duties

1. Receive all communications in reference to persons proposed for membership.
2. Consider all proposed candidates.
3. Carefully examine all membership candidates.
4. Treat all communications confidentially.
5. Vote upon each candidate separately.
6. Submit approved names to the board through the president.

Office Structure

The committee meets monthly. It consists of three non-board members who are known only to the president and secretary of the board. Each member serves a term of one year.

Bylaws

The following bylaw directly affects this position:

IV.5.e   The membership committee shall receive all requests for membership into the club and shall carefully and conscientiously investigate the qualifications of all candidates and their spouses, if any, to assure compatibility of all parties with the objectives of the club.

Club Policies

This position is expected to understand and enforce the following policies:

1. The club should maintain a level of 675 active members, 45 junior members, and 25 senior members.
2. Each board member will fill out a rating sheet on each candidate he or she meets. This sheet will be submitted to the secretary with any additional comments. A prospective member must receive ratings from seven or more board members. The rating sheets are then sent to the membership committee to review. The committee submits a recommended list to the board for consideration.
3. Screening shall include sending confidential questionnaires to sponsors to be completed and returned by them, normal investigation with references and a check on the candidate's credit record. It is the responsibility of the sponsors to introduce their candidate to one or more of the volunteer leaders. The volunteer leaders shall prepare a written report about the candidate. These volunteer leaders' reports, questionnaires, reference reports, credit checks and other such available information

shall be transmitted to the president or secretary who will then transmit them to the membership committee for consideration. The membership committee shall then recommend candidates for membership to the board of directors through the president or secretary based upon the information provided to the committee, and when it can do so, shall submit two candidates for each available new membership. Volunteer leaders will make every effort to be available for personal contacts with candidates as arranged by sponsors.

4. All voting shall be by secret ballots. Ballots shall be furnished to the members of the board, each ballot containing two boxes for checking, marked "for" or "against." All ballots received on any candidate must be marked "for" before he is approved for posting, and in the event of any vote "against" being cast, the candidate shall be placed on the suspension list. Any such person who fails to be elected shall not again be proposed for membership until after the expiration of twelve months from the time of such failure of election. No volunteer leader may vote "hold" on any secret ballot and may only vote "hold" orally, stating the reason therefore before voting.

Strategic Plan Goals

The membership committee is expected to take ownership of the following strategic plan goals:

1. The club will have a membership that is representative of the most successful people in our community.

2. The club will maintain its exclusivity while seeking to diversify its membership in terms of gender, race and age.

Position Description for Recreation Committee Member

This position description and its format are reproduced directly from a contributing club.

Purpose

To regularly review the adequacy and effectiveness of all recreation facilities (tennis, aquatics, day camp and exercise) and equipment, and recommend improvements or alterations to the board of directors.

To determine from time to time the adequacy and efficiency of employees in the recreation departments, and consult with management on any pertinent issues resulting therefrom.

To provide a comprehensive tennis program of instruction, based on the age and competence of the players. To include group competitions, social competitions and inter-club competitions and facilities for member participation and enjoyment.

To provide a swimming program that includes maintaining adequate and healthy pool facilities.

To ensure that the club meets the fitness/exercise needs of the members, including facilities, equipment and time opportunity.

Coordination/Reports

The committee coordinates with the volunteer leader of tennis, volunteer leader of aquatics, volunteer leader of fitness and recreation and the general manager. The chairperson reports directly to the board of directors.

Meetings

The committee meets on the third Wednesday of each month, or as otherwise called.

List of Duties

1. To develop an annual schedule of intra-club events for members.
2. To coordinate with other clubs in the production of inter-club competitions, as appropriate.

Committee Members

All types of membership holders are eligible to serve on this committee. Of course, they should be active in the various programs and knowledgeable in at least one of the areas. The chairperson should serve on the board of directors. The committee shall consist of twelve members with three-year terms. Diverse gender and age representation should be fostered. Active tennis players, members who swim or have children involved in swimming programs, or members interested in fitness, competitive/lifetime sports and those with administrative or competitive experience would be most appropriate.

Position Description for Centennial Committee Member

This position description and its format are reproduced directly from a contributing club.

The centennial committee is an ad hoc committee engaged in researching club history and making preparations for the centennial in 199X. The committee makes recommendations to the board of directors through its chairperson and liaison volunteer leader.

The committee is generating interest among the general membership by including requests for information along with the club's billing statements; with the "Centennial Moment" feature in the club magazine; and the "Centennial Moment" board in the garage lobby.

The committee investigates local history in the early club magazines, local libraries, newspaper archives, museums and photographic collections.

The committee is videotaping the recollections of longtime members to recapture part of the history of the club.

The committee is exploring ways to fund the centennial celebrations, the written history and the video projects.

The chairperson of the centennial committee is appointed by the board president and approved by the board of directors.

Template for Position Description

Position Description for

_____

_____

_____

_____

List of Duties

1.

2.

3.

4.

5.

6.

7.

8.

Structure of Office

_____

_____

_____

Prerequisites

_____

_____

_____

Bylaws and Rules

_____

_____

_____

_____

Club Policies

_____

_____

_____

_____

_____

_____

_____

_____

_____

_____

_____

Club Budgets

_____

_____

_____

_____

_____

_____

_____

_____

_____

_____

_____

Strategic Plan Goals

This position is expected to take ownership of the following strategic plan goals:

_____

_____

_____

_____

Contracts and Legal Agreements

The following contracts and legal agreements affect this position:

Traditions

_____

_____

_____

_____

_____

_____

_____

_____

Relationships

_____

_____

_____

_____

_____

_____

_____

Meeting Agendas

_____

_____

_____

_____

_____

_____

_____

_____

_____

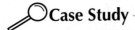**Case Study**

Too Many Managers

Simon Westerman recently became the General Manager at the Overlook Country Club, a small club that's been going through some growing pains in the past few years. Simon formerly worked at a number of very successful clubs and has a reputation for turning clubs around in difficult times.

Since coming to the Overlook a few months ago, Simon has noticed little consistency or control in the levels and types of responsibilities held by committee members and chairs. No committee roles or guidelines outlining specific responsibilities and limitations existed for any of the club volunteer positions. Various committee chairs, under the previous general manager, frequently took actions that impeded the work of the general manager. Some committee chairs did too little, others overstepped their authority. All in all, things just didn't seem to work the way Simon believed they should.

Simon decided to talk with Mr. Carpenter, the board president about some of the problems he'd seen develop.

"Mr. Carpenter, I realize the previous general manager had a strong relationship with the committee chairs, and allowed them a lot of latitude in the decisions they made. Did anyone ever outline actual roles and responsibilities, as well as limitations for each volunteer?" asked Simon.

Mr. Carpenter chuckled. "Are you kidding? When you've been around as long as the last general manager, Tom Dillard was, everybody just understands what the responsibilities for a position are. Why? Is there a problem?"

Simon paused and said "Well Mr. Carpenter, actually there does seem to be a problem. A lot of the committee chairs are making decisions without getting input or approval from me. In some cases they're even authorizing expenditures without notifying me. It's starting to affect the club's operations and our bottom line."

"Give me specifics. And don't beat around the bush," ordered Mr. Carpenter.

Simon gave a quick summary of one situation he was dealing with. "Okay. Here's an example of what I'm talking about. The chair of the golf committee, Fred Jarvis, has started to micromanage the golf staff and Brian, our golf pro. Mr. Jarvis seems to think he's actually Brian's boss, and he doesn't like the way Brian was managing the golf staff. Mr. Jarvis wants to change tee times and has actually started giving directions to the golf staff that contradict Brian's." Simon continued. "He's also decided that slow play is not to be tolerated. Mr. Jarvis has demanded that Brian penalize anyone who breaks four hours by restricting their access to the course. I might point out that our course is rated at four hours and ten minutes. Brian is really upset with the entire situation."

"Well, slow play *is* an issue, Simon." Mr. Carpenter interjected.

Simon nodded, "Of course it is, but we can't be so heavy-handed in how we deal with the issue. All we'll do is upset our members."

"Good point. We want to maximize course time, but our members won't be very happy if they feel they've been herded through a golf game like cattle." Mr. Carpenter continued, "Are Fred's complaints about mismanagement of the golf staff valid?"

"One or two issues, maybe, but a lot of Mr. Jarvis's concerns are his own opinion and don't consider the big picture." said Simon. "I don't discount Mr. Jarvis's responsibility to be concerned with these situations; however, any actions should be taken by me."

Mr. Carpenter asked with a frown, "Any danger of losing Brian?"

"I think it's a possibility if the situation continues." Simon shrugged, "We were lucky to get him in the first place."

"Yeah, we can't afford to lose our golf pro, especially at this time of the year." Mr. Carpenter agreed. "But Fred Jarvis is a long-time and well-respected board member, too. We can't just ignore his concerns." Mr. Carpenter was interested in hearing how the new general manager would handle the problem. He asked Simon, "So what do you plan to do about the immediate situation with Fred?"

"I'm going to meet with Mr. Jarvis to discuss his concerns about Brian's management of the golf staff and tell him I'll communicate his concerns to Brian at the right time." outlined Simon. "If I approach Mr. Jarvis tactfully, he'll let me handle the situation. I'm also going to speak with Brian and tell him I understand his frustrations and I'm working on resolving the problem. That should help him to be more patient with Mr. Jarvis."

Mr. Carpenter smiled and said, "Sounds like a good idea. You don't want to make an enemy out of Fred, but I agree you've got a point about committee chairs overstepping their bounds."

"Well, you could really help in this situation. With your influence, you get people to listen to you. I think it would be really helpful if you spoke with Mr. Jarvis to set the stage for me. What do you think?" Simon asked.

"I'd be glad to, Simon. I think I'll hand out an organization chart and make a blanket statement to the entire board at our next meeting before I speak with Fred. If I reinforce the idea that part of your job is to mediate between the board and club staff, they should get the picture." Mr. Carpenter laughed. "I'll appeal to their egos and remind them that they are all too busy with other things to waste their valuable time on those kinds of tasks. Then, if the situation hasn't changed, I'll speak to Fred directly and prepare him for a meeting with you. That way, neither of us will step on any toes or hurt any feelings with one of our members."

Discussion Questions

1. What could Simon do to prevent committee chairs from misusing responsibilities?

2. What obstacles might Simon encounter from members when he implements his plan to create job descriptions for the volunteer positions?

3. What actions should Simon take to overcome those obstacles?

4. How would formulating committee roles and guidelines help the club?

The following industry experts helped generate and develop this case: Cathy Gustafson, CCM, University of South Carolina; Kurt D. Kuebler, CCM, Vice President, General Manager, The Desert Highlands Association; and William A. Schulz, MCM, General Manager, Houston Country Club.

Effective Board and Committee Meetings

The bane of every GM/COO is the board meeting that lasts for hours and accomplishes little. While some GMs/COOs simply stifle inner groans and tolerate whatever contortions the board or committee wants to make, other GMs/COOs have identified and implemented ways to make meetings more meaningful for the participants and the club.

This Topical Reference Series issue will outline a number of ways to make your meetings more effective so that they better benefit club operations. GMs/COOs play a significant role in helping a board or committee run more effectively. However, it is often the President rather than the GM/COO who is in charge of meetings. In this issue, we will explore the benefits of effective meetings, identify roadblock warnings, look at tools for conducting more successful meetings and then examine the roles of the participants and club staff members.

Types of Meetings

Let's eavesdrop on three fictitious GMs/COOs who meet on a regular basis for lunch:

"I don't know why I bother going to board meetings," Charlie complained. "Except that once a year or so there is a meeting where they accomplish something. And it's not as though they keep minutes so I could read about it the next morning."

"That sounds dreadful," Jane said. "Ours take forever, but at least we have minutes."

"Last night's meeting was five hours — and that wasn't including the dinner," Charlie said. "It took my board an hour to decide what they were going to talk about and then another ten minutes to figure out what order to discuss things in."

"Five hours? That sounds about right," Jane laughed. "Actually, ours usually only lasts three to four hours. Don't you prepare an agenda beforehand?"

"We used to," Charlie shrugged. "But some board members complained that it was too restricting and was limiting their discussions. Of course, it didn't help that the president at the time had purposely left off a rather controversial building inspection report."

"I could see a board getting upset about that, but no agenda?" Jane asked. "I would think that would make things challenging. Our board has an agenda that makes sure every committee gets to report at every meeting — whether it has something important to say or not. However, I wouldn't want to miss a meeting, they do get a lot done."

"What about you, Tony? What are your board meetings like?" Charlie asked.

Tony smiled sheepishly. "Our meetings go quite well. They usually last 90 minutes, and run like clockwork. Our board really helps make the club a better place — and the meetings are a big reason why."

"Efficient meetings?" Jane asked. "How do you do it?"

"Actually, I don't. It was the idea of the board president when I first arrived at the club, and the other board members liked the new system so much, they've kept it. And the board is pretty disciplined. I'd be happy to show you how."

Although few clubs are as deeply mired in disorganization as Charlie's club, many can closely identify with Jane's club — a board that meets with good intentions but is unsuccessful in using meeting tools to their fullest extent. Tony's club comes closer to the ideal that most clubs strive for — efficient meetings that are well-organized and effective.

GMs/COOs report that the board and committee meetings at their clubs range from very efficiently to very poorly run. Most meetings tend to fall somewhere within that spectrum. Three basic types of meetings that GMs/COOs report are:

- Rambling and unstructured
- Rambling, but structured
- Focused and structured

The goal of this TRS issue is to offer tips on how to make board and committee meetings be both focused and structured — in short, be effective. What is meant by effective meetings? An effective meeting is one that:

- Takes only as much time as is needed to accomplish its goals
- Sticks to the subject
- Meets its objectives or goals

An effective meeting is not necessarily measured by the length of the meeting. An effective meeting might last several hours if there are many important or controversial items of business on the agenda. Likewise, a meeting that lasts only an hour cannot be considered effective if nothing was accomplished.

Benefits of Effective Meetings

Few people would argue that effective meetings are a bad idea. However, with so many other demands on the time of GMs/COOs and board and committee members, is the commitment to make meetings more effective worthwhile? After all, if an extra hour or two is spent in preparation for each meeting, why not just have longer meetings? The answer is that all involved can gain more than just time by having effective meetings. Also, it is still more efficient for one or two people to invest an extra few hours than it is for an entire group to be committed to a longer meeting. Ideally, those extra hours of planning will reap a greater return of time for all involved. Effective meetings reap benefits for the club, the participants and the club's GM/COO.

Club Benefits

A club's success often depends on the success of its board. An active, dynamic board can translate into an active and dynamic club. A commitment to effective meetings is a commitment to greater accomplishments for the club.

One club member credited her club's active volunteer structure with the success of the club: "Our members are pretty significant members from very powerful think tanks and corporations who have knowledge and are willing to share. They like their membership in the club enough that they're willing to put in the volunteer time to make the club even better and help the staff in any way possible." So when boards and committees consistently hold productive meetings, the club will benefit from more ideas, greater member participation and a higher level of excitement about the club's activities.

One GM/COO specifically cited effective meetings as one of the reasons his club is so successful. "We try to treat our members well when they volunteer their time, make their board or committee service worthwhile and interesting and efficient. And from that, we get really good volunteers. It didn't happen by accident. There's a lot of work involved in it, but boy when it clicks, it's tremendous."

Participant Benefits

Board and committee members are the first to benefit from effective meetings. There are two primary benefits that participants glean from having more effective meetings:

- Better use of their time
- More enthusiasm about their service

Better Use of Volunteer Time

Many club members are wealthy in money, but time-bankrupt. This is especially true for people who serve on boards and committees, as many nominating committees follow the maxim, "If you want something done, ask a busy person."

One of the worst things that can be done to a time-deficient person is to waste his or her time. By making meetings more effective, participants feel that the time they give is of value. If meetings are inefficient, participants may feel that they can get better value out of their time by devoting it elsewhere.

One GM/COO said he immediately tells all new board and committee members that he values their time. During their orientation, he asks them to calculate the cost of a meeting. "You look at a volunteer's time, and if that volunteer is a lawyer and makes $200 an hour, which is low-end for a lawyer in some cities, for an hour and a half for her time you're talking $300. Multiply that by the 12 people on the committee — because the other people are probably highly paid, successful people too — and you've spent $3,600 in volunteer contributions for that hour and a half meeting. You'd better get out of that meeting $3600 worth of decision-making from those 'volunteer consultants' or you've wasted their time."

More Enthusiasm About Volunteer Service

When board and committee members feel they are getting a high return on their time investment, then they are generally willing to increase their commitment. Members become more enthusiastic when they can see immediate results from their work.

One GM/COO warned that inefficient meetings are one of the quickest ways to drive good volunteers away from service. "If members come to a meeting that has been poorly called, with no agenda, and no organization, they've wasted their time. The next time someone says, 'Come over to XYZ committee,' the volunteer goes, 'Hey, sorry, I'm busy, I've got a lot going on, I can't do it.' Your best volunteers jump out real quickly, and what you have left are people who have nothing better to do with their time than to show up for a free lunch. They're the *worst* ones you want making decisions."

GM/COO Benefits

Although the GM/COO sits in on meetings only as a staff liaison and resource, the effectiveness of the meetings can make a difference to his or her performance. When meetings are run efficiently, the GM/COO has a better relationship with the board and committees. He or she can be more efficient and can spend more time implementing what the board dictates.

If the GM/COO fulfills his or her role of providing board and committee members with the information they need *before* the meeting, then the GM/COO will face less pressure at the actual meeting. As one GM/COO said, "If you're giving board members the information and they don't use it, shame on them. If a board member doesn't know or doesn't understand something, the onus is on him to find it out, as opposed to the onus being on management."

That same GM/COO said that working closely with the board — and especially with committees — can increase his success as a manager. "I feel very strongly that, in a nonprofit organization, working through and with the committees is much more effective than viewing them as a necessary evil. If a manager uses his committees correctly, he'll be a lot better off. A lot can happen that he couldn't possibly accomplish on his own."

Why Meetings Fail

Few people actually plan to have an inefficient meeting. More often, meetings are inefficient because participants have given up hope that things can be run better. Professional meeting planners typically cite four main reasons why meetings are ineffective:

- Inexperienced meeting leaders
- Lack of planning or objectives
- Lack of an agenda
- Meetings held at the wrong place or time

These next few sections take a look at how each of the above reasons apply to club meetings.

Inexperienced Meeting Leaders

Although most of the time board and committee chairpersons will be successful people with a wealth of business experience, they may not all have expertise in running efficient meetings. Or a chairperson might be reluctant to apply business principles to his or her social club.

A skilled meeting leader is able to keep all of the members on track, deal with difficult personalities or disruptive meeting behaviors and keep all participants actively interested in the proceedings. This can be a herculean task no matter what the setting.

Figure 1: Tips for How To Be a Better Meeting Chairperson

The following tips can help chairpersons no matter what their level of meeting experience:

- Never compete with group members
- Listen to group members
- Don't let anyone be put on the defensive
- Don't allow negative comments
- Use every member of the group
- Keep the energy level high
- Keep the members informed about where they are and what is expected of them
- Keep your eye on the expert
- Don't manipulate the group
- Work hard at the technique of chairmanship
- Find a unifying item with which to end the meeting
- At the start of the discussion of any item, make it clear where the meeting should try to get to by the end
- At the end of the discussion of any item, give a brief and clear summary of what has been agreed on
- Start meetings on time
- Close on a note of achievement
- Check with the group from time to time with "Can everyone hear me OK?"
- If you don't know the answer to a question, be frank and say so
- Smile a lot — it helps ease tension
- Know the material you are presenting
- Don't belittle individuals in front of the group, even if they deserve it

In one club, the GM/COO and board president worked together to deal with a few committee chairpersons who were consistently putting their committee members to sleep. They developed a series of pamphlets and committee chair handbooks that outlined ways to run effective meetings. When elections and appointments came up, they made it clear that all committee chairpersons would be expected to follow those guidelines. They also gave copies of the material to all committee members so that they could help keep their chairperson on track. Figure 1, "Tips for How To Be a Better Meeting Chairperson," offers some suggestions that can be shared with anyone leading a group meeting.

Lack of Planning or Objectives

Meetings held with no preparation are doomed from the start. A meeting can no more run itself than a golf tournament can. The meeting leader and the GM/COO should always get

Figure 2: Roles of Key Personnel

The chairperson	The GM/COO	Members
• Starts the meeting • Is the key decision-maker, although this responsibility can be delegated to the group • Handles disruptive behavior • Manages conflict • Seeks consensus • Ends the meeting • Checks and distributes the minutes • Monitors follow-up	• Assists the chairperson in meeting planning • Takes notes and makes them visible during the meeting • Models and coaches members in process behavior • Models key communication skills • Checks the group for direction and progress	• Do prework • Remain attentive and participate in discussion and other meeting activities • Provide accurate and complete information • Commit to action plans • Avoid disruptive behavior

Peter Tobia and Martin Becker, "Making the Most of Meeting Time" *Training & Development Journal*, August 1990, p. 36.

together before a meeting and plan what they want to accomplish and how they plan to do it. For some committees, the GM/COO might assign a staff liaison to attend meetings in his or her place. Later in this issue, the roles of the chairperson and the GM/COO will be examined in greater detail.

However, the planning of a meeting is not limited to just those in charge. Every member should be able to come to the meeting prepared to work with the issues at hand. This can be facilitated by pre-mailing the agenda. See Figure 2, "Roles of Key Personnel," for a general list of the tasks each participant must complete before a meeting.

When a meeting first starts, one of the best things that the meeting leader can do is state the objectives of the meeting and make sure that participants agree with him or her. If the meeting starts with everyone agreeing about what should be accomplished, it is more likely to stay on track.

At one club, the GM/COO prints the board's mission on placards and has one sitting in front of each board-meeting participant. It acts as a constant reminder of what the board is supposed to be accomplishing. Another GM/COO said that club staff members, typically the committee liaisons, should keep a schedule of when to send out memos, notes, or letters about board meetings; keep track of whom they should notify; and know when to reserve meeting rooms. This helps ensure that board and committee meetings will run more smoothly.

Lack of an Agenda

Consistently, GMs/COOs and meeting experts cite the agenda as the single most important tool for making a meeting successful. Every meeting needs a road map. Every participant needs to know what the route is going to be. Without an agenda, participants are likely to turn off at every interesting side street, which results in some interesting sight-seeing, but rarely a successful road trip.

This issue will examine meeting agendas in greater detail in a later section.

Wrong Place or Time

Often, the physical environment can detract from the effectiveness of a meeting. Participants can get distracted by the room that they are in and the way it is set up. If a group has a choice among several rooms, it should select a room with the following characteristics:

- A room that is as close to square as possible. The length of the room should not exceed its width by more than 50 percent.
- A room with heating, ventilation and air-conditioning system controls inside the room.
- A room whose main entrance is on a wall away from where the chairperson sits. People shouldn't have to pass by the leader to enter or leave the room.
- A room without pictures and other materials on the walls that might distract participants.

Many clubs have rooms that are designated as board rooms and have few practical alternatives. However, there may be a few things in those rooms that they can alter:

- Make the room as bright as possible. This encourages more informality and an exchange of ideas.
- Avoid having light shine into the eyes of the participants from mirrors, glass or metal. This can cause fatigue.
- Reduce the amount of outside noises.
- Provide comfortable chairs.

Generally, a rectangular table works best for board meetings, with the president sitting at one end. Seating at meetings may sometimes be based on a chart, follow a club tradition, or be based on seniority.

Tools for More Effective Meetings

There are several practical tools that GMs/COOs and meeting chairpersons can use to make their meetings more effective. The tools described in this issue have been assembled from suggestions of GMs/COOs, meeting experts, association resources and books and articles on the subject. They are meant to be practical resources that clubs can use immediately to make meetings more effective. The following tools will be examined:

- Agendas
- Communication rules
- Meeting calendars
- Controlled environments

Figure 3: Sample Meeting Agenda

5 min	Greetings from the chairperson with a statement of the objective(s) of the meeting
1 min	Roll call — either oral or observed
5-10 min	Review dates of future meetings and minutes of previous meetings
35 min	Discussion of agenda topics
30 min	Unfinished business and new business
2 min	Adjournment with thanks from the chairperson for the time and effort that the members devoted to accomplishing the meeting's objectives

- Staff liaisons
- Meeting procedures
- Consent agendas
- Straw votes
- Discussion-only items

Agendas

It is nearly impossible to talk about effective meetings without discussing agendas. As one GM/COO said, "If a manager can create an agenda with his president that does not waste the board's time and that's to the point, board members will have a lot of information up-front so that they can be prepared for the meeting. I think that's really the more effective way of doing things." See Figure 3 for a sample meeting agenda.

A properly prepared agenda can have a tremendous influence on the meeting's outcome. Some agendas are more effective than others. Figure 4 contains several tips offered by GMs/COOs for preparing an agenda.

Cyril Houle, author of *Governing Boards*, says that a meeting agenda should be carefully planned: "The items listed should not be merely sketchy notations indicating generally what is to be discussed but should be described at such length that the board will know what to expect. The person responsible for the presentation of each item should be noted, as should the expected length of time for its consideration at the meeting. Due care must be given to keep the agenda of the board meeting from becoming too full. If matters can be handled outside the meeting, they should be." (Houle, *Governing Boards*, Jossey-Bass, San Francisco, CA 1989.)

Many GMs/COOs recommend that the meeting agendas be as detailed as possible. For example, one GM/COO said that instead of simply listing "Treasurer's Report" on the agenda, he would write the following:

Treasurer's Report

Financial Review. (See the attached statement.)

Figure 4: Checklist for Preparing a Meeting Agenda

When preparing an agenda, check to be sure the following elements are present:

- ❑ The agenda contains a clear indication of why the meeting is being called
- ❑ The agenda is written
- ❑ It is sent out several days in advance to everyone expected at the meeting
- ❑ It contains routine reports and agenda items
- ❑ Relevant supplementary material is attached (e.g., reports, statistical information, proposals)
- ❑ Time is reserved for announcements
- ❑ It says who is running the meeting
- ❑ Time is budgeted for each agenda item
- ❑ Time is reserved for breaks during long or unusually difficult meetings
- ❑ It includes an explanatory line or two after each agenda item to set the tone of the discussion
- ❑ It follows a consistent visual format for each meeting
- ❑ It identifies the type of action that must be taken on a given agenda item when necessary (e.g., a recommendation, assignment, expenditure)
- ❑ It clearly identifies the location, starting time and ending time of the meeting
- ❑ It clearly notes the names of individuals making reports
- ❑ It avoids technical terms that might not be understood by all members (or explain any technical terms used)
- ❑ It places guests making presentations early on the agenda so that they can leave when their presentations are complete

Capital Requests. The grounds committee is requesting a supplemental air conditioner for the Kaiser Building.

Information Item. The accounting department has just completed a self-audit. (See the attached report.)

Delinquent Accounts. This month we have four delinquent accounts. (See the attached report.)

The GM/COO said that just putting down "Treasurer's Report" is too vague. "If it's too open-ended, you never know what questions will come up during the meeting."

Another tip from GMs/COOs: only list committees on the meeting agenda that have something to report. Traditionally, an agenda might list every committee in the club. With that format, all committee chairs feel they have to stand up and give some sort of report — even if they don't have anything to say. At least one GM/COO said that this change was enthusiastically welcomed by his board. "They were very pleased that they didn't have to report at every meeting."

Agendas should also list the length of the meeting, with a starting and an ending time. "It helps when working with volunteers to let them know how much time they will have to devote," said one GM/COO.

Determining in what order to place items can also present a challenge. There are many ways to arrange an agenda. Traditionally, agendas have started with the approval of minutes, then moved on to committee reports, old business, then new business. Some club managers have suggested a more meaningful agenda model, one that facilitates the flow of discussion and schedules the more difficult items for when people are freshest. This "action" agenda model looks something like this:

- *Announcements* (15 minutes or less). These are quick items that require no debate. Announcements could include everything on the consent agenda (consent agendas are discussed later in this issue.) By quickly dealing with these items, the facilitator helps the participants start to focus their attention on the group and away from their outside concerns.

- *Easily discussed items* (15 minutes). These are black and white issues that can be addressed quickly. Dealing with these items early in the meeting helps the group feel like progress is being made and can establish a sense of teamwork.

- *Most difficult item* (25 to 40 minutes). This is the hardest or most controversial item on the agenda. It's usually something that needs a lot of discussion or relates to a long-term need. The facilitator should first state what the expected outcome is — either discussion or a decision. Participants then have a chance to air their viewpoints.

- *Break* (10 minutes). This is a chance for everyone to take a break and think about the current discussion. It also allows for some behind-the-scenes persuasion or politicking. Participants can also smooth over any hackles raised during the debate.

- *Most difficult item, continued* (20 minutes). After the break, the discussion of the most difficult item is continued. Important points can be repeated and written down. This is the time to make decisions.

- *Discussion-only items* (30 to 40 minutes). This is the time to introduce new topics or present reports. Placing committee reports at the end of the meeting, when people are getting eager to leave, can keep the reports succinct and to the point. Placing reports near the end of the meeting leaves participants with the feeling that the behind-the-scenes work is being carried out satisfactorily and effectively. (Discussion-only items are examined later in this issue.)

- *Least difficult items* (10 minutes). These items are ones that can be quickly voted on. Putting least difficult items at the end of the meeting can leave group members with the feeling that they can decide things efficiently and quickly. It ends the meeting on a high note.

Most GMs/COOs feel strongly that a meeting's agenda should be mailed out ahead of time. This gives each board or committee member a chance to review it and do any necessary research ahead of time. Mailing the agenda out ahead of time can save a lot of time at meetings — members are able to find out how each issue on the agenda affects them.

Clubs that follow this practice have discovered that they have to table fewer issues, get quicker action and have members arrive with more creative solutions to the challenges they face.

Communication Rules

A basic rule concerning communication between club managers and boards that many GMs/COOs cite is a simple one: No surprises. A detailed agenda will help reduce the chance of surprises. In preparing the agenda, the GM/COO — working with the president or committee chair — should try to anticipate any problems that might need to be discussed.

However, communication does not begin and end with the agenda. Club managers and meeting leaders should be in frequent contact to make sure they get all necessary information to the board. One meeting expert suggests that managers and meeting leaders get together immediately after each meeting in order to plan the next one. This gives them a chance to review what went well in the just-concluded meeting and what could have been improved. It also allows them to identify who should be contacted before the next meeting for reports or other actions.

One GM/COO said he asks his golf pro and golf course superintendent to attend each board meeting with him so that they can answer board questions. He says, "There is nothing better than an informed board — if you want that, you have to bring in the superintendent and the golf pro. The GM/COO can't answer all of the questions that come up."

Another GM/COO encourages club managers to be honest with their boards, even though that may sometimes be difficult. "If there's a problem, don't try to hide it, bring it out in the open." GMs/COOs should also make sure that they are always available to board and committee members to answer questions and provide information. Boards and committees will be much more effective if they have access to important operating information.

Meeting Calendars

A meeting calendar can help a GM/COO set up an annual schedule for committee reports according to the needs of the club. This helps meeting leaders and the GM/COO plan meetings and set up agendas. For example, if the pool opens on May 15, the calendar would show the pool committee making its report on the pool program in March.

One GM/COO said the meeting calendar helps impose discipline at meetings. Very few committees report except when they have something that needs board approval. He said at his club a preliminary schedule is written up at the beginning of the year that shows when each committee should report. A few weeks before each board meeting, the GM/COO contacts all committee chairpersons to see if they are going to make a report or are going to defer to another month. If they are going to report to the board, he asks if they need any help in preparing their report. Then, right before the meeting, he'll call to confirm that they are still going to report at the upcoming board meeting. At the meeting, any committee is allowed to make a report during the committee report section, but few do so unless they are on the agenda.

Controlled Environments

GMs/COOs frequently find that they can manipulate the meeting's physical environment to have a positive effect on the efficiency of meetings. They cite a major difference in the length and efficiency of meetings based on when they are held, where they are held and the amenities available. For example, the physical atmosphere in the room can affect a meeting's efficiency. Is there enough light? Is the temperature comfortable? Two other environmental issues cited by GMs/COOs are:

- The time meetings are held
- Food and beverages available

Time of Meetings

Clubs must schedule meetings according to the availability of participants. However, some considerations should be given to when a meeting is held and how the time affects the effectiveness of the meeting. "I think the timings of meetings are pretty important," said one GM/COO. "A manager should review when the meetings are held. Do you want them over prior to dinner? Before dinner, you might be less likely to have to deal with someone who has drank too much. Also, people are fresher earlier in the day."

Food and Beverage Available

Although meeting meals have traditionally been one of the few perks that board and committee members are allowed, many GMs/COOs say that offering dinners can interfere with the effectiveness of a meeting. One GM/COO said he doesn't provide any food or beverages to meeting participants until *after* the meeting is over. He said that there are fewer tangential conversations when participants are hungry. Another GM/COO said that he forgoes the meal altogether. "If you don't have a set dinner for the board, people will have to plan their own dinner. Since they've planned their own dinner, chances are they'll end the meeting on time." One GM/COO warns against providing drinks without food. He said his president works hard to get everything done by 7:30. However, before the meeting, members typically have a martini or some wine. "If they haven't eaten since lunch — and dinner isn't until 7:30 or 8 p.m. — then the conversation can get a little skewed."

Staff Liaisons

In order for a meeting to run efficiently, participants must have all of the information they need to make intelligent decisions. That's why a staff liaison is a productive addition to any governance meeting. The staff liaison is able to answer a variety of operational questions and provide information to board or committee members on an as-needed basis. The staff liaison is also able to execute board or committee directives without having to wait for written or second-hand instructions.

Typically, the staff liaison for the board is the GM/COO. Some clubs also assign staff liaisons to every committee. For example, the golf pro might be assigned to the golf committee, the clubhouse manager to the house committee. Several GMs/COOs said they attend every meeting, board or committee.

Meeting Procedures

Every meeting must have some sort of procedure by which it is run. General Henry Robert developed meeting procedures in 1876 by adapting the rules followed by the U.S. House of Representatives. Since that time, Robert's Rules of Order have been generally accepted

Figure 5: Order of Motions

The precedence of motions according to Robert's Rules of Order are:

1. Fix the time of the next meeting
2. Adjourn or recess
3. Question of privilege
4. Call for orders of the day
5. Rise to point of order
6. Appeal
7. Suspend the rules
8. Create special orders
9. Withdraw
10. Voting "division" — motion to ballot
11. Objection to consideration
12. Lay on the table
13. Close debate
14. Postpone to a certain date
15. Refer
16. Amend
17. Postpone indefinitely
18. Main question
19. Reconsider and have entered on the minutes for action at the next meeting
20. Reconsider
21. Rescind
22. Elections (nominations)
23. Order of business

as an efficient way to run a group meeting. Figure 5 shows the motions used under Robert's Rules in their order of precedence.

Some board members may resist Robert's Rules of Order as too stifling or because they inhibit debate. However, when used correctly, Robert's Rules can do just the opposite. They are ultimately meant to ensure that the majority is able to accomplish its goals while the views of the minority are protected and heard.

A danger to Robert's Rules of Order is what Edward Scannell, director of the University Conference Bureau of Arizona State University and past president of Meeting Planners

International, calls "motion sickness." He points out that not all items require motions. If participants can agree to something quickly, then they should do so and save the procedures for when they are needed.

Consent Agendas

For every item opened for discussion, someone will feel obligated to say something. However, not all items that come before a board or committee need to be discussed. There are always routine actions that must be voted on due to club tradition, bylaws, or policies. These might include contract renewals, ceremonial decrees, setting meeting times, etc. One way to reduce the amount of time spent on these routine items is for the chairperson to develop a consent agenda.

The consent agenda is given to all participants before the meeting. When the meeting starts, any participant can request that an item be removed from the consent agenda and opened for general discussion. All other items are voted on together, without further discussion.

Richard Chait, author of *How to Help Your Board Govern More and Manage Less*, encourages consent agendas as a means to help participants recognize priorities. "Consent agendas signal to trustees that certain items are ordinary transactions that do not merit board discussion and, by implication, that other issues do. Yet, almost inevitably, if such mundane items are placed before the board for action, one or more trustees will have questions, concerns and even amendments to offer. Soon hours have lapsed. A consent agenda imposes a little more discipline, raises the ante slightly for trustees inclined to discuss routine operations, and thereby lessens the chance of an extended discussion of an essentially extraneous issue." (Chait, *How to Help Your Board Govern More and Manage Less,* National Center for Nonprofit Boards, Washington DC, 1993.)

It is important to note that the consent agenda should be used only to save time, not to push something through on an unaware board. The only items that should be placed on a consent agenda are those that are highly likely to pass unanimously without discussion or amendment. Any chairperson or GM/COO who places a controversial item — or any item that obviously needs discussion — on the consent agenda risks his or her credibility.

Straw Votes

A straw vote is as much a consensus-building tool as a time-saving tool. A straw vote involves introducing an issue and allowing a moderate amount of discussion. When the chairperson senses that there is a majority or consensus on an issue, he or she can ask for a non-binding — or straw — vote on the issue using a show of hands. This enables members to see whether there is a consensus and how other people are voting. If there is a clear majority, the chairperson can ask, "Are you ready to vote?" If there is not a clear majority, the chairperson can say, "OK, do we need to keep talking about this or should we set it aside for another meeting?"

One board member said that a straw vote cuts down on discussion time, because "often, board members are ready to vote, but they don't know it yet. However, it takes a good chair to know when to call one."

Discussion-Only Items

Some boards have found that they can save time by bringing up an item at separate meetings. The first time that an item is brought up it is either introduced without discussion (preferably at the end of a meeting) or introduced for discussion only. At the next meeting — if the issue did not need further research or information to be reported — it can be brought up for a vote without any discussion.

"If you abide by it, it's a real time-saver," said a board member. "The few times we've used it, the vote has gone very quickly."

This method allows members to work out any problems they have with the item between meetings instead of on the spot. They can then come to a meeting more prepared and comfortable with their vote. Members are able to absorb new information better this way before making a decision. Items that can be covered in this manner might include program information or committee reports.

Role of Board or Committee Chairperson

The responsibility for a meeting's effectiveness rests on the meeting leader — whether that be a board member or committee chairperson. All participants will take cues from the leader and are subject to the procedural expertise of the leader.

To ensure an effective meeting, the meeting leader has two main responsibilities — preparing for the meeting and facilitating the meeting. These responsibilities typically include:

- Preparing for the meeting
  - Work with the GM/COO or other staff liaison
  - Conduct orientations for new members
  - Inform participants of meeting time and place
  - Become familiar with all agenda items

- Facilitating the meeting
  - Guide discussions
  - Deal with dysfunctional behaviors
  - Keep the group focused
  - Seek consensus
  - Manage conflict
  - Take votes
  - Close the meeting
  - Manage the physical environment
  - Follow up on action items

The next several sections of this issue will explore these responsibilities in detail.

Preparing for the Meeting

As mentioned earlier, lack of planning is the bane of effective meetings. Truly effective meeting leaders will usually spend as much time preparing for a meeting as they spend in the actual meeting. Some of the things that a meeting leader can do to prepare for a meeting include:

- **Work with the GM/COO or other staff liaison.** Shortly after each meeting, the meeting leader should meet with the GM/COO or other staff liaison to plan the next meeting. Houle encourages leaders and staff members to "review together what happened so that they can gain insights into the motivations of members and the dynamics of processes, identify potential danger points, reflect on their own actions to see whether changes would be desirable, identify all follow-up actions they need to take and note all the items that should appear on future agendas." The meeting leader also needs to meet with the staff member to produce the meeting packet for the next meeting. The meeting packet typically includes the agenda, any reports, a consent agenda and any other necessary resources.

- *Conduct orientations for new members.* Imposing meeting discipline after the fact can be a tricky and thankless task. It is much more effective to instill good habits in new members immediately than to try to correct bad habits later. A proper orientation session will let new members know what to expect in their first meeting so that they can come prepared to participate. It will also help prevent new members from covering issues the board has already closed on. For more information on orientations, see the first Topical Reference Series issue, "Club Board and Committee Orientation."

- *Inform participants of meeting time and place.* While the meeting leader may delegate the notification task to a secretary, he or she still retains the responsibility to ensure that it has been done.

- *Become familiar with all agenda items.* Meeting leaders need to acquaint themselves thoroughly with every issue before their board or committee. Otherwise they run the risk of having the meeting spin out of control. Also, the meeting leader and staff liaison will be expected to provide resources and guidance on everything the board or committee is dealing with.

Facilitating the Meeting

The actual facilitation of the meeting is the most visible and crucial aspect of meeting management. Hours of preparation will not profit the meeting leader who is unable to keep control of the actual meeting.

Although meetings will differ, depending on the participants and tasks to be accomplished, there are some basic responsibilities that every meeting leader must assume in order to have an effective meeting. The next several pages will examine some of these responsibilities.

A meeting facilitator's first responsibility is to start the meeting on time. Figure 6 contains some tips for starting a meeting on time.

Guide Discussions

A meeting leader's first responsibility once the meeting gets started is to guide the discussion. Typically, the meeting leader is expected to be reticent about his or her opinion, but active in his or her control of the meeting. The chairperson of a group should make sure that everyone who has something to say is recognized and has a chance to give input. The chairperson should also make sure that, while there is sufficient discussion on each topic for an intelligent decision to be made, the discussion does not continue endlessly or needlessly.

Some meeting leaders have had to get creative to encourage participation from all members. Some ideas that they have shared for increasing participant involvement include:

Figure 6: Ways to Get People to Meetings on Time

It can be difficult to end a meeting on time if it doesn't start on time. Some suggestions for getting people to the meeting on time include:

- Schedule meetings at odd times
- Start on time no matter who's missing
- Close the door at the appointed time
- Cover the most important items first
- Items of interest to habitual latecomers should be raised early
- Speak privately to offenders

- *Devil's advocate.* The facilitator selects participants to take opposing points of view to fully discuss a given topic.
- *Meeting themes.* A meeting is given a particular theme, such as a political convention, where every participant is considered a state delegation, or an Olympics team, where everyone represents a sport. This makes the meeting a little more light-hearted and might be used for the first meeting after an election to help participants get to know each other and form working relationships.
- *Buzz groups.* The group divides into small groups to discuss a given topic or agenda item for ten to twenty minutes.
- *Brainstorming.* This technique can be used to generate ideas, goals, or solutions. Basic brainstorming ground rules include: No criticisms of ideas can be made; free-wheeling or wild ideas are welcome; quantity — not quality — is desired; and combining or improving ideas is encouraged.

Deal with Dysfunctional Behaviors

One of the more difficult things for a meeting leader to do is to deal with disruptive or dysfunctional behaviors. However, the ability to handle these behaviors is a key skill for meeting leaders. As one meeting expert said, "Nothing can sandbag a meeting faster than a person who chases tangents or refuses to keep quiet."

There is no single right way to handle all disruptive behaviors. Usually, meeting leaders must tailor their actions to the types of behavior being displayed. One general solution that avoids direct confrontation but does not evade the issues is to provide feedback. When giving feedback, a few basic rules should be followed:

- Limit feedback to the specific behavior that has been observed
- Specify the effect of that behavior on the group or on the objectives of the meeting
- Restrict comments to behaviors that can be changed

See the appendix for more specific strategies that can be used when dealing with certain dysfunctional meeting "types."

Keep the Group Focused

It is the task of the meeting leader to make sure that the group stays focused on the item at hand. It is easy, especially for a group accustomed to socializing together, to bring up side issues that may be distantly related to the agenda item. However, these side issues rarely help bring the agenda item closer to resolution. Some tools for keeping the group focused include meeting agendas and flip charts with key points noted from the current discussion.

To keep a group focused, the meeting facilitator must have excellent communication skills. A meeting facilitator should have solid skills in both of the following types of communication:

- *Nonverbal communication.* Meeting facilitators should understand that their nonverbal communication can be misunderstood. They should also work hard to keep their verbal and nonverbal communication in sync. If verbal and nonverbal messages contradict each other, listeners are more likely to believe the nonverbal message. Meeting facilitators should ensure that their nonverbal communication is positive, not negative. A smile and direct eye contact are good examples of positive nonverbal communication. A meeting facilitator should also avoid being distracted by the negative nonverbal cues of the meeting participants.

- *Verbal communication.* The following are basic tips for good verbal communication: identify the main point of the message, use examples or repetition, use concrete language, state things positively, say why the message is important and check for understanding.

Seek Consensus

Ultimately, the goal of each meeting is for the group to reach consensus on the items it is considering. Until consensus is reached, little action can be taken. A group leader must hone his or her skills to bring a group to consensus.

Active listening is the most important skill a leader needs to get a group to agree on an issue. The leader must be able to discern all of the messages being given by participants. Some basic guidelines for active listening include:

- *Listen for the total message*. Every message has two levels — the idea level and the feeling level. Ideas are the thoughts or opinions a person has; feelings are the emotions related to the ideas. To get the most out of any message, listen for the total message — both ideas and feelings.

- *Don't interrupt.* Interrupting is the most damaging thing a listener can do. On the other hand, one of the finest compliments that a listener can give is to hear another person out.

- *Ask questions.* Ask questions so that the speaker will provide more information or clarify a confusing point. Asking questions is especially useful when the listener is seeking to understand something or trying to make a decision.

- *Paraphrase.* When listeners paraphrase, they restate to the speaker in slightly different words what they thought the speaker said. This lets the speaker know that they are really listening. This reassures the speaker that he or she has been understood, so that he or she can move on to the next point. The speaker also gets a chance to reevaluate his or her ideas by hearing them in different words. Paraphrasing allows the listener to check how accurately he or she understands the speaker. When paraphrasing, meeting facilitators should try to identify the feelings they picked up on as well as paraphrase the ideas they heard.

- *Recognize diverse needs in diverse groups.* Listening can promote good interpersonal relationships among people of different ages, backgrounds, cultures, or interests. Avoid rushing speakers for whom English is a second language. When meeting facilitators are unable to understand what a speaker said, he or she should politely ask the speaker to repeat the idea. Meeting facilitators should relax and have a sense of humor. It conveys goodwill and smooths over frustrations.

- *Adapt to different listening situations.* During a meeting, the facilitator will usually have to deal with three different types of listening: informational, evaluative and empathic.

(For more information about listening skills, see the "Interpersonal Communication" workbook in the *Hospitality Management Skill Builders.* [East Lansing, Mich.: Educational Institute of the American Hotel & Motel Association, 1994.])

Meeting facilitators also need to be careful that they don't mistake silence for agreement. A person's silence does not necessarily imply that the person agrees with the prevalent opinion on an issue being discussed. If a facilitator is truly seeking consensus, he or she should draw out quiet members by asking for their opinions.

Manage Conflict

If all agenda items are immediately adopted unanimously at a meeting, there was probably little reason to hold the meeting. Meetings are usually called because there is a need to exchange information or ideas before a consensus can be reached. The consensus-building process can sometimes produce conflict. Conflict is not necessarily bad. Conflict can lead to more creative solutions to the challenges a club faces. However, productive boards and committees stay focused on their goals, are cooperative and supportive, are energetic and are comfortable with sharing responsibility. If there is too much conflict, some of these characteristics may start to break down and meetings could become gripe sessions or meetings where participants air personal disagreements.

Conflict among participants can occur for many reasons. It might be the result of:

- Communication problems
- Limited club resources
- Different goals
- Social relationships
- Individual differences
- Organizational problems or poorly-defined roles and responsibilities

One of the most successful approaches that a meeting facilitator can take to conflict is an assertive win-win approach. A win-win outcome usually guarantees that the conflict won't keep cropping up at meeting after meeting. Whenever someone loses as the result of a conflict resolution, the conflict is likely to be resurrected at a later date.

There are some basic steps that a meeting facilitator can take to keep conflict productive:

- Summarize the disagreement
- Confirm the accuracy of the summary
- Discuss the conflict's effect on the primary meeting objective
- Reconfirm the points of agreement
- Clarify different points of view
- Involve the group in resolving the disagreement

Take Votes

The method by which a meeting facilitator takes votes will be determined by the types of parliamentary procedures to which the group adheres. It takes an astute meeting facilitator to determine when a vote should be called and what type of vote should be taken.

There are several methods by which a meeting facilitator can take votes:

- *Voice vote.* If a facilitator is relatively certain that an issue is going to be passed by a wide margin, he or she should ask for a voice vote. A voice vote is a quick and convenient way to take a vote, but it is not accurate.

- *Show of hands.* This is also a quick way to collect a vote, but is not accurate. It is not appropriate if the vote is close.

- *Rising vote.* This may also be called a "division." The meeting facilitator asks everyone in favor of the motion to stand. He or she then counts everyone standing. He or she then asks them to be seated and for everyone opposed to stand and be counted.

- *Ballot or roll call.* For a ballot vote, each person writes down his or her vote, and the votes are collected and counted by "tellers." A roll call vote entails someone calling out each person's name and then recording an "aye" or "no" as the person's vote. Both methods can be time consuming, but are the most accurate way of counting votes on issues that are close or require a record of how people voted.

Close the Meeting

The final task of the meeting facilitator is to close the meeting. This may be accomplished by a movement to adjourn. However, in the interest of future meetings, it is very effective if the chairperson takes the time to summarize what was accomplished in the meeting to be sure everyone agrees. A positive summary can help set the tone for the next meeting.

Manage the Physical Environment

There are a few more tasks that meeting leaders can do to help make their meetings effective. The first is to arrive early. This allows the leader to check the room set-up and make sure it is correct and all needed supplies are present. It also makes the leader available to participants who might have questions they want answered before the meeting begins. If there is time, the meeting leader can review all agenda items one more time with the GM/

COO or other staff liaison before the meeting starts. He or she can also make sure that refreshments are ready and that any guest speaker is present, in the right place and properly set up.

Follow Up on Action Items

After the meeting, the meeting facilitator and GM/COO or staff liaison should review what actions the board or committee agreed to take. They need to determine who will follow up on each action item and establish a timeline for completion. It is then their responsibility to inform the appropriate people and give them whatever support they need to accomplish their tasks.

Role of GM/COO or Staff Liaison

Making sure the meeting runs effectively is not the sole responsibility of the board or committee chairperson. The GM/COO or staff liaison also bears some of the burden of making meetings run smoothly. The staff person's role generally consists of the following tasks:

- Support functions — communicating with the chairperson, preparing meeting agendas, compiling and distributing reports, establishing schedules for reports and notifying members of meeting times and places
- Orientations — preparing orientation materials and conducting orientations with board or committee chairpersons
- Meeting attendance

The next three sections will examine these tasks in greater detail.

Support Functions

The GM/COO or staff liaison is expected to do much of the board or committee's legwork. One of the most important functions is to communicate with the board or committee chairperson. Meeting facilitators rely on their staff resource person to let them know about all important operational factors that affect their groups.

One committee member talked about how the committee needs to work very closely with the staff so that the committee is not trying to run the club. "Members want the volunteer structure to augment what the staff is already doing."

Typically, the GM/COO must be available to all committees. However, appointing a staff liaison for each committee — especially in clubs where there are a lot of committees — can require more attention than the GM/COO would be able to give. Their staff liaison then becomes the first point of contact with club staff for the committee chairperson. Whenever the chairperson needs something, he or she can go first to the staff liaison. The staff liaison would also attend all committee meetings. One GM/COO said he attends all board meetings and tries to attend all committee meetings, "but it's hard to be everywhere at once. You have to make some kind of provision to cover meetings that you can't attend."

The GM/COO or other staff liaison also plays an important role in preparing meeting agendas. Some GMs/COOs say that they are the ones who originate the agenda, working closely with the meeting leader. Even if the agenda is prepared by the group's president or secretary, the GM/COO still needs to know what is planned and be active in duplicating and mailing out the agenda.

Another task that typically falls to the club staff is compiling the various reports that will be handed out at the board meeting. The staff may format, duplicate and distribute any of the printed resources needed for a meeting.

If the club uses a calendar to schedule committee reports, the GM/COO needs to establish the schedule and inform the appropriate people of when they are expected to make a report.

Finally, it may fall to the GM/COO or staff liaison to set up the meeting room and notify members when and where the meeting will be held.

Orientations

The GM/COO also plays a major role in the orientation of new board and committee members. It is typically the GM/COO who prepares orientation materials and schedules orientations. When the GM/COO runs an effective orientation program for new members and for new board and committee chairpersons, meetings are much more likely to be effective.

When holding an orientation meeting with new meeting leaders, GMs/COOs should ensure that the orientation accomplishes the following:

- Provides background information on past board or committee decisions
- Reviews ongoing projects
- Clarifies governance issues
- Helps the leader develop a plan for the year
- Reviews effective meeting techniques

Meeting Attendance

The GM/COO should attend all board meetings except ones where his or her salary, contract, or job performance is being discussed. At committee meetings, either the GM/COO or a staff liaison or both should be in attendance.

The staff person's role in a board or committee meeting is not to vote or lead the meeting. Instead, he or she should take a very low-key role, speaking up only when he or she can add value to the discussion. Houle says, "Though she (the staff person) does not need to impose a vow of silence on herself, and indeed should speak up on any matter on which she feels strongly or believes that she has special knowledge not possessed by the board, she is usually wise to leave participation to the members themselves .... She is a reporter, presenting not only her own opinions but all other facts necessary for the board to reach a judgment."

The staff person's role is to help meeting participants engage in an intelligent dialogue that is useful for the club. To fulfill this role, a staff person might:

- Ask questions

- Record key points
- Identify conflicting points of view
- Summarize any actions, messages or orders of the board or committee
- Draft a resolution, based on the discussion, for the board or committee to vote on

Other Factors Affecting Board and Committee Meetings

The effectiveness of a meeting also depends on several other factors that the participants may or may not have much control over. Some of these factors include:

- Parameters of the board or committee
- Terms of office
- Minutes of meetings
- Degree of informality

Parameters of the Board or Committee

Every governing body needs to have a well-defined scope of concerns. If a board tries to manage the club as well as govern it, the board will spend hours in ongoing minutiae. However, the line between what is governance and what is management is often hard to draw.

Chait gives several reasons why a board might become active in management instead of restricting their duties to governance:

- Sometimes boards are legally required to act on such managerial issues as the acceptance of gifts; signature authorizations; and leases, contracts and easements.
- Some governance issues involve board and committee members in operations, which blurs the line between governance and management. Some of these governance issues include raising money or recruiting and evaluating the GM/COO.
- If the club's staff lacks people with specialized skills or the resources to hire well-trained employees, board or committee members may provide their talents on a voluntary basis. However, boards in these cases should work to expand the club staff's expertise so that they can withdraw from administrative duties.
- If a board lacks confidence in the GM/COO, board and committee members will become more involved with day-to-day operations to determine whether they want to replace him or her.
- Boards may intercede during times of crisis to help restore the status quo.
- Management offers more instant gratification than governance, because management is usually involved in immediate decisions and actions. Governance is much more long-term and requires more analyses, discussions and knowledge.

Chait also recommends that GMs/COOs and boards structure meetings to direct the participants' attention to issues of policy and strategy. This can be done by highlighting issues of policy and strategy. It can also be done by the use of a consent agenda that includes all routine actions. Also, setting priorities for agenda items can let all participants know what is important and on what they should focus.

Also affecting the conduct of a meeting is whether the board or committee is a policy-making body or whether it is strictly advisory. Policy-making and advisory meetings require slightly different approaches. It is always important for participants to understand what they should and should not be doing.

Terms of Office

The terms of service for members can also have an effect on meetings. There are different challenges involved with conducting a meeting that has 75 percent new members than there are with a meeting of only 25 percent new members. The longer a member serves, the more likely he or she is to maintain established meeting discipline. However, the flip side is that the longer people serve, the more likely they are to resist change.

Clubs should carefully evaluate length of service, rotation of officers and any term limits for how they affect meetings.

Minutes of Meetings

Keeping minutes can aid the effectiveness of a meeting in progress and all future meetings. Minutes, in their simplest form, can help keep participants informed of prior decisions, pending issues and repeating agenda items. At a slightly more complex level, minutes can be used as a living document to help facilitate the current meeting. "Living document" minutes should be kept on a flipchart or chalkboard. As discussions are held, the "recorder" writes down key words or main points. When necessary, he or she can ask "Is this what you're saying?" or "Is this OK?" As the flipchart pages fill up, they can be hung around the room as a reference to help keep the discussion moving and prevent repetitiveness.

See Figure 7 for some tips on keeping minutes during a meeting.

Degree of Informality

Although most of this issue has focused on adding structure to meetings, meetings should not be overly formal. Formalization does not have to be the end result of good meeting planning and execution. In fact, formalization tends to be the enemy of effective meetings.

"There should be as much informality as possible," Houle encourages. "Boards with good social relationships among the members are more likely to have good board meetings than those where the members do not know each other well. Board members who are unacquainted with one another feel stiff and constrained, reluctant to talk, awkward and over formal."

For the most part, members of club boards and committees are already accustomed to socializing together. Nonetheless, sometimes informality can take an effort. There may be factors that lead a board or committee to behave in a very formal manner. Some of these might include:

- Strong factionalism

Figure 7: Tips for Minute Taking

When recording minutes, keep the following tips in mind:

- Don't worry about spelling while recording information.
- Listen for key words and phrases to capture basic ideas.
- Interrupt the discussion and ask for clarification if you get behind.
- Focus on ideas rather than names. The group speaks as "one" so it is not necessary to record the names of who said what.
- Use names in the minutes to indicate assignments given to group members. Names may also be used when thanking a person or group.
- Read back your notes to the board or committee at the end of the meeting to make sure there aren't any additions or corrections.
- Finish your notes by outlining the agenda for the next meeting.
- Write clearly.
- Underline for clarity.
- Change colors for visual relief.
- Star, box and circle for emphasis.

- Members who aren't used to working with one another
- A highly controversial issue that splits the group

If one or more of the above factors exist, the meeting may have to be conducted in a more formal manner just to get things accomplished. However, boards and committees should strive to make those instances the exception.

Putting It All Together

The reward to implementing the tools discussed in this issue can be a more effective meeting style that can contribute to more effective club governance. Understanding the factors of presenting a successful meeting can help meeting leaders and the GM/COO perform better and help all meeting participants feel that they are contributing to the welfare of their club.

ACKNOWLEDGEMENTS

The following individuals generously donated their expertise and time to make this issue possible:

Albert Armstrong, CCM
George Carroll, CCM
Emory Daniels
John Foster, CCM
Terry Gilmer, CCM
John Jordan, CCM

Mariana Nork
William Schulz, CCM
Jim Troppman, CCM

Additional Resources

Chait, Richard, *How to Help Your Board Govern More and Manage Less*, National Center for Nonprofit Boards, Washington DC, 1993.

Davis, Daniel T. and Wachsberger, Ken, "Handling Problems and Conflict," *Supervisory Skill Builders*, Educational Institute of AH&MA, East Lansing, MI: 1996.

Houle, Cyril O., *Governing Boards*, Jossey-Bass, San Francisco, CA 1989.

Jones, O. Garfield, *Parliamentary Procedures At a Glance*, Penguin Books, New York, New York, 1971.

Prince, George M., "How to be a Better Meeting Chairman," *Harvard Business Review*, January-February 1969.

Scannell, Edward, "We've Got to Stop Meeting Like This," *Training & Development* January 1992.

Seelhoff, Karen, "Interpersonal Communication," *Management Skill Builders*, Educational Institute of AH&MA, East Lansing, MI: 1994.

Discussion Questions:

1. Who benefits from effective meetings? How?
2. What are some reasons that meetings fail?
3. What are some tools to make meetings more effective and how are they used?
4. What roles are taken by the board president/chairperson? the GM/COO?

Additional Activities

1. Develop two agendas for a board meeting. The first agenda should illustrate how *not* to run an effective meeting. The second agenda should facilitate an effective meeting.

2. Form a group of six to eight people. Assign a "participant type" from the table in the appendix to each person. One person should be assigned the role of board president. Conduct a 20-minute meeting about dining room dress codes. Each person should play their assigned role. After the mock meeting, discuss how the "president" responded to each problem person and what the result was.

Participant type	Who they are	Ways to handle them
Complainers	Professional gripers with a pet peeve. They always have something negative to say about the issue at hand.	Try to prevent them from speaking until others have offered positive comments. Ask them questions such as, "How would you handle it, Pat?" Or, "Can you think of one or two ways we could make improvements?" Avoid negative words when you phrase these requests. Even if complainers have a legitimate complaint, point out that policy can't be changed here, and that the objective is to operate as best as possible under the system. Discuss the problem with them later or ask a member of the group to respond.
Silent Sams/Sallys	They won't talk, because they are bored, indifferent, timid, or insecure.	Your response will depend on why these people are quiet. Draw them out with statements such as, "We value everyone's input." Ask them to introduce a speaker or read a report. Ask for their opinions directly. Draw out the person next to them and then ask the quiet people for an opinion on the view expressed. If the quiet person is seated near you, let him or her talk to you, not the group. If a Silent Sam/Sally is sensitive or timid but joins in anyway, compliment him or her — and be sincere.
Know-it-alls	These people are constantly trying to impress others with how much they know on every topic.	Don't discourage them, but don't let them off easy. Probe them for specific information that supports their position. Be sure to make use of their knowledge and thank them for their contributions. Sometimes they really *do* know it all. Make sure they don't turn into Barkers or Biters. Sometimes you will need to talk to them in private about respecting others.

Participant type	Who they are	Ways to handle them
Actors and Actresses	People who take a long time to say very little because they love the spotlight or are naturally wordy.	Ask them questions that start out broad, but narrow down to specifics. Don't embarrass these people or be sarcastic, because you may need them later. Try to slow them down with difficult questions.
Boxers	These people have a combative personality; some are professional hecklers.	Keep your temper in check and don't let the group get excited either. Try to find honest merit in one of the person's points. Express your agreement, or let the group do so, and then move on to something else. When a boxer says something obviously wrong, throw it out to the group and let them respond to it. If necessary, talk to this person privately during a break.
Tongue-tieds	These people lack the ability to express their ideas properly.	Don't say, "What you mean is..." Say, "Let me repeat that..." then put the idea into better language. Don't get impatient or interrupt them.
Left-fielders	People who can't stay on the subject. They're not rambling, just off-base.	Take the blame. "Something I said must have led you off the subject — this is what we should be discussing." Restate the topic or refer to the agenda. Before the meeting, you might want to ask one of the participants to speak up and point out when and if the discussion starts to wander or get off track.
Opinion solicitors	People who are trying to put the leader on the spot.	Point out that your view is not as important as the view of the group as a whole. If you are backed into a corner, be direct about giving your opinion. However, first try to determine why this person is asking for your view. Suggest getting opinions first from other members of the group.

Participant type	Who they are	Ways to handle them
Hatfields and McCoys	Two or more participants who have a personality clash.	Emphasize the points where they agree and try to minimize the points of disagreement if possible. Draw attention to the objectives of the meeting. Interrupt them with a direct question on the topic. Bring an objective member into the discussion. As a last resort, frankly request that personalities be omitted from the discussion at hand.
Stubborn sticklers	People who won't change their minds and refuse to acknowledge other people's viewpoints.	Throw these people's opinions to the group and let the other participants respond. Say that time is short and you'll be glad to discuss the point later. Ask them to accept the group's consensus for the time being.
Chatty members	People who are holding their own conversations on the side — whether they are related or personal.	Don't embarrass them. Call on one by name and ask him or her an easy question. Or, call one by name and, after restating the last opinion given, ask him or her for a comment on it. If you normally move around the room, casually stand behind members who are talking, but don't make it too obvious.
Barkers and biters	They throw temper tantrums, trample on other people's opinions, and make cutting and often personal remarks. Barkers are insensitive but harmless; biters are mean.	Hold your ground with barkers and biters. Wait out their outbursts and then say something like, "If you're through letting off steam, let's try to talk about this calmly." Sometimes you have to confront biters with questions like, "That sounded like a dig. Was it?"
Wet blankets	Mention any change to these people and they'll have 100 reasons why it can't or shouldn't be done.	Introduce changes slowly if you have a lot of wet blankets. Tell them what you have in mind. Let them criticize it. Then ask them how they would solve the problem. Keep prodding until you can get some cooperation.

Participant type	Who they are	Ways to handle them
Poppycock artists	These people pose as know-it-alls, but they don't know what they're talking about.	Recognize that poppycock artists are often insecure and overly sensitive. When it's necessary to call their bluff, leave them an out so that they can save face.
Wafflers	These people can't make a decision or don't want to make one.	Try to make the environment friendly and secure. Sometimes wafflers are distracted by a desire to please.
Old-timers	These people don't want to believe there is any way to do something other than the tried-and-true way of their 130 years of experience.	Kill them with kindness. Stress the good points they make and ask them if there *might* be more than one way to respond. Then open it up for group analysis.

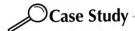

Case Study

Bored by the Board

Tom Frost has recently become the general manager of the Leisure Resort Club, a private, residential, golf course community at which the average age of members is 65. Most of its members are retirees. Many members used to be CEOs or in the upper management of large corporations. They previously led very hectic lifestyles and are now learning to unwind.

Tom used to be the general manager of the Vertigo Club, a large downtown club. The average age of members there was 45—many members were hardworking professionals. Board meetings for the club were typically held for no more than an hour over breakfast one day a month. The president of the Vertigo Club was known for his efficient meeting-time management with the board; he would mail out agendas in advance that included timeframes for each item on them, and he knew how to diplomatically keep discussions on schedule.

In the course of his orientation, Tom learned from the Leisure Resort Club president that monthly board meetings typically start at 3:00 P.M. and vary in length. Sometimes they finish by the dinner hour, sometimes they do not. Tom has met with each of the board members, and he has been impressed with the warmth and cooperative attitudes they exhibit. His understanding from the president is that he is to conduct a review of club operations, so he reviews human resources records and gathers reports from the accounting division, the food and beverage outlets, the golf and greens operations—all the branches of the club's operation. He puts tremendous effort into reading minutes from previous board meetings, internalizing the club's goals and organizational structure, and reviewing, analyzing, and reformatting reports. His goal is to give a "State of the Club" address at the upcoming board meeting, which will be his first, and receive feedback on his observations from board members.

The day arrives for Tom's first board meeting. He learns at 10:00 A.M. that there is a schedule conflict for the boardroom, so he has the board meeting moved to the Smith Room, a private room off the main dining room. Tom has his staff spread the word to the board members while he calls to inform the club president. When Tom asks whether the board members will be badly distracted by the unusual setting of the meeting, the president tells him not to worry about it. Tom arrives at the Smith room at 2:30 P.M. and arranges his presentation materials. Tom hands the president a copy of the meeting agenda, complete with time frames for each agenda item. The president comments, "Wow, we've never had anything this detailed before. This should really help us stay focused." Tom places copies of the agenda and of his report summaries at each place around the table. At 3:00, as members start to arrive and look at the materials before them, Tom hears many comments about how organized his handouts are and how helpful they are sure to be.

The president opens the meeting with a welcome to Tom. The board members offer a hearty round of applause, and Tom beams, thinking to himself, "This bunch of people makes it worth all the effort I put in last week." The president continues with his own report: "One of the most pressing issues we are facing here, Tom, is the renovation of the main clubhouse. All of you know how it has been a mixed blessing for us in the past months. I feel that it is important that Tom know the depth of this board's struggles and feelings over our extensive but necessary renovation enterprise. Wouldn't you say so, Bill?"

Bill jumps in. "You're right, Reynold. Why just the other day a member came to me and said she had seen what she feared was asbestos hanging down from a section of ceiling..." As they talk, two servers come in, looking for a contact lens a member has supposedly lost in that room earlier.

Three hours later...

Tom has been taking notes from time to time, but has been getting more and more anxious. The board has discussed the renovations, slow play, the renovations, their most recent golf games, the renovations, cigar smoking, the renovations, soft spikes, and the renovations. Two board members are on their hands and knees, helping the servers look for the contact lens. The president is just summing up the discussion on the renovations when a dining room employee enters and whispers in Tom's ear. As the president takes his seat, Tom says, "I'm terribly sorry, everyone, but there's another group scheduled to meet here in fifteen minutes, so we need to wrap things up."

Tom eagerly begins to cover agenda item 3 of 11, the general manager's report. He quickly outlines the results of his analysis. A board member interrupts and says her copy of a particular page is too light to read. Two other members start talking about how shameful it is that they are the most important decision-making body in the organization and they can't even have a meeting room for an adequate period of time. The president steps in and says, "I think Tom has done an excellent job at taking the pulse of our club, and I encourage all of you to take these report summaries home and read them. It's just about time to go. Tom, do you have any more comments to share?"

Tom says, "I thank you in advance for the effort you will put into reading these materials."

Floyd, a committee chair whose report is always last on the agenda, asks the president for a chance to speak. The president gives him the floor, and Floyd begins: "Tom has obviously put a lot of work into these summaries. He will need to hear our feedback and to begin to know what actions to take on his conclusions. If we leave him to muddle through the next month, we'll have only ourselves to blame if he takes actions we don't like. Let's all be timely in reading these reports and giving Tom our feedback." The president agrees and hears a motion to adjourn the meeting. After a quick vote, the board members file out. Bill finds the contact lens on his seat cushion, and the board members nearby hail him as a hero.

By the time Tom has gathered his belongings and vacated the conference room, the next group is almost ready to start their meeting. On the way out, Tom sees a copy of his report on the bar counter. He grabs it and hopes the bartender hasn't read anything, especially the section about poor liquor control on the part of the bar staff.

"What a disaster," Tom thinks to himself as he shuffles back to his office. He feels too exhausted to think, but he makes himself call the general manager of the

Schenkles Club, a sister club to the Vertigo Club. The manager listens carefully to his story and gives several ideas.

Discussion Questions

1. What more does Tom need to know to conduct an effective board meeting? What skills does he need to exercise and develop if future board meetings are to be effective?

2. In terms of the setting, interaction with board members, and the agenda, what went wrong at Tom's first board meeting?

3. In terms of the setting, interaction with board members, and the agenda, what should the Schenkles Club GM suggest that Tom do differently at the next board meeting?

The following industry experts helped generate and develop this case: Cathy Gustafson, CCM, University of South Carolina; Kurt D. Kuebler, CCM, Vice President, General Manager, The Desert Highlands Association; and William A. Schulz, MCM, General Manager, Houston Country Club.

Ethics

In a recent National Public Radio broadcast, a commentator said he overheard two college students talking about their business ethics class — a class they resented being mandatory. One student summed up the day's lesson by saying, "Sometimes in business you'll have to do things you know are wrong, but you should think about them first."

Many people would call these students misguided. The commentator certainly did. And yet, when spoken against the backdrop of increasing corporate illegal activities, political shenanigans and even charity scandals, the comment may be a realistic reflection of today's business environment. Are ethics absolute? Only the most dogmatic would say yes. But neither are they transitory ideals, to be referred to only in esoteric settings and quickly discarded when they cost money, membership or prestige. Pure ethics is defined as "knowing what ought to be done and having the will to do it."

Implicit in a member's satisfaction with a club is the belief that he or she belongs to an organization with integrity. Because of this belief, all clubs must put a high priority on ethics and ethical behavior. This can mean tough decisions when clubs are faced with "gray" issues that each member might define differently. What one member considers an ethical response, another might consider an overreaction that wastes money. Therefore, a club's managers and officers must work hard to determine the ethical code of their members and learn how to consistently practice it.

This issue of the *Topical Reference Series* can help club managers build a foundation for making ethical decisions. It examines the definitions of ethics, describes ethical situations that arise in clubs and presents a few models for ethical decision-making. This issue also examines codes of ethics and discusses how to develop and use them. Throughout the issue you will find "Ethical Entanglements," which can be considered mini-case studies. Use these ethical entanglements in a way that best meets your needs. One way to use them is to share them with your staff and board.

What Are Ethics?

The word "ethics" comes from the Greek *ethikos* and *ethos*. The Greeks also used the word *ethos* to mean character. Ethics has been defined as the science of behavior by William Barclay, "the bit of religion that tells us how we ought to behave." It is more difficult to find a pragmatic definition of the word. Any given person's ethical code is based on his or her own conscience, upbringing, culture and values. When perspectives are so vastly different, how can anyone reconcile theory with practice?

Rather than settle for a simple definition, this issue will explore several aspects of ethics and the different interpretations put upon them. David Whitney, an associate professor of marketing and hospitality services, identifies the following aspects of ethics: the utilitarian principle (do the greatest good for the greatest number), the principle of rights (individuals have certain moral rights) and the principle of justice (everyone should have access to a level playing field).

Figure 1: Compliance with Laws vs. Ethics

Compliance with Laws	Ethics
Prevents criminal misconduct	Encourages responsible conduct
Externally imposed standards	Self-imposed standards
Motivation is to avoid penalties or punishment	Motivation is self-actualization and self-improvement
Legal reinforcements, emphasis is on restrictions	Principle-driven reinforcements, emphasis is on personal responsibility

Also worth discussing are:

- Ethics and the law
- Social responsibility
- Ethics and labor relations
- Obstacles to ethics

It is important, however, not to look at the different aspects and philosophies of ethics as simply a multiple choice question. Stephen S.J. Hall, a quality expert, put it succinctly when he said, "Do not allow the stratification of ethics to mislead you into believing that there are different types, forms and intensities of ethics. 'Doing what is right' is the solid bottom line of ethics and is not mitigated by the fact that we are talking about interactions with the public, the guests, the employees and those who support these interactions." (Stephen S.J. Hall, "The Emergence of Ethics in Quality," in *Ethics in Hospitality Management: A Book of Readings*, East Lansing, Mich.: Educational Institute of the American & Motel Association, 1992, p. 17)

Ethics and the Law

The practice of ethics is not merely a feel-good proposition. Increasingly, ethics are becoming codified in law, and violations of those laws often carry severe penalties. Ethics regulations increased in the past decade as the public responded to unethical business behavior with demands for greater regulatory oversight. Yet, laws provide only a minimum standard for ethics. They do not demand that any business behave ethically, only that it not behave unethically.

Michael G. Daigneault, former president of *Ethics, Inc.*, stressed the difference between compliance with laws and ethics at the Club Managers Association of America's 1995 Annual Conference. His illustration of the differences between the two is shown in Figure 1. Compliance is that which must be done to prevent predetermined penalties. Ethics is what is done to ensure integrity and quality. A club that stops at compliance with the law is only giving its members partial service.

Social Responsibility

One of the more controversial areas of ethics for clubs is that of social responsibility. Social responsibility involves taking actions for the good of society as a whole. There are two aspects of social responsibility: one is closely associated with corporate charity and the other involves everyday operational decisions.

The first type of social responsibility, corporate charity, was originally the only form of social responsibility practiced by businesses. In the mid-1960s, managers became more active in responding to the social ills of society. Today, nonprofit foundations provide an outlet for club members who want to give back to their communities through their club.

A second aspect of social responsibility is making sure that the everyday decisions made by the club are good for society as well as for its members. Are the practices of the club socially sound? Are they environmentally sound? Clubs traditionally have been some of the better employers in the food service industry — partly because club managers and members have made socially responsible decisions to provide sufficient and stable employment to their workers.

Many clubs embrace the practice of social responsibility wholeheartedly, participating in social programs in order to give their members a safe outlet to influence society. As Robert Greenleaf said, "There is no other way that as few people can raise the quality of the whole American society as far and as fast as can trustees and directors of our voluntary institutions, using the strength they now have in the positions they now hold." (J. W. Nason, *The Nature of Trusteeship*, Washington, D.C.: Association of Governing Boards of Universities and Colleges, 1982, p. 12.)

Many clubs are just beginning to reach out to the public by selecting charities to which they want to contribute money. There are many club members who want their club to get involved in the community. A general manager/chief operating officer (GM/COO) said that "if members can do it through the auspices of the club, everyone benefits. The club gets a little better reputation in the community and the members satisfy their need to do some good."

For the past four years, CMAA members have had the opportunity to involve their clubs in the association's *Clubs Collecting for Communities* campaign. This campaign involves hundreds of club managers around the country who lead their clubs in food and clothing drives for local charities and toy drives for the Marine Corp's Toys for Tots. CMAA provides each participating club with pre-written press releases, newsletter articles, flyers, posters and campaign schedules. For more information about the program, contact Tamara Tyrrell at (703) 739-9500 or at tyrrellt@cmaa.org via ClubNet.

However, there are some clubs that back away from most charitable work, saying they do not want to put an added burden on already busy and generous members. At a recent CMAA Business Management Institute III, a board member participating in a guest panel told managers that he didn't want his club to be socially active. He said he participated in charities enough at work and that he went to the club to escape.

Ethics and Labor Relations

Another sometimes stormy ethical area concerns labor relations. Harold Morgan, in his article "Ethics and Labor Relations" (*Ethics in Hospitality Management: A Book of Readings*, East Lansing, Mich.: Educational Institute of the American Hotel & Motel Association, 1992), said the only way to have ethical labor relations is to make informed decisions based on:

- Laws

- Union contracts
- Organizational goals
- Ethical principles

One of the biggest arguments for treating employees ethically is that employees typically will treat members and guests the way they are treated. In clubs the issue is compounded because members usually want long-term employees who they recognize and who recognize them. One GM/COO says, "Members want to have that home away from home, they want to have that name recognition. But there's a cost to that. What about when long-time club waiter old Harry gets a little forgetful and brings the meal to the wrong place and doesn't know how to figure out the guest check? Yet the members don't want you to get rid of old Harry, he's an institution." This GM/COO said that he's had to create new jobs for some long-term employees in order to keep them at the club without having them lose their status as senior employees with a lot of credibility. "Somehow," he said, "you have to protect the membership in the club by putting long-term employees into positions that are going to complement their experience and their worth and not have a negative impact on operations."

Treating employees ethically, then, becomes a factor in member satisfaction. Members want club employees treated well, so that they will stay. Clubs must also be ethical in their treatment of unions. No club wants a union picketing in front of its doors or complaining in headlines about unfair labor practices.

Obstacles to Ethics

Since few people would argue against the necessity for ethical behavior, why is it still an issue? One would think that all unethical practices would cease because of everyone's positive intentions. Unfortunately, unethical behavior does persist. There are many reasons why this occurs. Just a few include:

- *Ego.* A person with a large ego may feel threatened by an attempt to improve ethical processes. That person may see the improvement as an attack on his or her integrity, not realizing that ethics and ethical processes require constant vigilance and improvement.

- *Time.* Club managers are constantly on the go, constantly responding to crises and member demands. There is rarely adequate time to analyze a situation from every conceivable angle. However, well-structured ethical standards can reduce the number of ethical blunders by employees, which reduces the amount of time managers must spend undoing the damage these blunders cause.

- *Bad information.* It is difficult to make an ethical decision if that decision is based on false information. How can a manager ethically discipline an employee for theft if the information given by the employee's supervisor is false or exaggerated? In order to make ethical decisions, decision-makers must question the validity of information and seek out the facts.

- *Ignorance.* Sometimes, unacknowledged ignorance prevents managers and board members from making ethical decisions. Often, this ignorance takes the form of cultural biases or narrow-minded clinging to a particular business philosophy, exclusive of all other considerations. A person raised in a sexist environment, for example, may be unable to recognize sexual harassment or unequal treatment based solely on a person's sex.

- *Greed.* While the GM/COO and board members have an ethical responsibility to be sound financial guardians of member dues and income, paying attention to only the bottom line causes its own ethical dilemmas. If a club is too focused on its bottom line, it may neglect the human side of its business and the ethical treatment of members and employees.

Ethical Issues in Clubs

The ethical issues that clubs face vary somewhat among different club areas. A board member has slightly different ethical concerns than the GM/COO, the tennis pro or the grounds superintendent. Each will find him- or herself in unique situations.

Ethical Issues for Board Members

Board members take on an awesome responsibility when they assume office, and they usually have very high member expectations to live up to. The members of the club rely on board members to represent their interests, act with integrity and make decisions based on the club's needs and desires. Harold Koontz of the University of California, Los Angeles, compiled a list of ethical questions that individual board members should ask themselves (Harold Koontz, *The Corporate Director: New Roles, New Responsibilities*, Boston: Cahners Books, 1975, pp. 141–142). Those questions are listed in Figure 2.

Some of the ethical issues that board members must deal with include the following:

- Conflicts of interest
- Human resources issues
- Supplier/vendor issues
- Membership issues
- Environmental issues

In the following sections we will examine each of these issues in greater detail.

Conflicts of Interest

Perhaps the most common area of concern for board members — and the one that requires the most personal vigilance — is conflict of interest. Cyril O. Houle, in *Governing Boards* (San Francisco: Jossey-Bass, 1989, p. 139), defines three levels of conflict of interest:

- *Potential conflict of interest.* A potential conflict of interest exists when a board member has interests other than the board's. This is among the most common areas for potential conflicts of interest, for boards typically select people to serve who are active in the community and have many commitments. There is also a potential for conflicts of interest when a board member is related to a staff member or has a set agenda that overrides all other issues.
- *Actual conflict of interest.* Actual conflicts of interest occur when opposing loyalties are directly involved in a situation. This might happen, for example, when a board

Figure 2: Questions for Board Members to Ask Themselves

1. Why was I selected to be a board member?

2. Why am I serving as a board member?

3. Does my position on the board involve any serious conflict of interest with any other board membership, corporate position, investment or friendship? Have I disclosed any significant actual or potential conflict of interest to the other board members?

4. Do I understand which decision areas are reserved to the board and which are delegated to the club's managers?

5. Do I resist meddling in operations areas that are not the province of the board?

6. Do I have a clear understanding of what my legal and ethical responsibilities are as a board member?

7. If I am an insider with a divisional or functional operating responsibility, do I lay aside the prejudices of my operating position and make decisions as a board member with the entire club's interest uppermost in my mind?

8. If I am an insider, subordinate to the chairperson or president, do I feel I must support his or her positions on a board matter, even if I believe them to be unwise?

9. Do the minutes accurately reflect the actions of the board? Am I given an opportunity to review these minutes before final approval?

10. Am I willing to put in a reasonable amount of time, interest and commitment to discharge the responsibilities of a board member?

11. Am I willing to resign, after notice and attempting to obtain desirable changes, if I feel that the board is not being effectively used, if the club is not being well managed or if the actions being taken not in the best interest of the members?

12. Do I insist on receiving adequate information so that I may be assured that the club is being effectively managed?

13. When matters are submitted for board action, do I insist on well-researched and analyzed recommendations being presented?

14. Am I willing to ask probing, discerning and even embarrassing questions to assure myself that recommended courses of action have been thoroughly thought through?

15. In a matter before the board, do I attempt to identify the critical factors in a decision and satisfy myself that these have been adequately considered?

16. Do I attend meetings regularly?

17. Do I come to board meetings prepared on reports and other information sent me in advance of the meetings?

18. Do I feel a sense of commitment to the club and its objectives?

19. Am I willing to give a reasonable amount of assistance to the GM/COO and the club outside of board meetings?

20. Do I help in recruiting and evaluating qualified new board members?

21. Do I recognize that, while the board represents the members, the long-range success of the club requires also being responsive to the external economic, technological, political, social and ethical environment in which the club operates?

member is advocating the hiring of a golf pro who is also a personal friend of his or hers.

- *Self-interested decision.* This is perhaps the most dangerous of conflicts. In the first two, the potential for conflict exists and can be confronted. In a self-interested decision, the board member has already made the decision to act in a way that is advantageous to him- or herself or someone close to him or her.

Left unchecked, conflicts of interest can cost a club money, goodwill and membership. For individual board members, refusing to correctly address conflicts of interest could result in disgrace or a lawsuit. Even in cases that are not so extreme, conflicts of interest can create distrust and cause the morale of the board to plummet.

How can a board prevent conflicts of interest? There are many options that can help steer a board away from the morass of cross-cutting loyalties. The most obvious, and often least practical, option is to avoid nominating people for the board who might have any conflicts of interest. This would mean not nominating the president of the company that supplies the club's baked goods, for example, or not nominating a member of the club who also happens to be the daughter of the golf pro. However, the issue becomes more tangled when a club must decide if it should make it a policy to bar a member from board service who also belongs to a neighboring club and would be involved in looking at competing bids for tournaments. Or should a club prohibit board membership to a member who is an employee of one of the club's suppliers?

A more effective way of preventing conflicts of interest is to encourage self-monitoring on the part of each individual. Each board member should inform the rest of the board of any potential conflicts and refuse to participate in any decision-making that could involve or even appear to involve a conflict of interest. Some questions that a board member might ask him- or herself are listed in Figure 3.

Aside from encouraging individual monitoring, the board can also act to prevent conflicts of interest by creating policies that help avert potential ethical problems. For example, a club could require that any major purchases be made by competitive bid. Another example of a club bylaw that can help prevent conflicts of interest is the following:

> No solicitation of funds for charitable or other purposes shall be made in the Club or from any roster of Club members, except as the Board of Governors may authorize.

This bylaw prevents members from using club proprietary information in the interests of other organizations.

Another way to help stem conflict of interest problems is to adopt a conflict-of-interest statement and ask board members to read and sign it annually. The statement could include the club's policies for dealing with vendors, for nonpreferential treatment of members and their families and for doing business with the club.

Also, the board can deal openly with potential conflicts of interest by discussing them during a board member's orientation and whenever the need arises. The board should make it easy for a member to withdraw from a discussion or decision when he or she feels it might pose a conflict-of-interest problem. Some boards may choose to put a member in charge of reviewing possible conflicts of interest. Boards should also be vigilant and prepared to confront — however gently — a member who is stepping out of line. Sometimes a warning comment made early on can prevent a formal inquiry later into inappropriate actions.

Figure 4: Ethical Entanglements: Who Decides?

One of your fellow board members, John, is going through a painful and messy divorce. Your club bylaws state that:

In the event of the dissolution of marriage of a Member by divorce, the member's spouse may be eligible to become a member. A written application for membership must be made to the Board of Directors by the member's spouse. If the Board of Directors approves such application, upon payment of all amounts then due the Club, the former spouse shall succeed to the membership category of the member, without the payment of an initiation fee.

You notice on the board meeting agenda that John's ex-wife has applied for full membership status and the board will be reviewing her application. On the way into the meeting, John pulls you aside and says, "Hey, you'll vote with me, won't you? There's no way I want to see my ex-wife have full membership in this club. I already come here to get away from her, let alone once the divorce is final!"

What is your response?

Figure 4 is an Ethical Entanglement that illustrates a conflict-of-interest scenario.

Human Resources Issues

Although most human resources issues fall under management's responsibility, the board must handle a select number of cases, primarily those dealing with the employment of the GM/COO. The board is responsible for the following human resources issues:

- Selecting a GM/COO
- Assessing the GM's/COO's performance
- Arbitrating in conflicts between staff members and the GM/COO
- Ensuring that all legal and ethical responsibilities are being fulfilled

Among the most challenging of board responsibilities is selecting a new GM/COO. The board is responsible for establishing a selection procedure; determining the qualifications needed for the position; searching for, screening, and interviewing candidates; and then selecting a candidate. This task can be onerous to board members because of all the pressures brought to bear on them by club members. Cyril O. Houle quoted one board member who had just been asked what he would do differently in the next executive search. The answer: "I'd resign. I very honestly never would want to live through such an experience again. It was tedious; it was full of conflicts … exceptional pressures were brought upon members of the board. It was a dirty game, a haphazard game, a game without a rule book." (Cyril O. Houle, *Governing Boards,* San Francisco: Jossey-Bass, 1989, p. 104.)

Ethical considerations when selecting a GM/COO include the following:

- Allowing staff members to be involved
- Carefully selecting candidates
- Honestly dealing with candidates

Figure 5: Ethical Entanglement: A Bone for the Assistant

You are the head of the executive search committee. During the search, an assistant manager, David, has been acting as temporary chief operating officer. Although David is a very talented assistant manager, the consensus of the committee is that he is not ready for the top position yet — especially since you have many other strong candidates. However, the committee members think they should let David into the final round of interviews because he is the only internal candidate. One member says that it would be a way of throwing David a bone for the hard work he's been doing since your last COO left. Including David in the final list would mean eliminating another candidate — who would otherwise have a legitimate chance at receiving the position — and submitting David's name to a board vote.

What is your response?

Although many boards want to keep all of the GM/COO selection proceedings secret, it is important to involve the people who will be most affected by the selection — the club's staff. Often, staff members can provide valuable input into the qualifications needed to perform the job. Not actively involving the staff in determining selection criteria will leave them feeling disenfranchised and unwanted. Once input has been obtained from staff members, however, their role will probably end. The board will probably not want to include staff members as part of the selection committe, and it certainly should not allow staff members to have a vote in the final choice.

When selecting candidates, the board must be careful not to end the application period too early or let it go on too long. Many would argue that the board has an ethical responsibility to be active in the selection of candidates — even when it has hired an outside search agency. Likewise, the board must be careful who it selects as finalists. The National Center for Nonprofit Boards, in its Governance Series Booklet "Finding and Retaining Your Next Chief Executive: Making the Transition Work" (Thomas N. Gilmore, Washington, D.C.: National Center for Nonprofit Boards, 1993, p. 10), warns against including a weak internal candidate in the final group of candidates, even if the board is certain that he or she will not be selected. Doing so could cause the weak internal candidate to not support the candidate who is ultimately chosen. The booklet suggests that the board's chairperson have a frank discussion with the internal candidate about the board's thinking, rather than give him or her false hopes by putting him or her in the finalist group out of "kindness."

Finally, a board should be honest with all of the candidates about the conditions of employment. It is best if everything is in writing, but even if it is not, the board should strive to give complete and honest answers to all of the questions candidates ask. Honesty during the selection interviews will set the stage for the board's future relationship with the new GM/COO.

See Figure 5 for an Ethical Entanglement on GM/COO selection.

Another human resources duty of the board is to establish a grievance procedure for staff members. Labor laws in the United States make it absolutely essential that boards set up a process for employees to air their complaints when the GM/COO is unable to resolve them. While no board wants to be a court of appeals, it can sometimes act to keep a case against the club from going to court. Most boards shy away from this duty because they do

Figure 6: Ethical Entanglement: He's Not Fresh!

You are the president of the board. One evening, you get a call at home from the dining room captain. He tells you that the GM/COO has been ordering frozen vegetables to be used in the gourmet dining room, even though the menu descriptions of the vegetables always say "fresh." You know that the dining room captain has been reprimanded recently by the GM/COO and you suspect he carries a grudge.

What is your response to the captain? Do you do any additional follow up? If so, what?

not want to get involved with disputes between a staff member and the GM/COO, especially if they fear the disputes are of a personal nature. One way to reduce the number of cases a board must arbitrate is to require that all personnel policies be put in writing.

When forced to arbitrate a case, the board must consider all factors carefully. It is not uncommon for a board to make arbitration decisions based solely on its opinion of the GM's/COO's integrity or personality. However, a board committed to behaving ethically will find a way to justly resolve each situation while still being supportive of the GM/COO. A board should refrain from using an arbitration as an opportunity to harass an unpopular GM/COO or put him or her on the spot. Likewise, boards should not automatically rule against employees in an effort to support their GM/COO and ensure that he or she does not quit to go elsewhere. (See Figure 6 for a human resources Ethical Entanglement.)

Although board members can usually leave compliance with personnel laws in the hands of a capable GM/COO, they still retain certain legal responsibilities. If a personnel law or code is being violated, the board can be held responsible. It is therefore incumbent on the board to periodically audit club operations to make sure personnel decisions are being made in a legal and ethical manner.

Finally, the board is responsible for a regular assessment of the GM's/COO's performance. Kenneth N. Dayton, former chairman and chief executive officer of the Dayton Hudson Corporation, said, "It has been my observation over the years that most CEOs spend an inordinate amount of time worrying about whether they are doing a good job or not, and whether they are satisfying their board. If they know where they stand, they would waste a lot less energy in worrying and could therefore exert a lot more energy in doing an even better job."

In the club environment, boards have been known to appraise the work of a GM/COO only when they are firing him or her. This lack of feedback harms not only the GM/COO but also the club itself, which must live with a manager who has been given little board direction. More typically, boards give GMs/COOs yearly evaluations, or at least an evaluation at every contract renewal session.

Boards must avoid several ethical traps during the evaluation of the GM/COO:

- *Favoritism.* It is important that the GM/COO have a cooperative and friendly relationship with the board. However, if the relationship grows too intimate, there is a danger of favoritism. The board must be vigilant so that the assessment it gives the GM/COO is fair and the feedback useful. Favoritism can lead board

Figure 7: Ethical Entanglement: Award-Winning Scandal

Your GM/COO recently won an Idea Fair award for a caddy training program he said he created. Since you are proud of him, you obtain a copy of the program and read it. You discover that everything in the program — from the introduction and objectives to the wrap-up activity — is identical to a copyrighted program produced by a small training/consulting firm that your business has used in the past. The only change is that the GM/COO added some case studies. You call the firm and find out that the club has never hired it, and the firm is unaware of the plagiarism.

How do you respond?

members to rate personality traits above performance. If the favoritism is on the part of a single board member, it can cause resentment among other board members. Typically, a board chairperson can deal with this situation in a subtle way, unobtrusively letting the board member know that the relationship may be out of line.

- *Subjectivity.* Board members, like anyone conducting an employment evaluation, must be wary of substituting their own likes and dislikes for objective standards.

- *Dramatic incident effect.* This trap occurs when board members rate a GM/COO on a single event, not on his or her total performance.

See Figure 7 for an Ethical Entanglement involving a GM's/COO's job performance.

Supplier/Vendor Issues

One of the most commonly discussed ethics issues for board members involves purchasing. Many GMs/COOs have stories to tell about board members who have put pressure on club purchasing agents to use their businesses as suppliers. One GM/COO reported that a member insisted that "if you won't spend your money with me, I won't spend my money with you."

While many clubs take member products and services into consideration, few rely exclusively on member businesses. After all, clubs must treat the vendor community fairly. When a club seeks bids, it must accept all bidders as true competitors for the contract. It should not use the bidding process only to give the appearance of competition.

In *Purchasing: Selection and Procurement for the Hospitality Industry,* Second Edition (New York: Wiley, 1985, pp. 44–46), author John Stefanelli outlines objectives that a hospitality purchasing operation should meet:

- Provide the goods and services required to sustain operation
- Maintain inventories at a level that minimizes investment and operational expenses
- Sustain qualitative standards by procuring only those items that meet the standards and specifications established by appropriate operating managers
- Focus on lowering consumption costs
- Maintain the competitive position of the unit [club] through the continual implementation of measurable cost-avoidance and cost-savings programs

Figure 8: Eleven Purchasing Standards

Standards of Purchasing Practice

1. Avoid the intent and appearance of unethical or compromising practices in relationships, actions and communications.

2. Demonstrate loyalty to the employer by diligently following the lawful instructions of the employer, using reasonable care and only the authority you've been granted.

3. Refrain from any private business or professional activity that would create a conflict between personal interests and the interests of the employer.

4. Refrain from soliciting or accepting money, loans, credits or prejudicial discounts and the acceptance of gifts, entertainment, favors or services from present or potential suppliers which might influence, or appear to influence, purchasing decisions.

5. Handle information of a confidential or proprietary nature to employers and/or suppliers with due care and proper consideration of ethical and legal ramifications and governmental regulations.

6. Promote positive supplier relationships through courtesy and impartiality in all phases of the purchasing cycle.

7. Refrain from reciprocal agreements that restrain competition.

8. Know and obey the letter and spirit of laws governing the purchasing function and remain alert to the legal ramifications of purchasing decisions.

9. See that all segments of society have the opportunity to participate by demonstrating support for small, disadvantaged and minority-owned businesses.

10. Discourage purchasing's involvement in employer-sponsored programs of personal purchases that are not business related.

11. Enhance the proficiency and stature of the purchasing profession by acquiring current technical knowledge and maintaining the highest standards of ethical behavior.

Source: Adapted from Stephen S.J. Hall, ed., *Ethics in Hospitality Management: A Book of Readings* (East Lansing, Mich.: Educational Institute of the American Hotel & Motel Association, 1992), p. 162.

If using a member's business will cause the club to be in conflict with these goals, then the club needs to resist caving in to pressure. While the club wants to encourage the success of all of its members, it cannot afford to give one member beneficial treatment that will be costly to all of the other members.

Some GMs/COOs say that their clubs have responded to these pressures by writing policies forbidding members from pushing onesupplier over another whenever the members have a vested interest. Another GM/COO says he deals with purchasing issues on an individual level. If a member is putting pressure on a club purchaser, this GM/COO asks the board president to talk to the member and discourage the behavior. Many clubs have bylaws that deal with these issues.

The National Association of Purchasing Management put together a code of standards (see Figure 8) for making purchases, based on three principles:

Figure 9: Ethical Entanglement: Paper Trail

You are the chairperson of the house committee. You are reviewing several bids that have come in for supplying wallpaper. All of your committee members have made comments on each bid. You notice that the last bid to come in — and one of the lowest — is from a company where a fellow committee member is vice president. The fact that she is a committee member was not disclosed in the bid, nor had she excluded herself from the review process.

How do you handle the bid? the committee member?

- Loyalty to your company/club
- Justice to those with whom you deal
- Faith in the profession

See Figure 9 for an Ethical Entanglement in the purchasing area.

Membership Issues

Because the board is the policy-making body of the club, it has the power to determine what members can and cannot do. The board can determine the personality of the club by the way it responds to membership issues. One GM/COO commended his board for encouraging a diverse membership: "To me the club that is most interesting is a club that is multidimensional. Like one of our past presidents said, this club is fabulous because we're like an interesting tapestry that's woven together of a lot of different people, colors, nationalities and religious and political beliefs."

Guiding a club ethically means responding to a number of different membership issues:

- *Admitting members.* Policies for admitting individuals to the club have the highest risk of getting the club into legal or publicity problems. The original British social clubs popularized the use of a blackball approach to member selection. A single member had the authority to keep someone else out. Recently, clubs in the United States have been examining that concept and asking whether one person should have the right to veto the wishes of the majority.

  Although some clubs have only responded to antidiscrimination movements to avoid crippling negative publicity, other clubs have addressed discrimination as an ethical issue. These clubs have examined whether their membership admission policies discriminate based on race, gender, national origin or religion.

- *Enforcing rules.* Enforcing club rules can be a delicate issue. It is expected that club members are ladies and gentlemen who will uphold the rules in the interest of the entire membership. When they do not, the club must make uncomfortable decisions. Failing to enforce a rule in one instance compromises the credibility of staff members who must enforce it in other instances, and compromises the authority of the remaining rules. (For more information about enforcing rules, see *Club Rules*, the third issue in the *Topical Reference Series*.)

- *Allowing participation.* Boards also need to determine ways to allow the membership to have a voice in the policy-making decisions of the club. If no system exists for filing complaints or appealing policies or rules, members may create their own system — and it may not be one that the board likes.

- *Changing with the times.* As court rulings and state laws have made it illegal in some locations to have a "men's grill" or a "ladies' card room," clubs have had to make internal changes. One GM/COO said that several years back, when his club was renovating, some members wanted to make it very difficult to ever change the men's grill into a mixed grill. They had the architect design the room so that the only access to it was through the kitchen or the men's locker room. Later, when the legal and social environment nudged the club toward making the room a mixed grill, it had to add an outside door. The club is now looking at ways to provide easier access to the room for all its members. At other clubs, the switch to a mixed grill or a mixed card room is in name only, and social pressures and tradition keep the opposite gender from entering. Each club board must evaluate what the most ethical response is for the club.

Environmental Issues

Most clubs are meticulous in their care of club grounds, but environmental standards are constantly being raised and clubs may struggle to keep up with them. Boards may find that establishing a policy to deal with environmental issues can keep them from shirking because of costs when environmental issues arise.

Perhaps one of the more common environmental issues that board members face is the authorization of pesticide use on club grounds. Clubs may struggle to find the right balance between providing a comfortable and enjoyable golf course and using too much or the wrong kind of pesticide.

Another environmental issue clubs face involves water usage and presence on their grounds. There are many laws protecting wetlands, and often there is a high member interest in preserving the bird sanctuaries found in those wetlands. However, the presence of a wetland on club property can limit the development of a club or the restructuring of a golf course. Likewise, the use of water can also provide many quandaries for a club board. How does a club respond during times of draught? Should the club invest in a water recycling system so that the club can use its recycled water to irrigate the golf course?

One GM/COO described a water problem his club ran into when it sold some of its land to members to be developed as a member community. All of the community's sewage drained into the club's septic system, causing constant overload problems. The club's board members, though aware of the problem, put it on the back burner because they felt they had no alternatives to explore. Finally, when the city expanded its sewer system, the club decided to spend the money to co-finance the building of a pump station to pump the community's sewage into the main sewer system. It cost the club money on a short-term basis, but reduced the overload on the club's septic system, which ran through many environmentally sensitive areas. "A lot of clubs that got into the development business in the '50s and '60s are going to find hidden skeletons in their closets," the GM/COO said. "They're going to be facing the need to change things done 50 years ago."

See Figure 10 for an environmental Ethical Entanglement.

Figure 10: Ethical Entanglement: Oily Problem

During her report to the board, the new grounds manager says that in the past, maintenance staff members used to dump used oil into the ground outside a little-used maintenance shed. She says she has put an immediate stop to the practice, but the dumping has contaminated the groundwater. Preliminary estimates show that the cost of cleaning it up would require a membership assessment to pay for it. Last year the board levied an unpopular assessment that led to most of the board being recalled. One board member suggests keeping quiet about the contamination until enough money can be saved to pay for it. Later, the grounds manager tells you she will quit if the problem is ignored.

What do you do? What do you say to your fellow board members? the grounds manager? members?

Ethical Issues for GMs/COOs

For GMs/COOs, the practical issues of ethics often are in sharp contrast to their theoretical application. The most upstanding and moral managers can still be put in a quandary when an ethical decision threatens their employment. Most GMs/COOs are in the precarious position of employment-at-will, and if a board demands that they act in a manner that they consider unethical, then part of the decision becomes, "Am I willing to lose my job over this issue?" For the major issues, the answer may be clear. But it may be less certain if the issue is a repeated but relatively minor one.

Employee Issues

The type of ethical issues that most frequently arise for GMs/COOs are employee issues. Some of these issues are addressed by policy, because club managers cannot afford the time to make decisions concerning these issues individually on a daily basis. Even if they did have the time, it would be unfair to leave employee standards undefined and uncertain.

However, there is also a danger that because GMs/COOs are so familiar with these employee/human resources issues, they might fail to ask the ethical questions associated with them. Employee issues include equal opportunity, the minimum wage, working hours, sexual harassment, employee rights, employment-at-will, drug and alcohol abuse, employee theft, health and safety codes, workers' compensation and scheduling.

One GM/COO talked about the expense of making sure there are enough employees to provide proper service to members. He pointed out that when there's a wedding or other function, the club may need an extra 20 people. "But what do you do with them when you don't have the wedding? You've got to integrate them into the staff somehow. So there's always going to be an extra expense involved that you try to minimize the best you can. But all these workers need a livable wage. You can't just pull them out of the hat. You've got to employ them to make it worth their while to stay with you. Otherwise you're just holding the ladder for somebody else. You train them and then they go somewhere else."

A club that has highly cyclical business struggles with this issue even more. Is it fair to hire employees with the intention of laying them off in three months? Most managers would say yes, it's a business necessity. However, many would also stress that the ethical thing to

Figure 11: Ethical Entanglement: A Recipe Deal

You are interviewing an executive chef who is currently working for the club across town, Country & Golf Club. He comes highly recommended, with 15 years experience. Your board has been pressuring you to get a good chef since your last one left nearly four months ago. You have just about decided to make him a job offer when he says, "And if you hire me, I'll be bringing all the recipes with me. Including the one for CGC's trademark peach pie." CGC is well known for its peach pie. Some of your former members switched to CGC because of the better meals and desserts.

What do you say to the chef? Would you hire him? Would you tell the other club that the chef offered to bring recipes?

Figure 12: Ethical Entanglement: To Tell or Not To Tell

You get a call from a former assistant manager who is now managing a club in another part of the country. You were a mentor to him and helped him get the position he has now. After catching up on old news, he tells you that he is looking at a candidate for golf pro that used you as a reference. He says that Sue has a great resume, but he's concerned about how many different places she's worked in the last two years. He asks you if you know why she's moved around so much. You have heard rumors that Sue has a history of mental instability and takes a lot of sick days.

What do you say to your former assistant manager?

do is to be very up-front with applicants before they are hired. This also provides the club with an opportunity to recruit among populations that are often only interested in seasonal, temporary employment, such as teachers, spouses of migrant workers, students or retirees.

A GM's/COO's obligation to employees does not begin at their hire date nor end at their termination date. Managers need to examine their recruiting and selection policies to make sure they are ethically representing the terms of employment to candidates. The GM/COO also has an ethical obligation to the club to make sure that the right person is hired for the job. And even after an employee has left the service of the club, the GM/COO may have ethical decisions to make surrounding references or future employment opportunities. Figures 11 and 12 are Ethical Entanglements that address some of these issues.

Purchasing Issues

Whenever a discussion on club ethics begins, it is not long before issues of purchasing arise. As mentioned earlier, one of the more frequently addressed ethical problems is when a board or other club member begins putting pressure on the staff to use him or her as a supplier of goods or services to the club.

The GM's/COO's role in purchasing is to ensure that all transactions are conducted ethically and to adhere to the policies established by the club. If a member is putting too much pressure on the staff, the GM/COO can appeal to the board president to remedy the situation. A GM/COO can also encourage the board to create policies that could help prevent uncomfortable situations.

Figure 13: Ethical Entanglement: Changing the Sheets

> Your clubhouse manager comes to you with a complaint. She says that a board member has been putting a lot of pressure on her to switch laundry services to the one that he owns. The member's service charges slightly more, though it does make deliveries more often. The clubhouse manager is concerned that the member's company could not offer the same quality service that the club is getting now. The member's company does not have any other clubs as clients. The clubhouse manager asks you whether the club should switch services. Currently the club does not do business with any member-owned businesses.
>
> Do you recommend switching services? What do you say to the clubhouse manager? the board member?

Figure 14: Ethical Entanglement: You may already have won ...

> Your purchasing manager comes back from a convention and tells you that he put his business card into a drawing and won a trip to Hawaii. You congratulate him. The next year, he comes back from the same convention and tells you that he "won" the same trip again. He's suspicious about how random the drawing is.
>
> What do you tell him? How do you respond to the situation?

Another aspect of the GM's/COO's role in purchasing is his or her relationship with vendors. The GM/COO must be careful to treat these relationships with the highest degree of professionalism. Accepting perks or kickbacks can compromise a GM's/COO's impartiality. Yet, it is standard practice among many vendors to give small gifts to their customers during the holidays. GMs/COOs may want to determine in advance what they will do with these gifts. At some clubs, they donate all such items to local charities. Some GMs/COOs make the food gifts they receive available to club members in lounges or other areas.

In maintaining an ethical relationship with vendors, GMs/COOs should aim for the following:

- Treat vendors with honesty and courtesy
- Meet promptly with vendors at appointed times
- Call vendors back promptly
- Keep bids and quotes confidential, and protect other proprietary vendor information
- Safeguard fair and open competition without favoritism
- Make sure requests for proposals, purchase orders and terms and conditions are clear and easy to understand
- Do not expect to acquire goods at a price so low that the vendor's profit is eliminated

See Figures 13 and 14 for Ethical Entanglements addressing vendor ethics.

Food and Beverage Service Issues

A club can thrive or wither based on its food and beverage service. Members have extremely high expectations for what they will receive and attention they will get while in club dining rooms. This raises the importance of ethics in the club's food and beverage operations. A violation of ethics in the club's food and beverage department, if detected by members, could well lead to decreased activity in the food and beverage outlets or even a decrease in membership.

Some of the specific ethical issues that managers face in food and beverage departments include the following:

- *Alcohol service.* Alcohol service has had a tempestuous history in this country. While some clubs have epitomized classy alcohol service, others have given beverage service an almost sleazy reputation. It is these types of establishments to which temperance activists a century ago, and Mothers Against Drunk Drivers today, have reacted. Private clubs are typically very careful not to contribute to the negative reputation of alcohol service. However, a club manager still must determine what to do when a drunken member insists on leaving the club and driving home.

  Club managers should provide proper training and support to staff members who serve alcohol. If a server is not trained, he or she may not properly track drinks served or be able to monitor signs of intoxication. This situation has the potential to land a club in court. Likewise, if servers feel that their judgments will not be supported by management, they may be less vigilant about protecting the safety of members when it comes to recommending that drinks be cut off. The Educational Institute has produced an award-winning program, *CARE* (*Controlling Alcohol Risks Effectively*) for Servers, that can be used to help create responsible beverage service. A companion program, *CARE for Guest Contact Staff,* helps train employees who are not serving alcohol, but who might come into contact with intoxicated guests.

  There are positive returns for ethical alcohol service. In his article "Ethical Concerns in Food and Beverage Management" (*Ethics in Hospitality Management: A Book of Readings,* East Lansing, Mich.: Education Institute of the American Hotel & Motel Association, 1992), H. A. Divine says, "Certainly one of the primary elements of judging service quality is the attentiveness of the server. An important component of instituting a good monitoring program to ensure that individuals do not over consume alcoholic beverages is to encourage server attentiveness to the guest. Thus, the idea of paying attention to the guest and his or her needs, which is essential to providing quality service, is found also to be essential to ensure a safe environment."

- *Truth-in-menu.* As mentioned earlier, club members have extremely high expectations for the food they receive at the club. Frequently, a club subsidizes its food and beverage service to provide high-quality items to club members at low prices. Because of the commitment to high quality, controlling food costs becomes a pertinent issue. The pressure to contain food costs might lead a manager to cut corners wherever it is possible to do so without compromising quality. Nonetheless, if a club advertises that something is "fresh," then a manager does not have the option of substituting something frozen.

- *Sanitation.* No club wants to have its kitchen shut down for a sanitation offense, no matter how minor. Typically, providing a sanitary kitchen goes hand-in-hand with providing quality food. Most clubs are proud to show off their kitchens, even during busy meal periods. Most clubs don't struggle with the major ethical sanitation issues of whether to spend the extra money to ensure the kitchen is clean. It is

Figure 15: Ethical Entanglement: Out of Line

You are working late one night and a server comes to your office in tears. She tells you that Pete, the board's treasurer, just yelled at her. Pete had drank three Manhattans in an hour and she had cut off service after clearing it with the dining room captain. Pete got angry after being refused service and called her several obscene names in a loud voice. He then told her she was fired and that he'd better never see her in the club again. You have had some complaints about Pete drinking too much in the past and making improper suggestions to your servers. When you call the dining room captain, he tells you there wasn't much he could do about it.

What do you tell the server? the dining room captain? Do you say anything to Pete? If so, what?

more often the smaller questions that plague clubs. Is the staff properly trained in sanitation? Are the water temperatures in the dishwasher high enough, even during times when the club is trying to save on energy costs? Are employees sent home when they have a cold?

Figure 15 is an Ethical Entanglement addressing food and beverage ethics.

Golf Course Issues

Golf continues to grow in popularity. As the competition from public courses grows, members are demanding more of club golf courses. There tend to be three primary ethics issues surrounding golf course management:

- *Overbooking.* Clubs with a high rate of cancellations or no-shows may turn to overbooking as a solution. These clubs maintain that overbooking is a sound business practice that gives a greater number of members the opportunity to use the course. Problems arise, however, when there are no cancellations or no-shows and the golf course becomes overcrowded.

- *Tee time reservations.* In a club with a popular course and a lot of avid golfers, reservations can become a volatile subject. While the person taking reservations may not see any harm in reserving a prime spot for the board president before he or she calls in, if this were known it might cause resentment among other members.

- *Gender issues.* Many clubs are currently struggling with gender issues surrounding tee times. It is not unusual for clubs to set aside different times for men and women to golf — reserving the weekend morning times for men, for example, based on the old-fashioned assumption that men work during the week and women don't. In some states, courts have ruled that clubs may not deny equal access to club services based on gender. In states where there has been no ruling, clubs must make the decision internally. Several managers have said that it is not an issue of gender, but an issue of overcrowding. Others say that men and women aren't interested in golfing together anyhow. Questions surrounding scheduling according to gender include the following:

  — If a female member is paying the same dues as a male member, shouldn't she receive equal services for her money?

Figure 16: Ethical Entanglement: Money Trap

A major professional golf tournament is being held at your club. One of your club members is sponsoring a reception for all of the golfers participating in the tournament. This is the first time a professional tournament has been held at your club and you want everything to be perfect. The reception is a major bonus for the club because the member is picking up all of the associated costs. Just before the reception, the member asks you to combine the food and liquor totals. If you do this, he will be able to deduct the entire total as a business expense, but his company won't let him deduct anything for liquor. He winks at you and says, "Besides, the club will get paid the same, it can't harm you at all!"

How do you respond?

— When a club attempts to manage overcrowding on the golf course, should the determining factor be gender?
— How does the scheduling of tee times affect club recruitment of new members?
— How comfortable would the club feel defending its gender and golf policy publicly or in a courthouse?

Figure 16's Ethical Entanglement addresses golf course ethics.

Facilities Issues

Although often taken for granted, a club's facilities are one of the biggest trusts given over to the care of the GM/COO. Members expect to be safe and free from hazards while on the club's premises. It is sometimes difficult for GMs/COOs to get their boards to approve capital expenditures, however. In those cases, the GMs/COOs may be tempted to hide certain hazards and push back maintenance work.

However, the club's management and board have an ethical duty to protect members and employees from facility hazards. Managers and board members should make sure the club is properly maintained and staff members are trained in the following areas:

- Cleaning chemicals
- Fire prevention
- Flooding
- Electrical hazards
- Prevention of trips and falls
- Contaminated air
- Security

See Figures 17 and 18 for Ethical Entanglements concerning facilities.

Accounting Issues

Clubs tend to have less pressure to create a profit than other hospitality businesses. This does not mean, however, that clubs do not have to be strong financial performers. Members are constantly demanding increased services, which all cost additional money. It is in the

Figure 17: Ethical Entanglement: Dried Up

There has been a drought in your region for the last several months. Most of your neighbors have been forced to ration water. The club, however, has its own artesian well and is not suffering from any water shortages. There is a message on your voice mail from a local reporter who wants to interview you about the club's use of water for the golf course.

Do you talk to him? If so, what position would you take at the interview? Does the club continue to use water at the same rate? What actions, if any, would you take?

Figure 18: Ethical Entanglement: Unwanted Extras

You have been renovating the golf shop during your slow season. Part way through the renovation, the contractor comes to you and tells you he's discovered asbestos in the ceiling of what will be an exposed area of the golf shop. Removing it would increase the cost of the remodeling by 30 percent. The budget is extremely tight this year and you would have to cut back on either staff or services in order to come up with the extra money. In addition, he tells you that it would add two weeks to the renovation schedule — which would mean the shop would be closed during the club's member-guest tournament. The contractor tells you that he could ignore it, but only if you signed a disclaimer saying that you instructed him to do so.

What is your response?

accounting department that there is often the temptation to distort "the numbers" so that they say what the board and membership want them to say.

Many times, accounting practices that are deemed questionable don't do outright harm to anyone. For example, a chef might overstate end-of-month inventories to increase the food and beverage profitability. However, taking a purely utilitarian view leaves unasked whether the practice was done with the intent to deceive.

In the article "Ethics and the Accounting Function" (Peter D. Keim, *Ethics in Hospitality Management: A Book of Readings,* East Lansing, Mich.: Educational Institute of the American Hotel & Motel Association, 1992, p. 173), Peter Keim says:

> Creativity in accounting ... while certainly within the bounds of legality (e.g., accrual basis vs. cash basis, or tax basis vs. financial statement basis reporting) can lead to misinterpretation of results unless it is clearly explained. Creative accounting can lead to trouble and unethical behavior when there is inadequate training or guidance for the accountant or when there is intent to deceive. In these circumstances, clearly wrong decisions can be made, either unwittingly or deliberately. For example, an accountant could easily distort the results of operations by overstating profits through capitalization of normal repair expenses or using LIFO (last-in, first-out) basis inventory valuation during inflationary periods, which would artificially increase period-ending inventory values and reduce the cost of sales.

Moral Issues

Moral issues are among the more difficult for GMs/COOs to address, as there are few absolutes. Eric F. Nusbaum defines ethics as "dealing with what is good and bad or duty and obligation from a perspective of culturally or generally accepted standards of conduct" and morality as "a system of principles of right and wrong as they apply to both beliefs and actions." (Eric F. Nusbaum, "Morality — the Rights of Guests, the Responsibilities of Management," *Ethics in Hospitality Management: A Book of Readings,* East Lansing, Mich.: Educational Institute of the American Hotel & Motel Association, 1992, p. 25.) So it may seem that while ethics are a pertinent issue, morality should be left to the individual.

Yet Nusbaum argues that a moral code will help encourage staff members to respond uniformly to situations, which can protect a club from charges of bias or discrimination. He argues that morals are the foundation of ethics and that some situations can be resolved only through a moral code. He suggests that the following statements should be the underpinning of a hospitality morality system:

- Service is an honorable profession, worthy of and deserving of respect and a code of moral conduct.

- A consequence of entering the service industries is that our guests entrust themselves to our care and we willingly and knowingly accept the responsibility to protect them.

- We have a moral as well as statutory obligation to our guests that can be drawn from the basic foundations of the Judeo-Christian concept of morality —the Ten Commandments.

- We have a similar responsibility to our employees, and its source may also be the Ten Commandments.

- We have a responsibility to protect and enhance the values of assets belonging to those who employ us.

- We have the capability to evaluate the moral consequences of our own choices and courses of action based on whether or not the outcomes of these actions are just.

- Our decisions must be made in a reasoned and consistent manner, because this simplifies the task and protects us from charges of discrimination.

There are certain moral issues that a GM/COO may face at the club and must be prepared to deal with. One pervasive example is the issue of gambling. How does a GM/COO respond when told that part of his or her job involves supervising gambling activities in a state where gambling is illegal? How should a manager respond if he or she finds out that a club employee is having an affair with a married member?

GMs/COOs also have a moral responsibility to their employers and fellow managers. CMAA's code of ethics addresses some of the moral responsibilities that managers have. By becoming a CMAA member, managers pledge, for example, to "always honor their contractual employment obligations" and to "conduct their personal and business affairs in a manner to reflect capability and integrity."

See Figure 19 for an Ethical Entanglement on this issue.

Responses to Ethical Issues

Once a situation has been identified as having ethical ramifications, the people involved may choose to respond in a number of different ways. After the situation has taken place, most responses are limited to reactive ones, such as:

Figure 19: Ethical Entanglement: "By the way ..."

You are applying for a general manager position at a prestigious country club. The morning you are to go in for your second interview with the board, you discover you are pregnant.

Do you tell the board? Why or why not?

- *Obstructive.* Some people choose to deny responsibility for a situation or problem, and claim that any evidence pointing to unethical actions is misleading. If the situation has not been made public, the people involved may choose to try to keep all word of it from getting out.

- *Defensive.* With a defensive response, people will admit to some errors or at least to the failure to act in a perfectly correct manner. However, they will do the bare minimum acceptable to correct the situation. The primary motives in a defensive response are to avoid lawsuits, membership loss and negative publicity.

- *Accommodating.* Some people accept responsibility when their unethical actions are pointed out. They will then try to fix the problem and meet not only their legal responsibilities, but their ethical ones as well.

Some people anticipate situations with ethical overtones before they happen. These proactive individuals tend to be ethical leaders, as they anticipate societal and club needs and respond to them before any actual situations arise.

Social Responsibility

One of the tenets of the CMAA code of ethics for managers is, "We shall promote community and civic affairs by maintaining good relations with the public sector to the extent possible within the limits of our club's demands." This statement forms the basis for practicing social responsibility.

As defined earlier, social responsibility means that a club acts for the good of society as a whole, not just for the good of club members. While social responsibility is not a new theory, it is one that has evolved.

Philosophies

There are three major philosophies of social responsibility. Each philosophy represents an evolution in behavior that has transpired during the last two centuries. These philosophies are:

- Traditional
- Stakeholder
- Affirmative

Traditional

The traditional philosophy of social responsibility is one that promotes no governmental regulation and an overriding sense of *caveat emptor.* Managers who work under this philosophy answer only to their superiors; in clubs, they answer only to their boards and members. Under this philosophy, a manager caters to the wishes of members even when members want something that is harmful to society or otherwise borders on the unethical.

Stakeholder

The stakeholder philosophy broadens the spectrum of the persons to whom managers must be accountable. This philosophy acknowledges that managers are responsible to people both within and without the organization. Some call this philosophy "enlightened self-interest." A common element of this philosophy is ethical responsiveness. Businesses subscribing to this philosophy attempt to respond to situations in a way that is best for all involved.

An example of stakeholder ethics in action was Johnson & Johnson's response to the Tylenol scare in 1982, when some extra-strength Tylenol tablets that had been tampered with led to the deaths of several people. Johnson & Johnson, the makers of Tylenol, issued a recall of all extra-strength Tylenol even though it was not mandatory to do so. Many have since argued that this voluntary action was in Johnson & Johnson's best interests. However, that ought not detract from the ethics of the decision. A company can act in its best interests and still behave in an ethical manner.

A private club has fewer stakeholders than a traditional business. Some club stakeholders might include the following:

- Neighbors
- The local community
- Employees
- College students
- Vendors
- CMAA and allied associations

Some club managers have trouble seeing how accountability to an outside group can have any benefit to a private club. After all, a club does not have transient customers that it must constantly attract. It would seem that only the treatment of members is of any importance. However, in these days of declining memberships, clubs have found that they need to shake the image of elitism that keeps many people from joining. A club that is accountable to all of its stakeholders may be more attractive to members and potential members with a highly developed social conscience.

Affirmative

A club with an affirmative philosophy toward social responsibility is a club that tries to anticipate changes in stakeholder and societal needs and voluntarily conforms its actions to that which is best for all involved. It takes social responsibility a step further than the stakeholder philosophy. Under stakeholder policies, a company reacts. Under affirmative policies, a company prevents and initiates.

This philosophy can be a little trickier to put into practice, as it requires an accurate reading of the moods of members and society. Clubs that voluntarily abolished race discrimination

Figure 20: Social Responsibility

Pros and Cons of Social Responsibility	
PROS	**CONS**
Clubs are a part of society and should work for it	Clubs have a responsibility to minimize expenses to give members the best value for their dollar
Clubs have technical, financial and managerial resources to help society	Time used on social responsibility could be better spent serving members
Improved society is good for clubs	Clubs should not engage in societal issues because it gives them too much influence
Clubs can help prevent future government regulations by being proactive	Club managers are not elected — therefore they can do what they want without answering to the public
Social actions can be profitable	Social actions are too difficult to measure
Social responsibility is ethical and moral	The cost of social responsibility is high and clubs cannot raise dues to pay for it
Social responsibility improves a club's public image	There are too many different issues from too many different groups
Today's societal norms require involvement	Today's societal norms are not the responsibility of the club to enforce
It is cheaper to prevent problems than to cure them	The club may never be confronted by problems faced in the outside community, so why should it spend money to do so

Adapted from "Ethics and the Building of Trust," by Robert Woods, created for BMI III.

clauses before they became illegal are examples of clubs that put the affirmative philosophy in action. A more contemporary dilemma involves the acceptance of openly gay men and women and their partners into club membership. Clubs practicing affirmative philosophies will find themselves challenged in trying to gauge how future public attitude will swing. Certainly, observing the current legal environment offers few clues as to whether gay men and women will be offered protected status, or even equal protection.

See Figure 20 for a pro-con chart addressing social responsibility.

Foundations

Foundations have long been a way for corporations to practice social responsibility. In the last several years, however, nonprofits such as clubs have also been forming foundations as a way to raise money that will benefit their communities. The Union League Club of Chicago is one of the most longstanding examples of clubs that support foundations. The club runs the Boys and Girls Club of Chicago and engages in a variety of other foundation activities, including sponsoring summer camps for youths.

One GM/COO said that foundations provide an outlet not only for the club to support its community, but for the members as well. "It's a wonderful way for members to meet their own philanthropic needs. You're not only asking them to give money, you're providing a vehicle to meet that personal need that they have. Members find it tremendous. Our members tend to be fairly affluent but they're time-bankrupt. They'd like to be able to make a contribution back to the city, but they'd like to do it in a way that is meaningful and safe. There are a lot of scams out there. And people don't want to give their money to something that hasn't been checked out thoroughly, but they don't want to check it out themselves. Or they'd like to do like Jimmy Carter, rebuild a house or go work on a park, but they want to make sure that whatever work they do is respected and appreciated and is going to be well-organized."

CMAA's Club Foundation will assist clubs that are interested in establishing their own private foundations. For more information, contact Marianna Nork at (703) 739-9500.

Ethical Decision-Making Models

Earlier, ignorance was identified as one of the obstacles to making ethical decisions. Decision-makers frequently lack the necessary tools to make the correct choice. An ethics model is one of the tools that decision-makers can use to weigh the factors of a situation and come up with an ethical solution.

Three-Step Test

A basic, user-friendly model for making ethical decisions is presented in Kenneth Blanchard and Norman Vincent Peale's book, *The Power of Ethical Management* (New York: Morrow, 1988). It is a three-step test to which all ethical dilemmas can be submitted. The questions are:

1. *Is it legal?* The decision-maker needs to make sure that his or her actions comply with all local, state and national laws. He or she must also make sure that all actions comply with the club's rules, bylaws and policies. If they do not, then the actions are unethical and must be avoided.

2. *Is it balanced?* The decision-maker must evaluate whether the actions would be fair to everyone involved. Blanchard and Peale talk about creating win-win situations. If the action would put someone else at an unfair disadvantage, then the action probably is not ethical.

3. *How will it make me feel about myself?* As ethics are always determined at a personal level, the decision-maker must finally turn inward. Is the action one that will keep the decision-maker up at night? Will he or she be able to live with him- or herself afterward? One question often posed is, "If your action was described on the front cover of the club newsletter, how would it make you feel?"

This model provides a pragmatic way to respond to any ethical dilemma.

Other Models

There are several other models that decision-makers can use for different situations. They include:

- Rule of reciprocity
- Moral rights
- Stakeholder analysis
- Organizational decision-making
- Balance-sheet approach

We will take a brief look at each of these models in the following sections.

Rule of Reciprocity

Perhaps the most commonly referred to ethical decision-making model is the rule of reciprocity. It is also known as "The Golden Rule." This model has the decision-maker evaluating his or her actions by reversing the situation and putting him- or herself in the other person's shoes. Neither the simplicity nor the age of this approach negate its usefulness.

Some experts have updated the Golden Rule slightly, so that instead of saying, "Do unto others as you would have them do unto you," it says, "Do unto others as they would have done to themselves." This variation recognizes the fact that not everyone wants to be treated the same way. Even if the decision-maker might be willing to tolerate a particular action done to him- or herself, that does not guarantee acceptance on the part of another.

Moral Rights

The moral rights model is based on the idea that there are absolute moral duties. Each person is expected to do the "right" thing. A key part of this model is that actions are based on principles, not on the consequences. This model says that there are no exceptions to moral and ethical behavior.

Supporting this concept are two additional rules. One is the rule of universality, or "Do only those acts that you are willing to allow to become universal standards." The second is the rule of respect: "All individuals are intrinsically important and an end unto themselves. Never treat others as a means to an end."

Stakeholder Analysis

The stakeholder-analysis model analyzes the consequences of an action and who the action affects. There are three steps to this model:

1. List all of the stakeholders who will be affected by the decision.
2. Choose ethical principles over non-ethical principles.
3. Violate an ethical principle only when necessary to advance another true ethical principle that will ultimately produce the greater good.

Organizational Decision-Making

The organizational decision-making model does not attempt to build a different model for every type of situation. Instead, it concentrates on developing standards of moral leadership for managers. In order to successfully implement this model, managers and leaders must respond to critical questions surrounding a situation. This model has the club adapting a

Figure 21: Organizational Decision-Making Model

Laura Nash, in "Ethics Without the Sermon" (*Harvard Business Review* 59, 1981, pp. 79–90), suggests the following organizational decision-making model for ethical decision-making:

1. Define the problem accurately.

2. Define the problem from the view of the person or group most likely to be adversely affected by your decision.

3. Determine how the situation occurred.

4. Determine to whom and to what you give your loyalties.

5. Examine your intentions in making the decision. Ask yourself why you are really doing it.

6. Compare your intentions to the likely results.

7. Find out whether your decision or action could injure someone.

8. Discuss the problem with the people your decision will affect.

9. Assess how confident you are that your decision will be valid over the long term.

10. Ask yourself if you could comfortably discuss your decision or action with your boss, board of directors, club members, your family or society as a whole.

11. Determine what the symbolic potential of your action is if it is misunderstood.

12. Decide under what conditions you would allow exceptions to your stand.

series of questions or steps that are consistently used by everyone in the organization. See Figure 21 for Laura Nash's organizational decision-making model.

Balance-Sheet Approach

The balance-sheet approach is a common model for any type of decision. It requires two columns of information. On one side, the decision-maker lists all of the positives to a contemplated action. On the other, the decision-maker writes all of the negatives to that particular action.

If a simple counting of items does not accurately reflect the factors involved in making a decision, try weighting some of the items according to their importance. Then add up the values on each side and make the decision accordingly.

Managing Ethics

Up to this point, this issue has discussed the forms ethics takes, the situations that arise and the models by which to monitor ethical decisions. There is one final area that must be addressed for clubs to take a pragmatic approach to ethics: managing and communicating ethical standards throughout the organization. As useful and necessary as it is for ethical issues to be pounded out at the boardroom table or the manager's desk, this work is lost without implementing ethical standards throughout the club.

There are several pragmatic tasks that a club can do to ensure all members and employees are moving in the same direction when it comes to ethics. These include:

- Creating a code of ethics
- Empowering others to be ethical
- Establishing a structure to monitor ethics

Creating a Code of Ethics

The process of creating an ethics code must be taken extremely seriously. Once it has been created, it must be strictly followed in order to be effective. There are many factors that should be in place before beginning to create an ethics code. For starters, board members and the club's top managers must be committed to the process.

Tarun Kapoor, a club and hospitality consultant, suggests taking the following steps to develop a code of ethics:

1. Survey employees and members
2. Develop the code
3. Communicate the code
4. Provide follow-up and feedback

A GM/COO suggests adding the following steps to the list:

- Define specific responsibilities for specific people, in both the development and the implementation stage
- Identify your current ethical standards by consulting:
  — The club's mission statement
  — A list of stakeholders and the club's obligations to them
  — Anecdotes that illustrate required or permitted behaviors
  — Sanctions that have been placed on people who made poor decisions
- Use ethics workshops to train the board, management and staff in ethical behavior
- Conduct an annual ethics audit

See Figure 22 for a sample club code of ethics.

While it is possible to secure many different samples of ethics codes from a variety of sources, it can be dangerous to adapt another organization's code wholesale. Each organization has its own character, and its ethical code needs to reflect that. Irving S. Shapiro, in a 1979 Benjamin F. Fairless Memorial Lecture (*Power and Accountability: The Changing Role of the Corporate Board of Directors*, 1979), said, "Corporate leaders seem to agree that no one piece of paper will fit universally, except one so couched in generalities as to be useless — that is to say, one that permits no tests for compliance and thus is incapable of enforcement. The conclusion is that each company must prepare its own list of do's and don'ts, citing specifics on the behavior that is out of bounds, and noting the punishment for stepping out of line."

Figure 22: Sample Code of Ethics

> ### The Beach Club Code of Ethics
>
> 1. Can the decision be published on the front page of *The Breeze*? [Note: *The Breeze* is the club's newsletter.]
>
> 2. Is the decision in the long-term best interests of the Beach Club?
>
> 3. Is the decision consistent with our mission statement?
>
> The mission statement is:
>
> We're in the happiness business. We're a home at the beach. We're the new neighborhood.

A club may decide that it needs more than one code of ethics. It is possible to have separate codes for managers, board members, members, employees and vendors. Club managers who belong to CMAA are also expected to abide by CMAA's code of ethics (Figure 23). According to a CMAA staff member, "We have a very strict code. For example, no manager can apply for the job of another manager without telling him or her first. And we enforce the code."

Empowering Others to Be Ethical

If ethical behavior is to truly permeate a club, each employee must be empowered to make ethical decisions. If an employee is expected to appeal to a supervisor every time an ethical question is raised, it might create the impression among members that there is doubt within the club's staff about whether to respond ethically or not.

Management should only empower employees who have been properly trained to perform adequately. A GM/COO at the 1996 CMAA annual conference suggested that clubs have ethical workshops to promote a code of ethics and to ensure everyone is following the same standards. He suggested that the workshop be held in an unconventional place and at a time where there will be no interruptions. He also encouraged the GM/COO and the president of the board to participate.

The GM/COO suggested that the following items be included in the workshop:

- Overview of the code of ethics
- Anecdotes or a case book that supports the code and provides practical applications
- Review of potential ethical dilemmas that might arise at the club
- Discussion of practical decision-making when confronted with the above dilemmas
- Identification of a support network that is available for decision-makers
- Discussion of the obstacles that decision-makers must deal with
- Discussion of the penalties for responding in an unethical manner

Training staff members to make ethical decisions will benefit the club, as those employees will be able to provide better service. Other benefits of empowering employees to make ethical decisions include:

Figure 23: CMAA Code

Code of Ethics

We believe the management of clubs is an honorable calling. It shall be incumbent upon club managers to be knowledgeable in the application of sound principles in the management of clubs, with ample opportunity to keep abreast of current practices and procedures. We are convinced that the Club Managers Association of America best represents these interests, and as members thereof, subscribe to the following CODE OF ETHICS.

We will uphold the best traditions of club management through adherence to sound business principles. By our behavior and demeanor, we shall set an example for our employees and will assist our club officers to secure the utmost in efficient and successful club operations.

We will consistently promote the recognition and esteem of club management as a profession and conduct our personal and business affairs in a manner to reflect capability and integrity. We will always honor our contractual employment obligations.

We shall promote community and civic affairs by maintaining good relations with the public sector to the extent possible within the limits of our club's demands.

We will strive to advance our knowledge and abilities as club managers, and willingly share with other Association members the lessons of our experience and knowledge gained by supporting and participating in our local chapter and the National Association's educational meetings and seminars.

We will not permit ourselves to be subsidized or compromised by any interest doing business with our clubs.

We will refrain from initiating, directly or through an agent, any communications with a director, member or employee of another club regarding its affairs without the prior knowledge of the manager thereof, if it has a manager.

We will advise the National Headquarters, whenever possible, regarding managerial openings at clubs that come to our attention. We will do all within our power to assist our fellow club managers in pursuit of their professional goals.

We shall not be deterred from compliance with the law, as it applies to our clubs. We shall provide our club officers and trustees with specifics of federal, state and local laws, statutes and regulations, to avoid punitive action and costly litigation.

We deem it our duty to report to local or national officers any willful violations of the CODE OF ETHICS.

- Ensuring that the code of ethics will be effective
- Saving the club time and money by not involving supervisors in every decision
- Increasing member and guest satisfaction
- Giving employees a sense of worth and ownership

Some clubs have found it effective to include ethical behavior as part of employee performance appraisals. This way, employees know that they are not only expected to behave ethically, but will be judged on it.

Conducting an Ethics Audit

Knowing how to respond to individual dilemmas is only the first half of ensuring ethical behavior on a personal and organizational level. Experts encourage club staffs to undertake an overall audit of where they stand in ethical decision-making. This overall approach will help club staff members determine whether ethics has become a habit or whether additional development or training is needed.

One way to conduct an ethics audit involves a three-stage approach:

1. Make sure the club has communicated ethical principles among club employees and members. This can be done through codes of ethics, newsletters or other forums.
2. Make sure club staff, board and committee members apply ethical principles to actual situations as they occur.
3. Provide case studies for discussion and example.

Some of the Ethical Entanglements in this issue can be used to help a club with the final step of the three-stage approach. There are many additional sources of case studies that are written in a much longer form. Also, managers or board members may wish to write their own case studies or hire a consultant to write them.

Another way to conduct an ethics audit can be called the critical-questions approach. This approach asks decision-makers to set aside some time, perhaps once a year, to question themselves about how well they are adhering to ethical principles when they make decisions. Some of the questions board members, managers and staff members may want to ask themselves include the following:

*   What are our existing agreements with stakeholders?
*   Do we currently have conflicts over any ethical issues?
*   Which of our rules and policies address ethical issues?
*   What is our attitude about theft, work ethics, volunteerism, diversity?

Establishing a Structure to Monitor Ethics

Although the cornerstone of empowerment is allowing employees to make decisions, there is another brick that must be added in order to have a solid foundation. All employees must have freedom to report ethical violations and be protected from retribution for doing so. This issue often causes discomfort, as the specter of a disgruntled employee distorting situations for his or her own personal reasons makes many managers uneasy. Yet, if there is to be a commitment to an ethics code, employees must be able to turn in managers and others who engage in unethical behavior, and not be punished for doing so.

Putting into place a structure to monitor ethics will help keep the ethical culture vibrant and dynamic. This structure will tell each manager, employee, board member and member where they can go if they have an ethical problem. The structure can be formal or informal, as long as it is understood by everyone who needs it.

Conclusion

Philosophers will continue to debate ethics and its meaning in society. Within the walls of higher education, ethics will continue to be expanded into increasingly esoteric realms. But no matter how far the theorists stretch our thinking, there will always be those practical basics that will help board members and managers run a more effective club.

Why be ethical? Why take all the time in a time-starved industry to make sure that every decision is an ethical one? Ultimately, because if no time is taken, and some decisions are unethical ones, the board member or manager might end up with surplus time, as he or she is deserted by members, without a job — or worse, sitting in a jail cell.

Fortunately, few club managers or board members have suffered from that bleak scenario. Perhaps this is because private clubs have long been committed to quality, and quality and ethics go hand in hand. When a person thinks of a club, they think of a welcoming, comforting, friendly and gracious environment. A club is committed to the well-being of its members, and ethics is merely the art of ensuring the well-being of everyone involved with the club, either internally or externally.

ACKNOWLEDGEMENTS

The following individuals generously donated their expertise and time to make this issue possible:

Albert Armstrong, CCM
Willmoore "Bill" Kendall, CCM
Marianna Nork
Gregory J. Patterson
Edward Shaughnessy, CCM
Timothy A. Walker, CCM
Robert Woods

Additional Resources

Blanchard, Kenneth, and Norman Vincent Peale, *The Power of Ethical Management*, New York: Morrow, 1988.

Gilmore, Thomas N., "Finding and Retaining Your Next Chief Executive: Making the Transition Work," Washington, D.C.: National Center for Nonprofit Boards, 1993.

Hall, Stephen S.J., ed., *Ethics in Hospitality Management: A Book of Readings*, East Lansing, Mich.: Educational Institute of the American Hotel & Motel Association, 1992.

Houle, Cyril O., *Governing Boards*, San Francisco: Jossey-Bass, 1989.

Koontz, Harold, *The Corporate Director: New Roles, New Responsibilities*, Boston: Cahners Books, 1975.

"Leadership" module of *Hospitality Management Skill Builders*, East Lansing, Mich.: Educational Institute of the American Hotel & Motel Association, 1994.

Nason, J. W., *The Nature of Trusteeship,* Washington, D.C.: Association of Governing Boards of Universities and Colleges, 1982.

Shapiro, Irving S., *Power and Accountability: The Changing Role of the Corporate Board of Directors,* 1979.

Stefanelli, John, *Purchasing: Selection and Procurement for the Hospitality Industry,* Second Edition, New York: Wiley, 1985.

Web sites for more information on ethics:

The Desktop Guide to Total Ethics Management
http://www.navran.com/Products/DTG/DesktopGuide.html

Practical Management of computer Ethics Problems
http://poe.acc.virginia.edu/~jws3g/pp0.html

Hazardous Waste Conference 1993 Policy and Ethics
http://atsdrl.atsdr.cdc.gov.8080/cx2c.html

The Ethics of Yield Management
http://www.hospitalitynet.nl/events/file/08721800.html

The Business Ethics Network
http://www.bath.ac.uk/Centres/Ethical/EBEN/home.html

Business Ethics Magazine
http://condor.depaul.edu/ethics/bizsocl.html

The Centre for Applied Ethics
http://www.sun.ac.za/local/academic/philosophy/ethics.html

National Management Association Code of Ethics for Management
http://www.dyton.net/nma/nmacode.html

A Collection of Codes of Ethics
http://www.laurentian.ca/www/Psyclr/Prof_Ethics/compendium.html

Seventeen-Year Index of Environmental Ethics
http://www.cep.unt.edu/index17.html

Discussion Questions

1. How is compliance with the law different than ethics?
2. What are some of the major ethical issues club boards face?
3. What are some of the major ethical issues club managers face in their club duties?
4. How does the theory of social responsibility affect ethical decision making?
5. What models can be used to facilitate ethical decision making?
6. What steps can a manager take to foster an ethical club environment?

Additional Activities

1. Divide your group in half. Flip a coin to determine which team is the "pro" team and which is the "con." Each group should select a spokesperson. Another team member (or subgroup of team members) should develop opening arguments, another counter arguments, and another closing. Use the following statement for debate: "Clubs should not contract with members for services."

   Set up facing rows of chairs with each team's spokesperson in front. Other team members should sit in the second row. The spokesperson should give opening arguments. Stop the debate and strategize how to counter opening arguments. Resume the debate. Participants should feel free to pass notes to their spokesperson and to cheer or applaud their representatives. When appropriate, end the debate. Do not declare a winner. Instead, mix the group together and discuss what was learned. Identify what the group thought was the best argument on both sides.

2. Keep a journal to reflect on your experiences. Focus on how ethics connect with your professional life; how ethics are reflected in other things you read, see or do; and what you conclude from the ethical choices you and others make. The journal will help you reflect on your experiences and become conscious of what those experiences teach.

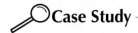

Case Study

Ethics

Charlie Davis is the manager of the Blue Creek Club. As he walks through the grill area one afternoon, someone from a nearby table calls his name. It's John Martinez, vice president of the club board. He has a guest with him.

Charlie approaches the table. "Hello there, Mr. Martinez," he says. "How are you?"

"I'm fine, thanks," Mr. Martinez responds. He pauses, then motions toward his guest, "Charlie, let me introduce you to my friend, Sam Jacobs. He's a board member of the Cherrywood Club, the most prestigious club in this area. And Sam, this is Charlie, the manager here at Blue Creek."

Sam and Charlie exchange hellos and shake hands. John continues. "You know, Sam, Charlie is quite a successful manager. He's been here several years, and the club runs like clockwork under his direction. He keeps costs down and keeps the place looking good."

Sam turns to Charlie. "Glad to hear it, Charlie," he says. "Boy, I wish we could have a manager like you at the Cherrywood Club. Sometimes the management there can't seem to get its act together. For example, last Saturday, two wedding receptions were scheduled at the club. From what I heard, it was quite chaotic. The second wedding was delayed and the dinner was late."

"I was at the second wedding," John says. "The guests had to wait in a holding room while the reception room was being set up. The holding room was too small for the number of people there, and we had to wait an hour for dinner to begin."

"And that's not the only thing that has happened recently," Sam says. "One member who owns a liquor store asked if he could bring his own champagne for his daughter's wedding reception, and the management wouldn't allow it. This man is a good friend of mine. He was pretty upset when he was told that he couldn't bring in his own champagne. He had to pay regular club prices to have champagne served at the wedding. In addition to those incidents," Sam continues, "the club operated with a $20,000 loss last month. And to top that off, ol' Ben Pilote was fired. He's been a favorite employee at Cherrywood for years. Lots of members are angry about that."

Charlie is silent. He doesn't mention that he and Henry Reed, the manager of the Cherrywood Club, have worked together in the past. On a few occasions, Charlie and Henry have shared staff and combined purchases. In addition, Charlie and Henry have been good friends for several years. They have dinner together with their wives every other month. Although Charlie would rather not say anything to Sam, he feels he must respond—especially since he is in the presence of John Martinez, who will be his board president next year.

A week later, Charlie receives a phone call from Sam Jacobs.

"Say, Charlie," he says. "Here at the Cherrywood Club, the manager position may be opening up soon. I was wondering if you'd be interested in coming over and talking to us about the position. A couple of board members and I would like to meet with you to discuss this further. I'm sure we could offer you twice the salary you're making now. But, don't mention anything about it to John Martinez. Again, we can discuss details later."

Charlie is surprised by the offer. The Cherrywood management job is an attractive one. The club is the most prestigious in the area, and the pay raise certainly would be nice. Charlie's thoughts are interrupted by another phone call just a few minutes later. This time, the caller is Henry Reed, Charlie's good friend and the manager of the Cherrywood Club.

"Hi, Charlie. It's Henry. I've got some great news! Susan and I are expecting a baby in December! We're very excited. And we've finally settled into our new house. Everything at the club's going great, too. Our revenue is up from two weddings last month, and I finally got rid of Pilote—remember me telling you about him? He's the server that couldn't get an order right to save his life. Things are really looking up. Whaddya say—how about you and Patty joining Susan and me for dinner this Friday? We've got lots to celebrate!"

CMAA Code of Ethics

We believe the management of clubs is an honorable calling. It shall be incumbent upon club managers to be knowledgeable in the application of sound principles in the management of clubs, with ample opportunity to keep abreast of current practices and procedures. We are convinced that the Club Managers Association of America best represents these interests, and as members thereof, subscribe to the following CODE OF ETHICS.

We will consistently promote the recognition and esteem of club management as a profession and conduct our personal and business affairs in a manner to reflect capability and integrity. We will always honor our contractual employment obligations.

We shall promote community and civic affairs by maintaining good relations with the public sector to the extent possible within the limits of our club's demands.

We will strive to advance our knowledge and abilities as club managers, and willingly share with other Association members the lessons of our experience and knowledge gained by supporting and participating in our local chapter and the National Association's educational meetings and seminars.

We will not permit ourselves to be subsidized or compromised by any interest doing business with our clubs.

We will refrain from initiating, directly or through an agent, any communications with a director, member or employee of another club regarding its affairs without the prior knowledge of the manager thereof, if it has a manager.

We will advise the National Headquarters, whenever possible, regarding managerial openings at clubs that come to our attention. We will do all within our power to assist our fellow club managers in pursuit of their professional goals.

We shall not be deterred from compliance with the law, as it applies to our clubs. We shall provide our club officers and trustees with specifics of Federal, State and Local laws, statutes and regulations, to avoid punitive action and costly litigation.

We deem it our duty to report to local or national officers any willful violations of the CMAA CODE OF ETHICS.

Discussion Questions

1. Given the fact that John Martinez will soon be the president of the club board, Charlie feels he must respond appropriately when Sam describes the conditions of the Cherrywood Club. What could Charlie say in response to the situations that Sam describes?

2. How should Charlie respond when Sam tells him about the management position?

3. What should Charlie say to Henry? Does Charlie have any obligation (according to CMAA code of ethics) to do anything?

The following industry experts helped generate and develop this case: Cathy Gustafson, CCM, University of South Carolina; Kurt D. Kuebler, CCM, Vice President, General Manager, The Desert Highlands Association; and William A. Schulz, MCM, General Manager, Houston Country Club.